Praise for
The Forager Chef's Book of Flora

"You see a sunny meadow. Alan Bergo sees a salad: all blue violet leaves and wild carrot tops. This accomplished chef cooks the wilderness. As he grinds flour from tree nuts, makes black walnut honey, braises sunflower heads like artichokes, and invents 'green electricity,' a magical lovage sauce, Bergo turns nature into food. With such stylish recipes and extraordinary photographs (Bergo's own), *The Forager Chef's Book of Flora* encourages a whole new world of cooks to explore the wild."

—**Dorothy Kalins**, founding editor, *Saveur*; author of *The Kitchen Whisperers*

"You haven't tasted most of the vegetables your ancestors ate. Today, everything is disdained that is too small or too green or doesn't keep for long on the produce shelf. We've been beguiled through generations into The Great Food Forgetting. But big, cheap, and easy have a profound cost: boring food, bad teeth, diabetes, and loss of the primal pleasure of interacting with the green world like a biologically normal human. How do we recover the birthright of perfect eating? By making forgotten food unforgettable. That's the dream that makes Alan Bergo's eyes sparkle, and sets his hands to work. As you'll see in these pages, his eyes and hands work very well together. Follow his guidance from the rediscovered culinary amusement park that surrounds you all the way to your kitchen, and your mouth will confirm everything that your heart suspected. This real, good food is worth remembering."

—**Sam Thayer**, author of *The Forager's Harvest, Nature's Garden*, and *Incredible Wild Edibles*

"This is so much more than a cookbook. Of course there are tantalizing recipes, but there are also walks in the woods, explorations of plant families, revelations of unusual flavors, well-crafted plant profiles, and explanations of why things work the way they do. In *The Forager Chef's Book of Flora*, Alan shares his philosophical and practical approach to making wonderful food, with exquisitely detailed flavor combinations and useful tips that could only come from a consummate pro. His passion for these wild and cultivated flavors is inspiring and will undoubtedly change the way you cook."

—**Ellen Zachos**, author of *Backyard Foraging*

"The joy and delight in Alan's writing are contagious. After reading just the introduction, I wanted to escape to the countryside to start foraging so I could cook his inspiring recipes. This book has so many layers. Not only does it contain an abundance of recipes and information about the plants, it provides us with a history from all over the world where people commonly cooked with these ingredients. His passion and enthusiasm are endless. I was instantly engrossed and keep going back for more. I feel like this book will continue to educate me every time I pick it up! I can't wait to start cooking from it."

—**Laura Jackson**, chef; coauthor of *Towpath*

"There's magic afoot! Edible green growing things we'd mistaken for weeds; everyday vegetables capable of far more than we'd give them credit for; and a most companionable, knowledgeable, and encouraging guide to help us see, cook, taste, and delight in it all."

—**Lori De Mori**, coauthor of *Towpath*

"There are a lot of reasons to love this book, but chief among them is its accessibility: Alan's recipes are approachable, and rooted in the various cultures that invented them. No pinkie-in-the-air foams or molecular whatnot here, just beautiful renditions of beloved dishes that hinge on the edible, wild world that lives all around us."

—**Hank Shaw**, cookbook author; owner of the James Beard Award–winning website Hunter Angler Gardener Cook

"Alan Bergo is one of the most talented and knowledgeable foragers and chefs of my generation. I've followed his adventures for many years now and am delighted to see all of his delectable food in this vastly inspiring and creative tome. Alan's journeys from the garden bed to the heart of the wilderness and back to your kitchen will instill in you the urge to forage for your food and the desire to learn about all the wonderful ways that you can use nearly any vegetable, wild or cultivated. *The Forager Chef's Book of Flora* is an indispensable guide to all the wondrous flavors, tastes, textures, smells, and sights of the wild foods of our world."

—**Jeremy Umansky**, chef/owner, Larder Delicatessen & Bakery; coauthor of *Koji Alchemy*

"Alan Bergo is one of the most important contemporary voices in the food of the Great Lakes North, and one of the most completely skilled wild-food chefs in America. He combines scholarship, science, vast curiosity, and a deep respect for the indigenous origins of American food. Through his efforts to reteach us how delicious our own food is, he is doing us an enormous and long-overdue favor. He is reintroducing us to our true native cuisine—a cuisine with breadth, flavor, and subtlety to rival the traditional cuisine of any other region on Earth."

—**Steve Hoffman**, James Beard MFK Fisher Distinguished Writing Award Winner

"I am wild about this book. I now carry a bag wherever I walk for gathering dandelions and purslane. I pick up acorns and hickory nuts, and am now thinking of so many new ways to make use of the immense larder that is nature. The sensibilities of the forager combined with that of the chef, truly inspiring."

—**Ken Albala**, PhD, professor of history at the University of the Pacific; author of food histories, cookbooks, translations and reference works, and video courses *Food: A Cultural Culinary History* and *Cooking across the Ages*

"This tome of a book, packed with a globally inspired fusion of playful recipes that have been gleaned during Alan's journey as a chef and forager, is loaded with practical tips for seeking out, storing, and serving your foraged greens. The book will serve the professional chef and home cook in equal measure. It is mind expanding, experimental and utilizes a magnificent diversity of plants."

—**Ben MacKinnon**, founder and codirector, E5 Bakehouse

"If you find wild foods as delightful as I do, and the act of foraging as empowering as Alan Bergo does, you will be charmed by the slew of wild recipes and unusual edibles in the pages of his much-anticipated *The Forager Chef's Book of Flora*. Even familiar garden plants like lilies, hyacinths, and hostas will begin to look distinctly appealing in terms of dinner. Dive in!"

—**Marie Viljoen**, author of *Forage, Harvest, Feast* and *66 Square Feet*

The Forager Chef's Book of
Flora

The Forager Chef's Book of
Flora

Recipes and Techniques for Edible Plants from Garden, Field, and Forest

Alan Bergo

Chelsea Green Publishing
White River Junction, Vermont
London, UK

Project Manager: Patricia Stone
Project Editor: Michael Metivier
Editor: Betsy Lancefield Lane
Copy Editor: Laura Jorstad
Proofreader: Angela Boyle
Indexer: Shana Milkie
Designer: Melissa Jacobson

Printed in the United States of America.
First printing June 2021.
10 9 8 7 6 5 4 3 2 1   21 22 23 24 25

Our Commitment to Green Publishing

Chelsea Green sees publishing as a tool for cultural change and ecological stewardship. We strive to align
our book manufacturing practices with our editorial mission and to reduce the impact of our business
enterprise in the environment. We print our books and catalogs on chlorine-free recycled paper, using
vegetable-based inks whenever possible. This book may cost slightly more because it was printed on paper
that contains recycled fiber, and we hope you'll agree that it's worth it. *The Forager Chef's Guide to Flora* was
printed on paper supplied by Versa that is certified by the Forest Stewardship Council.®

Library of Congress Cataloging-in-Publication Data
Names: Bergo, Alan, 1985– author.
Title: The forager chef's book of flora : recipes and techniques for edible plants from garden, field,
   and forest / Alan Bergo.
Description: White River Junction, Vermont : Chelsea Green Publishing, [2021] | Includes index.
Identifiers: LCCN 2021006945 (print) | LCCN 2021006946 (ebook) | ISBN 9781603589482 (hardcover)
   | ISBN 9781603589499 (ebook)
Subjects: LCSH: Cooking (Vegetables) | Wild plants, Edible. | LCGFT: Cookbooks.
Classification: LCC TX801 .B37 2021 (print) | LCC TX801 (ebook) | DDC 641.6/5—dc23
LC record available at https://lccn.loc.gov/2021006945
LC ebook record available at https://lccn.loc.gov/2021006946

Chelsea Green Publishing
85 North Main Street, Suite 120
White River Junction, Vermont USA

Somerset House
London, UK

www.chelseagreen.com

To Dorothy Bacon and her garden,
both of whom have taught me so much.

Contents

Introduction

In Japan, in the early spring, people might harvest various wild plants called sansai, which loosely translates to something like "mountain vegetables," some of the best known of these being shoots of the angelica tree (*Aralia elata*), Japanese knotweed (*Reynoutria japonica*) shoots, edible ferns such as common fiddleheads and the bracken ferns (*Pteridium aquilinum*, also loved in traditional Korean food), as well as things like hosta shoots (*Hosta* spp.). *Sansai* does not refer to one single plant; it's a colloquial blanket term for many plants regarded as being good to eat—not mushrooms, not fish or game, but plants. The sansai are known for being variable in flavor, and being intensely bitter is not necessarily a bad thing.

My girlfriend's father was Greek and would often exclaim when he saw a familiar plant, especially dandelions, things like, "We call that horta" and "We eat that." Wouldn't you know, in Greek cuisine, *horta* is a term not only for a dish but also for many different edible plants, exactly like sansai.

Across, Photograph by Mathew Hintz.

In Italy entire books have been dedicated to cooking piante spontanee, which translates to "spontaneous plants." Besides being fun to say, it's one of my favorite cultural descriptions for a variety of wild edibles—as if the plants have a mind of their own, popping up randomly as though in a game of Whac-A-Mole on top of every hillside and rural area in Italy. *Erbe selvatiche* is a synonym.

In Latin America people use the term *quelites*, a sort of diminutive, affectionate name for (you guessed it!) a variety of wild edible plants. Generally, quelites refers to, but shouldn't be limited to, purslane (*Portulaca oleracea*), orache (*Atriplex hortensis*), seepweed (*Suaeda* spp., an aquatic cousin to lambsquarters), and various species of lambsquarters (*Chenopodium* spp.) and amaranths (*Amaranthus* spp.). While thought of as everything from pesky to an outright plague in the case of Palmer amaranth (*A. palmeri*) in the United States, have been cultivated in South America as food plants for millennia.

Now let's look at the English-speaking world. We also have a catchall term for wild plants, but it's not a term of endearment. Inedible, dangerous, and poisonous, or delicious, edible, and valuable, it doesn't matter; the only term we have for our spontaneous plants is *weed*, and the relationship we have with them is one of eradication and chemical warfare.

Some people might think treating weeds as anything but an enemy is precious, or crazy, especially people who plant any sort of crop, food or otherwise—and that's understandable. A lot of work goes into tending the land in order for it to grow food plants, and I'm guilty of throwing the term *weed* around, just like anyone else. If I were to plant a row of tomatoes, or anything at all, you can bet I'd weed it to ensure the plants get the sun and nutrients they need to grow. The difference is that sometimes the weeds I pull from the garden would go straight into the house for dinner instead of simply being thrown away.

Working like that, I—and you—can harvest food continually from the garden during the entire growing season, sometimes enjoying multiple generations of food plants before the first tomato, carrot, or potato is ripe.

A few years ago, after years behind the stove in a variety of professional kitchens (and watching many of the restaurants I love get shuttered), I took a break from the constant pressure of running a restaurant to work as a consultant, which gave me more time to be outside discovering plants, mushrooms, and other ingredients I love. I started researching, consuming everything I could find on historical uses of wild plants, some of the most fascinating being ethnobotanical references to wild foods eaten in the Mediterranean, South America, and pre-contact North America. Here and there I'd stumble on things: a reference to an obscure regional dish calling for a specific wild plant, say (like Gazpacho Vuido, page 31), or an ethnobotanical account of a plant I'd never heard of (hyacinth bulbs / lampascioni). Each thing I uncovered felt like a treasure. There were references to storied regional dishes I'd never dreamed were possible, such as the Minestrella di Gallicano (page 33) that, depending which accounts you read, might include thirty, forty, or more individual species of wild plants. The Pistic of Friuli Venezia Giulia (page 35) was said to include even more—up to fifty! As a chef, I've made my share of fussy dishes with lots of components, but I would never have thought to conjure something like either of those. If I were to make a soup out of every plant I could find, it might not seem that special, but knowing the background of a dish, and the context of where and why it was created, gives it a name, and with a name comes a soul. Sometimes a recipe's history can be just as delicious as the dish itself; "eaten" together, the experience can be paradigm shifting.

Excavating a few antique recipes was only the beginning, though. As I cooked and ate my way through the landscape, I started to see not just food but also ideas and concepts. As a chef running a seasonal restaurant, I liked to think I was connected to the landscape by buying my food from local farmers and suppliers, but in honesty all my years behind a stove for twelve hours a day meant I was disconnected, in a way. Conversely, being outside nearly every day—seeing, watching, tasting, learning, and constantly looking out for the next new thing I could eat—fundamentally changed not only how I think about wild plants, but also how I see what we commonly conceive of as vegetables, too. After all, most vegetables we enjoy now were once wild plants themselves, carefully selected and bred over time by humans to enhance or remove certain characteristics to make them more useful to us in one way or another.

Watching wild plants grow and searching for new edible parts of familiar plants has transformed my culinary style, similar to how the nose-to-tail, grass-fed, and organic movements have affected the way chefs consider animals.

Understanding the properties of leaves, stems, roots, and flowers can inform how you cook something exotic (like the heads of immature sunflowers) as well as how you adapt the same techniques to cook something mundane (such as a broccoli stem or Brussels sprout). Now when I see squash in the garden, instead of waiting for them to ripen, I harvest some while they are still green and unripe, as well as the shoots, flowers, and seeds during the growing season, all before the first squash is "ready to eat."

As a society we've forgotten this type of old-school knowledge, including many brilliant culinary techniques that were born of thrift and necessity. For our own sake, and that of our planet, it's time we remembered. That idea, in a nutshell, is part of what this book is all about.

Monoculture has shaped, for the worse, what we think vegetables should look like. Broccoli is just a floret; we don't eat the juicy stem or thick, collard-like leaves. We think of beets as a root when in fact, cooked and put

Squash shoots were one of the first secrets about garden plants that foraging revealed to me.

on a plate during the summer, they're mostly stem and greens.

Foraging, in my mind, isn't just an act—it's a mindset and a healthy way of life. It's about the willingness to look beyond the status quo for exciting and unconventional ingredients; an eagerness to make the best possible uses of all the edible parts of plants and animals; and a desire to have a more personal, meaningful, and gratifying relationship with our food.

Plant Families and the Flavors They Share

Have you ever stopped to think about why one thing tastes like another? With meat we might say that something tastes like chicken if it's light-colored and doesn't have a lot of fat. Plants are a little more complex, though.

My journey down the rabbit hole of why certain plants share flavors started when someone sent me a video of people eating buds of mountain ash (*Sorbus americana*) trees, claiming they tasted of almond. I made a note to sample a small amount of the raw buds of my local mountain ash the next year, and, sure enough, they taste strongly of almond. Later I remembered famous French chef Michel Bras eating the seeds of an apple in a documentary (*Entre les Bras*, 2012) and mentioning that apple seeds—you guessed it—taste like almonds. And there's more.

Plum kernels are rich in oil, so much so that it's pressed and sold commercially, and that oil tastes faintly of almonds, not plums. The young tender growth of cherry trees and their leaves can have the same flavor and in Japanese cuisine are sometimes pickled, as well as being used in new distillation techniques by Empirical Spirits of Copenhagen to lend an almond flavor to spirits. Bird cherry flour, made from pounded, sun-dried wild cherries (*Prunus padus*) in Siberia, is used to make a cake with an almond flavor (Bird Cherry Cake, page 262) that is a cousin to Native American wojapi, originally a sort of dried, pounded cake of chokecherries (*P. virginiana*) and their stones, according to my friend Linda Black Elk, a Native American ethnobotanist. Mahlab, a type of Arabic almond seasoning, is made from the dried stones of cherries (*P. mahaleb*) and used to flavor baked goods. In France apricot kernels are crushed and used to infuse liquor for a sort of almond extract called noyaux. Interesting, right?

Now consider another flavor: artichokes. I'd wanted to cook immature sunflower heads like artichokes for a while after I saw the chef of Eleven Madison Park do it, and I wasn't disappointed when I did. After cooking (see Sunflower Artichokes, page 134) I thought it was interesting that the cooked sunflower not only looked like an artichoke but tasted faintly of one, too. Later in the same year, I was serving stuffed grape leaves filled with quickweed (*Galinsoga parviflora*) and was confused when multiple people asked how I was able to fit the artichokes inside the grape leaves. Guess what? There were no artichokes in my stuffed grape leaves.

There are more examples I could go into, but I think these already paint a pretty clear picture. Here's the big takeaway, as I see it: The flavor of almond, how almonds taste, isn't specific to almonds, but is a mix of flavorful compounds concentrated in different edible parts of plants in the Rosaceae family with many concentrated in the genus *Prunus*. The artichoke flavor is similar. Botanically speaking, artichokes don't taste like artichokes per se; rather, they share a taste that comes from flavorful compounds also found in plants such as sunflowers, Canada goldenrod, cardoons, compass plants, sochan, dandelions, and probably many others all found in the Asteraceae, or daisy, family. All of these plants acquire the tastes they share through heredity, passing the flavors down in their genes to the next generation of plants.

Clockwise from left: Unripe sunflower, prickly lettuce flower with bud, sunchokes and flowers, cardoon, galinsoga, artichoke, and sunflower seeds all share a similar flavor.

Safety

I'm a chef, not an herbalist, botanist, or mycologist, and it follows from there that this is, for all intents and purposes, a culinary book—not a foraging guide meant for identification of any plant. There are many books available on foraging and identification, the standard-bearers being anything written by Sam Thayer of Forager's Harvest. Besides helping me identify plants through his writing, Sam has influenced and inspired a lot of my work and perspective on wild food in general. I highly recommend his books, whatever your skill level.

Before you eat a new food, it is up to you to educate yourself on your local edible *and inedible or dangerous* flora, as some can be seriously debilitating, if not fatal. Confusingly, some of these plants might be one and the same; for example, parsnips and angelica (*Angelica atropurpurea*) can cause a skin rash if the plants' juices are exposed to skin and sunlight, but—even if you don't like parsnips—we can all agree they're a food plant. I've done my best to point out helpful or obvious safety tips here and there, but there simply isn't enough room in this book for in-depth conversations on every single solitary thing, so you need to use common sense. Take your time identifying new things. Eating wild foods is not a race, it's a learned skill developed gradually over time. When eating any edible wild plant for the first time, take it slow, and only eat a small amount until you know how it sits with you.

Simply eating too much of some plants can cause problems with some people, too. For example, milkweed pods are delicious but might best be eaten in small quantities by those who are sensitive to them. Certain aromatics, such as juniper (*Juniperus* spp.) and young pinecones,

As a chef I find it fascinating, and examining the botany of plants was the beginning of a paradigm shift for me about how I consider flavors: where they come from and why things might taste the way they do. Working with food gives me inspiration for new ways to cook and pair ingredients, using science and botanical families as a lens for understanding flavors. *How could anything like this be practical?* you ask. Well, for starters, applying my ideas here could be something as simple as garnishing cooked dandelion or other aster greens with sunflower seeds, or my favorite: Smude's sunflower oil. I would argue that we already do this on an almost subconscious level; it's hard to describe *why* the flavor of almond tastes so good with different fruit in the genus *Prunus*—especially cherries, plums, and peaches—but we know it does. For more examples of how you can apply botany to food, see "The Botany of Spices" (page 176) and "The Botany of the Garden" (page 73).

How to Use This Book

Think of this book as one part inspiration, one part instruction. Instead of an alphabetical list of obscure plants, herbs, vegetables, nuts, and other ingredients, I've organized the recipes into four chapters—"Verdant," "Abundant," "Aromatic," and "Nourishing"—roughly according to how the wild ingredients function in their respective dishes. An immature sunflower head is a lot less intimidating in the kitchen when you know to treat it like a familiar vegetable (the artichoke). Not sure what probably shouldn't be consumed in large quantities, either. Raw cherry seeds eaten in large doses could also be problematic, but don't let that scare you. Many common ingredients like nutmeg and cinnamon have toxicity thresholds, too, so it's important to consider dosage. For example, if you don't want a medicinal effect from nutmeg, don't take a medicinal dose by eating a whole nutmeg. Moderation in all things.

Along the same lines it's also important to take into account *where* it's appropriate to harvest food. As a general rule, I don't harvest any food from questionable locations, and it's good to remember that just because I consider a plant to be food doesn't mean that others do. Overly manicured lawns and golf courses could be sprayed with chemicals, as could plants along the side of the road, or aggressive plants that form large colonies such as Japanese knotweed.

Harvesting near railroad tracks, mines, and quarries where soil could be contaminated can pose similar risks. My advice is to only pick from areas you know well and can feel good about harvesting from.

Some ingredients, while few and far between, may also have medicinal properties. Carrot seeds and sweetgale (*Myrica gale*), for example, could potentially interact with pregnancy, so you wouldn't want to eat handfuls of them while you're pregnant, just as you wouldn't consume raw cookie dough, alcohol, or beef tartare. Bodies and tolerances vary, and the burden of proof is on you to fully understand something before you eat it. I've done my best to introduce my readers to the amazing array of foraged foods that are generally safe to consume, but I can take no responsibility for misidentification, misinterpretation, or culinary mistakes made while using this book.

to do with a basket of spruce tips? Cook with them as you would an herb or aromatic—to lend flavor to the rest of the dish. Similarly, the ingredients featured in "Nourishing" contribute earthy, nutty flavors and textures to both sweet and savory applications.

I've also tried to choose recipes where a variety of substitutions can be made, not only for conventional ingredients (say, spinach and chard in a recipe featuring lambsquarters) but also for other wild plants depending on your region and availability. For example, to make Spruce Tip Syrup (page 211), I might use Norway spruce (*Picea abies*), but you could use white spruce (*Picea glauca*) tips or a blend of whatever local species you have. If no spruce are available, you might try using the cones of balsam fir (*Abies balsamea*) or

red pine (*Pinus resinosa*). Since bird cherries are rare in the United States, you might harvest and dry chokecherries or black cherries instead to make your own Bird Cherry Cake (page 262), as I've done.

An underlying goal of this book is to help normalize wild plants by showing them alongside more familiar ingredients. I think one of the most valuable lessons here is how different plants and uncommon ingredients are used and consumed around the world (and have been, historically), and, again, how you can apply similar culinary techniques to what grows around you. In the United States purslane is a weed; in South America it's a beloved vegetable destined to be simmered with tomatoes and jalapeño, or cooked tender in a tangy sauce of tomatillos. Dandelions are seen

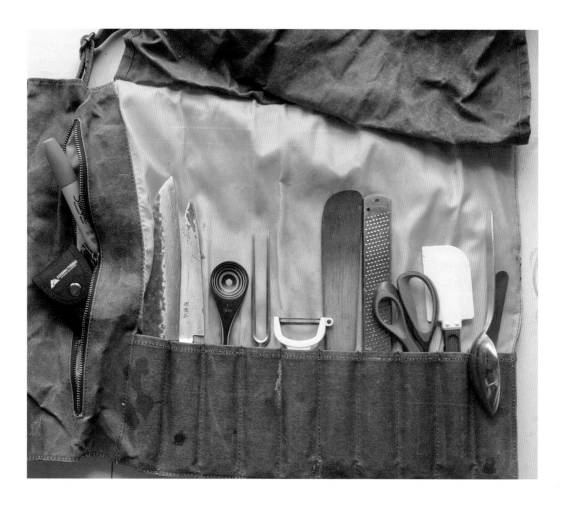

as a nuisance in American yards, but in Greece people who cook them tender and anoint them with olive oil and lemon juice see them a bit differently.

Another big takeaway I hope you get from the book is how the forager's eye and curiosity with which I look at a wild plant and wonder *Can I eat that?* can be applied to things you're familiar with, opening up new possibilities for old favorites. For example, many plants can be cooked before they're ripe. Most people will be familiar with fried green tomatoes, but what about unripe butternut squash or pumpkin, and from there, unripe walnuts or sunflower seeds? Questioning the status quo with regard to when

ingredients around you are "ripe" can be exciting and rewarding. In the "Abundant" chapter especially, you'll find lots of recipes that treat familiar vegetables as the whole plants they are, not just the select parts offered in supermarkets.

The recipes in this book have been carefully collected over the years, and I've included a mix I think both my chef friends and home cooks will find interesting and inspirational. Most recipes, even many with specific measurements, and especially conceptual dishes such as Carrot Family Soup (page 80), are less a formula than a suggestion of how to think differently about food. Other recipes, like Wild Herb Brioche (page 148),

Dehydrating makes certain flavors available year-round.

are best made using a scale and a stand mixer. Still other recipes, like a salad of wild greens, are best learned by creating them yourself with no recipe at all, though I've included a few tips I hope can be helpful.

I've intended this book to be a culinary toolbox filled with things I could make and enjoy easily and eat every day, as well as special-occasion projects or seasonal treats worth searching out. It's a big mix of things that I think are interesting in some way or another, and think you'll enjoy, too—wherever you live. I hope the book is approachable and useful to my seasoned, hard-core forager and chef friends, as well as the home cooks who, before picking up the book, might not have known stinging nettles are edible.

Many of the ingredients in this book I harvest wild, but some I don't, and I think it's fine to pick and choose according to your skill and availability. Most of the recipes can be made with substitutions from a grocery store, local co-op, or garden, although a few special ones cannot. Whatever place you're at in your local growing season, I hope you can open up to a section and find something useful, or maybe just an idea to inspire you to try something new.

CHAPTER 1

Verdant

Greens,
Bitter and Sweet

Seeing the first leafy greens poke up through the ground is one of the most exciting parts of the year, and a promise of many green meals to come after a winter where my frozen supply is dwindling or depleted. There are so many greens I love to eat, both cultivated and wild, that, instead of trying to share some sort of encyclopedic reference for many plants, I wanted to gather some of my favorite ways to cook greens as a sort of core sample of delicious ideas you can apply to many different greens—whether they came from the woods, your yard, or a supermarket.

After we cover some basic harvesting and cooking techniques, the first recipes are those in which just about any greens can be used, followed by those where you might reach for young, tender greens, and finally recipes that commonly call for greens with some bitterness, such as dandelions or mustards. Even so, you should know that plenty of examples within those categorizations are open to interpretation.

Where possible, I've noted historical combinations and recipes enjoyed by different cultures featuring specific species, but you should feel free to experiment with whatever plants are around you.

Harvesting Greens

Harvesting your own greens will quickly show you the incredible bounty of nature. Once you know a few plants, their sheer volume and variety can be intimidating in the best way, leaving you wondering, *What will I do with all this food?* No matter who you are or how much you know, if you don't take care of your food it won't taste good, and if it doesn't taste good you won't enjoy it.

Just as the people who harvest flowers in Provence for the perfume industry often work at a precise time of day (after the morning dew has evaporated and before the heat of the midday sun), harvesting greens in the morning is better than in the midday heat, especially if you have to travel any distance to get back home. Even so, if you find yourself someplace and uncover a patch of nettles begging to come home with you, you'll likely be fine, though the plants might need some refreshment when you get home.

If I can share only one secret about harvesting plants with you, this is it: When I harvest green plants, even if I'm just in the yard with a pair of scissors, I bring them inside and soak them in water as quickly as I can, not because they're dirty, but because it reduces their temperature and imbibes them—cleaning them in the process is just a bonus. Greens can be washed and dried any old time, but plants are living things and detaching them from their roots stresses them. Soak them in cold water, though, and they'll literally come back to life in your sink, typically in about 5 minutes (or longer, if they've started to wilt).

Soaking wild greens after picking removes grit but also refreshes them, making them crisp, as if they were just picked.

I guarantee you: A simple soak in cold water after picking can extend the life span of your fresh greens beyond what you've ever thought possible. Keeping cooking greens for weeks on end, as long as they're cared for, is possible, although I go through mine so quickly at home that it's never an issue. Depending on how long they've been out of the ground, or if they've been sitting in a warm car, soaking the greens until they come back to life can require some time, but 30 minutes is the longest it ever takes, and only in the direst circumstances (greens left on a dashboard—I didn't do it!) have they not come back to life. Just as a cutting can sprout an entire new plant, freshly clipped greens still have a strong will to survive.

This is the trick I've used to supply multiple restaurants with plants I pick by hand, driven into town in the heat of a midwestern summer not in the back of a refrigerated truck, but in the back of a jet-black Honda with a janky A/C unit from a farm 60 miles (96 km) away. *And I harvest alone.* Even after spending hours in bins and tubs in the warm air while I snip-snip-snip, pound after pound and bag after bag of fresh greens, sometimes piled on top of one another, will come back to life just like new, as long as they get soaked in cold water within an hour or two of picking.

Basic Ways to Cook Wild Greens for Storage

There are a lot of ways to cook fresh greens. I choose my methods based on the specific plant I want to eat, or whether I'm trying to cook large amounts at one time to preserve them.

Blanching

Blanching, or submerging something in boiling (typically salted) water for various lengths of time, is great for greens that may have a strong flavor like sochan or bitter mustards, or for when you want to preserve or quickly

Blanched wild greens. In some places (Italy) you might see balls of cooked greens like this at your local market or farm stall. They're space saving and convenient.

cook large amounts of greens without over-cooking them, as can happen with steaming. If you find a particular plant strong tasting in its raw state or when cooked from fresh, try blanching it before cooking. Some people are sensitive to compounds in certain plants, such as oxalates in spinach or amaranth; for these individuals, blanching the plant can mean the difference between being able to eat the plant and having to skip a serving of greens. Blanching usually yields 1 pound (455 g) of greens for every 1½ pounds (680 g) raw.

My favorite method for storing excess greens for use throughout the year is to blanch and freeze them. Here's a walk-through of my process:

I harvest as many greens as I can, usually about 10 pounds (4.6 kg) for a preserving batch, but you can do it with whatever quantity you like. From there, I fill the largest stockpot I can find with salted water and bring it to a boil. Meanwhile, I scrub and clean the sink or a large bowl, and fill it with cold water. Once the water boils, I cook the greens in large batches just until wilted—a few seconds—and immediately transfer them to the sink of cold water until cool. Next, I squeeze out the water and form the greens into balls, which I freeze in zip-top bags. Because the greens essentially get washed twice, this is a great way to prepare greens fresh from the garden that might have extra grit.

Blanching greens in salted water might not seem like a big deal, but besides making food taste more like itself, salt is a preservative, and a powerful one. Over the years I've seen the difference, and have scolded more than one line cook for not salting their water. I guarantee you, greens cooked in salted water will last at least twice as long as those simply blanched and shocked in a cold-water bath. This is a good thing if you have the habit of taking frozen greens out to thaw and not getting to them for a few days, as I do. As for the amount of salt, I generally season the water until it tastes like the sea—generally

1 tablespoon for every 4 cups (945 ml) of water (some of my friends will double that)—but even using a small amount of salt can make a difference in the life span and flavor of blanched greens.

Freeze-Wilting

Freeze-wilting is a good alternative to blanching. It involves putting greens in the freezer, which quickly wilts them. This is good for flavorful greens and herbs that would lose some flavor from blanching in water. Mild (non-bitter) mustard greens or strongly scented herbs such as lovage are good candidates for this method, as well as lacinato and other kales. It's also a great way to wilt greens for cooking, even if they won't be frozen later, since they take up less space in the pan.

Here's how to do it:

Put your leafy greens in a container, such as a grocery or other bag, and place the bag in the freezer for 30 minutes, then remove and thaw at room temperature. Portion the greens into your preferred containers for freezing, then label, date, and refreeze until needed.

Wild Green Cakes are great as a side dish, but if you dress them up and make them larger they can even go on a bun.

Wild Green Cakes

Makes roughly 10 cakes

There's a reason this is the first recipe in this book. It's a hybrid of a recipe by French Chef Jacques Chibois and one outlined by Sam Thayer in his third book, *Incredible Wild Edibles*, and it's a statement on the culinary dichotomy of these two chefs, since wild plants are high-quality ingredients sought after by chefs, but also available to anyone who takes the time to get outside and learn about them. Many different species of plants can be used, and no two batches I've ever made have been exactly the same. My favorite part of this recipe is how the greens continue cooking on the inside of the cake, almost as if they're cooked under pressure, retaining a bright green color, with a tender bite that eats almost like meat. The cakes are meant to be a mild side dish—a different way to get your greens. If you want to jazz them up, consider serving them with a yogurt-, tomato-, or mayonnaise-based sauce. Sometimes I add cooked onions, seeds, or other alliums and herbs if I have them, so think of this recipe as a blank slate you can make your own. Breakfast, brunch, lunch, dinner, or as an appetizer: I'd struggle to think of a meal that wouldn't welcome a few green cakes.

2 packed cups (455 g) blanched and shocked wild greens, or a mix of spinach, parsley, and kale
2 large eggs
¼ cup (30 g) flour or flour equivalent
Kosher salt, to taste
Fresh-ground black pepper, to taste
Fresh-grated nutmeg or your favorite spice mix (such as Dried Ramp Leaf Rub, page 168), to taste (optional)
Cooking oil, such as lard or grapeseed oil, as needed for cooking the cakes
Fresh lemon wedges, for serving (optional)

Squeeze the greens dry very well. Chop the greens fine and mix with the eggs and flour. Season the mixture with salt, pepper, and nutmeg to taste; it should be well seasoned. Ideally, you'll now let the batter rest for 30 minutes or so before cooking, but it can be cooked straightaway if needed. Cook a small piece of the mixture to test the seasoning and adjust to your taste. Shape ¼ cup (2 ounces / 55 g) into cakes with your hands, then fry on medium-high until browned on both sides. If your cakes seem loose or wet, mix another spoonful of flour into the batter. The cakes are sturdy and reheat well, so I usually make them in large batches. Serve with lemon wedges.

Variations

- Using different grain flours and seasonings can give you different themes. For example, Latin American–flavored cakes made from quickweed and fine cornmeal, scented with cumin, are great used to scoop up guacamole—a bit like fried plantains. By the same token, chard or wild beet green cakes bound with buckwheat or millet flour would be at home with Eastern European flavors such as sauerkraut and pork sausage. Middle Eastern–inspired cakes could be made with malva or violet leaves, seasoned with baharat spice mix, bound with ground wheat flour, and served with tahini sauce.
- Nutmeg is traditional here, but other spices, especially seeds from the carrot family, are really good in nutmeg's place.
- Play around with combinations of bitter and "sweet" greens. Horseradish greens can be unpalatable for some people, but mixed with other greens (1 part to 3 parts) they can add a nice depth.
- Use the cakes as vehicles for dips, sauces, and salsas.
- After the cakes are cooked, they're great in a lot of places you'd use a meat patty or ground meat.

Green "Meatballs" Stuffed with Chèvre

Makes about 15 "meatballs"

Think of these as Wild Green Cakes in a different form. Stuffed with a nugget of chèvre or your favorite melting cheese, they make a great vegetarian "meatball." You can finely chop the greens by hand if you have to, but you'll get the most even, dependable results from a food processor. They're great served with something acidic like a simple tomato sauce.

1 packed cup (225 g) blanched and shocked
   wild greens, or a mix of spinach, parsley,
   and kale
1 large egg
4 tablespoons bread crumbs
Pinch of kosher salt
2 tablespoons flour or flour equivalent
Fresh-grated nutmeg, to taste (optional)
½ cup (30 g) chopped cilantro or other
   tender herb, such as basil
2 tablespoons toasted sunflower seeds or nuts
2–4 ounces (55–115 g) fresh chèvre
   (depending on how much you can fit in
   each meatball)
Cooking oil, such as lard or grapeseed oil,
   as needed for cooking
Fresh lemon wedges, for serving (optional)

Squeeze the greens dry as well as you can, then squeeze them dry again. You want as much water to come out as possible. Chop the greens roughly, making sure to cut any long stems. Add all the ingredients except the chèvre to a food processor and process until well blended. Taste the greens so you can judge the seasoning, adjusting as needed. Portion out the greens mix into generous tablespoons, then flatten each mound into a cake in your palm and press ½ teaspoon of fresh chèvre into the middle. Close your hand gently to form a ball, rolling it between your hands to make it evenly round. Arrange the balls in a steamer basket and steam for 15 minutes, or until cooked through and tender. You can then either brown them in fat or serve as-is with garlicky tzatziki or a pool of tomato sauce, or tossed with melted butter and sage. If you don't have a steamer basket, you can pan-sauté the balls gently and finish in a 400°F (200°C) oven for a few minutes to cook them through, but they won't be as tender or evenly cooked. Serve with lemon wedges.

Green "Meatballs" Stuffed with Chèvre. Steaming is the key for tender, meaty dumplings.

Simple Chiffonade of Greens

Serves 4–6

Chiffonade, or just *chiff* in chef parlance, is the method of shredding greens into thin slices before cooking. It's a great way to switch up how you cook greens, especially if you don't feel like blanching them. It's also one of my go-to techniques for older, more mature greens if I don't feel like boiling them. This method also comes in handy if you forgot to cook greens and need some on the fly. Any leafy green can be cooked this way, and it cuts the cooking time down to a fraction of the time needed to cook whole leaves.

Many greens, especially hardy ones like lacinato kale, collards, or mature sochan (see the "Sochan" sidebar, page 46), will make a good raw salad after being cut into fine shreds. To do that, I massage the greens a bit by hand with oil, acid, and salt, letting them sit for a few minutes or up to half an hour before serving.

8 ounces (225 g) wild or cultivated greens, or enough to fill a large skillet
2 tablespoons cooking oil or lard
Pinch of kosher salt
¼–½ cup (60–135 ml) water or stock
Fresh lemon wedges, for serving (optional)

Remove the stems from any hard winter greens such as collards or kale; young tender greens and many wild greens can be used whole. Ball the greens up on a cutting board, then carefully shred them as thin as you can. Heat the oil on high in a pan wide enough to accommodate the greens (a 12-inch / 30 cm cast-iron skillet generally works). When the oil is hot and nearly smoking, add the greens and a pinch of salt, give it a quick stir, then add ¼ cup of the water and immediately cover the pan and cook for about 30 seconds. When the pan is nearly dry, turn the heat down and taste the greens. If you're using young, tender greens, they should be done. If you're using kale or another hearty green, add the additional ¼ cup water, cover, and cook for another minute or two. The greens should be just barely cooked. Any hearty greens should remain a little chewy. Serve with lemon wedges.

Finely shaving greens or cutting them into a chiffonade cuts down on cooking time and can be a great way to quickly cook a side of greens.

Wild Greens I Like to Cook

Virginia waterleaf (*Hydrophyllum virginianum*)

Common blue violet (*Viola sororia*)

Wild lettuces (*Lactuca* spp.)

Dame's rocket (*Hesperis matronalis*)

Amaranths (*Amaranthus* spp.)

Wild mustards (*Sisymbrium* and *Brassica* spp.)

Ground elder (*Aegopodium podagraria*)

Chickweed (*Stellaria* spp.)

Garden yellow rocket (*Barbarea vulgaris*)

Galinsoga (*Galinsoga parviflora*)

Garlic mustard (*Alliaria petiolata*)

Mitsuba (*Cryptotaenia canadensis*)

Miner's lettuce (*Claytonia perfoliata*)

Common nettle (*Urtica dioica*)

Lambsquarters (*Chenopodium* spp.)

Canada goldenrod (*Solidago canadensis*)

Green Sallet with Eggs

Serves 4

A simple dish of wild plants and eggs is a common preparation in the American South for poke sallet (*Phytolacca americana*). (To be safe, par cook before eating.) The plant is very uncommon in the cold American North where I live, but the preparation of cooking with eggs is great with any greens. As an aside, the word *sallet* is a precursor to our modern word *salad*, but the sallets of old were generally cooked. For a southern touch, serve some Hot Pepper Vinegar (recipe follows) on the side. I like a little avocado and hot salsa since the dish includes eggs, but don't tell the traditionalists.

2 packed cups (455 g) blanched and
   shocked wild greens, squeezed dry
1 tablespoon finely chopped garlic
½ cup (115 g) finely chopped onion
4 tablespoons bacon drippings, animal fat,
   butter, or cooking oil, divided
Kosher salt and fresh-ground black pepper
6 large eggs, beaten
Chopped avocado, salsa, or hot sauce,
   for serving (optional—not traditional,
   but tasty!)

Begin by tasting your greens to be sure they are of a tenderness you like before adding them to the pan. Sweat the garlic and onion in half the fat until translucent. Add the greens, mix, and stir to coat. Season with salt and pepper to taste. Push the greens to the side of the pan, add the rest of the fat, then add the eggs. Cook, stirring the eggs only, until they're mostly set, then mix with the greens. Double-check the seasoning for salt, adjust as needed, and serve when the eggs are just cooked. Garnish, if you like, with avocado, salsa, and hot sauce. Serve with Hot Pepper Vinegar on the side.

Hot Pepper Vinegar

Makes 2 cups (480 ml)

A basic recipe. For variation, I might add some herbs or other aromatics, such as crushed seeds of cow parsnip (*Heracleum maximum*/golpar). It's good on just about any wilted greens, but especially firm ones like collards and kale.

8 ounces (225 g) hot peppers, chopped
   (I like Thai chilies or habaneros)
2 cups (480 ml) apple cider vinegar
2 teaspoons kosher salt

Wearing gloves, pack the peppers into a clean jar large enough to accommodate them and the vinegar. Bring the vinegar and salt to a boil, then pour over the peppers in the jar, seal, and store for at least a week. Strain out the peppers and discard them, then bottle the vinegar. For the best flavor, keep the vinegar in the fridge.

Greens with Garlic and Chili (Erbe Selvatiche alla Romana)

Red pepper flakes, to taste
Kosher salt, to taste
1 tablespoon toasted pine nuts (optional)
1½ tablespoons raisins or other dried fruit (optional)
Fresh lemon wedges, for serving (optional)

Serves 2–4 as a side

To me, this is *the* Italian preparation for wild greens—I've probably made it more than anything else in this book. The key is how the garlic is cooked: sliced—never minced or coarsely chopped. Use the recipe below the first time to get the feel for cooking the garlic; after that, forget about the recipe and channel your inner Italian grandmother. The deep flavor that the slowly cooked, gently browned slices of garlic and their oil give to a simple bowl of greens is nothing short of transformative. Pine nuts and raisins are optional; garlic and chili are not.

2 packed cups (455 g) blanched and shocked wild greens
1 large clove garlic
2 tablespoons extra-virgin olive oil, plus more to taste

Squeeze the greens dry very well. If the greens are long, consider chopping them coarsely so they can fit on a spoon. Cut the root end off the clove of garlic, then slice as thin as you can (the long way or the short way—either is fine). Heat the oil and the garlic slices in a pan (an 8-inch / 20 cm skillet is good) over medium heat until the garlic is lightly browned and aromatic, about 4 to 5 minutes. The deeper the color you can put on the garlic, the better the flavor, but be careful it doesn't burn. Add a pinch of red pepper, stir, then add the greens. Season the greens, then stir to heat through and coat with the garlic oil. Add the pine nuts and raisins, if you're using them, and warm through. Taste the greens: They should taste pleasantly seasoned with salt and scented with garlic. Adjust the seasoning to your taste, then serve with lemon on the side.

Dame's rocket (*Hesperis matronalis*) makes a great substitute for spinach in this Italian classic.

Simple Wild Greens Saag

Serves 4–6 as an appetizer

Saag—the famous Indian preparation for greens—is a sort of hybrid between a dip and a stew eaten with flatbread, and is often made with amaranth. This version isn't that traditional—it's what I throw together at home. You don't need a big list of spices, and you don't have to make your own flatbread (sometimes I just serve it with toast—the heresy!). In the spring I'll make it with ramp leaves (in the U.K.: wild garlic or leek), but the rest of the year I reach for onions and garlic. Either way it's a great way to get your greens. Although it's often spicy, mine is pretty mild, relying on heat from ginger and a little black pepper. If you want some more heat, add a chopped serrano chili to the onion or ramp leaves as they cook. If you add bitter greens, I would keep them to no more than half of the mix, to keep the dish from becoming overpowering.

2 ounces (55 g) ramp leaves, chopped; or 1 small yellow onion, chopped, and 1 large clove garlic, minced
¼ cup (60 ml) ghee or coconut oil
½ teaspoon black peppercorns
¼ teaspoon salt, plus more to taste
1 teaspoon coriander seed
½ teaspoon cumin seed
1 can (13.5 ounces / 400 ml) coconut milk; or 1 cup (240 ml) water and ½ cup (110 g) yogurt
1 teaspoon grated ginger
½ teaspoon ground turmeric
2 packed cups (455 g) blanched and shocked greens, or 1½ pounds (680 g) fresh greens, preferably softer ones such as lambsquarters, dame's rocket, or spinach
Toasted nuts, for serving (optional)
Flatbread, toast, or crepes, for serving (optional)

If you're using whole spices, lightly crush them in a mortar and pestle. Chop the greens so that there are no stems longer than 1 inch (2.5 cm). In a deep pot, sweat the ramp leaves in the ghee for a few minutes, along with the pepper, salt, coriander, and cumin—it's okay if it gets a little color around the edges. Add the coconut milk, ginger, and turmeric; simmer for a few minutes. Add the greens, working in batches if necessary, then cover the pot and allow the greens to steam until wilted. Blend, working in batches with a countertop blender until you have a smooth purée, then transfer back to the pan. Continue cooking, stirring occasionally, until you can see the bottom of the pan when stirring, most of the liquid has evaporated, and the mixture is thick, about 15 to 20 minutes. Taste and adjust seasoning. Transfer to a bowl and serve, garnished with toasted nuts and flatbread, toast, crepes, or another starchy vehicle for scooping.

On Fermentation

Once I'd learned basic kitchen skills, I started to get bored and experiment with ferments. The first thing I ever fermented was simple sauerkraut, and I can still remember the fizz, tang, and crunch of biting into a spoonful of my first batch—completely different from the soft, lackluster stuff in a can. I was in love, but, if asked, I would have struggled to say why and would've probably told you something like, *It's fun to have a kitchen pet.* Years later I have a deeper appreciation of fermentation, especially for its historical context. Fermentation, drying, and salting are three of the most ancient methods of food preservation, lacto-fermented brine being literally the original pickle and one that still lives in kosher dill pickles and pickled grape leaves. As a bonus, besides being able to preserve food, fermentation also transforms it, creating new flavors. For years I kind of knew what I was doing, but I didn't unlock the true potential until I started using a scale to measure my salt. I'll cover the basic processes I use, but if you're new to fermentation, you'll want to buy a book to familiarize yourself with the process and best practices for safety. The canonical standard *The Art of Fermentation* by Sandor Ellix Katz and *The Noma Guide to Fermentation* by René Redzepi and David Zilber are two of my favorites.

Wet Versus Dry Fermentation

Here's the skinny: I ferment things a few different ways, but usually I ferment things with salt (for a saltless ferment, see Black Walnut Ketchup on page 258 or Wildflower Crème Fraîche on page 200). You can ferment without measuring your salt in teaspoons and tablespoons, but it's inefficient and potentially inaccurate. Measuring your salt gives scientific precision and dependable results; once you get used to measuring, it's also actually easier. To understand the concept, let's talk about the two ways I ferment using salt in this book: fermenting an ingredient in

Vacuum (dry) fermented ramp leaves (note the cut corner that's been resealed to release carbon dioxide), and fermented ramp leaves in brine.

brine (wet fermentation) or adding salt to an ingredient with no added water (dry fermentation).

Brine/wet fermentation is great for things that don't hold a lot of water—like grape leaves or seeds. I typically use a salt concentration anywhere from 3 to 5 percent of the weight of the ingredient in question along with filtered water to cover (3 percent in the winter and 5 percent in the summer). For example, for 3 percent fermentation, one widemouthed quart jar might hold about 850 grams of combined liquid and ingredients, so to find the amount of salt needed, I multiply the total weight of the liquid and ingredients in the jar (850 grams) by 0.03, to get 25.5 grams of salt.

For dry fermenting, which I might do if I want a stronger flavor from something (such as the Ramp Steak Sauce on page 174 or the CSA Fermented Giardiniera on page 71), I'll typically put in 3 percent of the ingredient's weight in salt, mix it up, and vacuum-seal it in a bag. From there, all I have to do is check on the bag occasionally and release any accumulated carbon dioxide by cutting off a small corner of the bag and resealing it. It's exactly the same process as the one you'd use to make sauerkraut, but there's no pounding and mashing, and no scents to offend the other people in your house.

The entire fermentation process takes at the very most two weeks for just about anything I make, the exception being long-aged sauces like Tabasco-Style Ramp Hot Sauce (page 173). One of the biggest benefits to dry fermentation is that there will be no mold or kahm yeast, as often happens with wet fermentation. Using an air lock or other tools, such as the special fermenting lids designed for

Mason jars, can work, too, if you don't have a vacuum sealer.

Storing in Brine / Slow Fermenting Under Refrigeration

Storage in brine under refrigeration is a great way to keep green unripe seeds and capers, especially from daylilies and nasturtiums or things I may need to collect a few times from plants in order to get full jars. The low temperatures slow down the fermentation and curb the mushiness that can happen with green vegetables such as fermented cucumbers or fiddleheads.

I make a brine solution in a jar (generally 3 to 5 percent, or 3 to 5 grams of salt for every 100 grams of water) and just add things to the jar in the fridge as I harvest them—especially the aforementioned ingredients, as well as aromatic seeds such as caraway. For a recipe using this technique, see DIY Fermented Capers (page 203). Items in brine will still ferment in the fridge and develop the sour lactic acid tang but at a very gentle pace that you can slow down or speed up by taking them out of the fridge for a day or two.

———

Now let's apply the dry and wet approaches to grape leaves. You can use this process for tons of things, but I use grape leaves as an example, since they're one of the easiest and most traditional. As a bonus, grape leaves won't get soft on you (unlike other greens), and to keep things crisp and ward off kahm yeast, you can throw a grape leaf into different ferments such as pickles and garlic scapes. Grape leaves are also the poster-child leaf to use in Roulades Verts (page 28).

Dry-Fermented Grape Leaves

Grape leaves
Kosher salt

Wash and dry the grape leaves, then weigh them in grams. Multiply that weight by 0.03, then add that number of grams of salt to the greens; mix to combine, then vacuum-seal. Leave the greens to ferment for up to 2 weeks in a cool, dark place at room temperature, slitting the corner of the bag to release carbon dioxide as needed during the process, resealing the bag each time. Refrigerate or freeze the leaves when they're sour to your liking.

Brine/Wet-Fermented Grape Leaves

Grape leaves
Water
3 percent salt (roughly 1.5 tablespoons salt for each quart/liter jar of water and leaves)

Wash and clean the leaves. Put your jar on a scale, tare it to zero, then roll the leaves up into bundles and pack them into the jar. Cover the leaves completely with water. Note the total weight of the ingredients in grams, then multiply that by 0.03 and measure out that amount of salt by weight. Pour a small amount of the water from the jar out onto the salt to dissolve it, mix well, then pour the salt slurry back the into the jar. Weigh the leaves down with something heavy (a clean stone is good), cover the jar with a lid, and allow to ferment in a dark place with a stable temperature, such as a pantry, opening the jar occasionally to release carbon dioxide, until you like the taste, about 7 to 14 days. The grape leaves will keep indefinitely and don't need to be refrigerated as long as they're under the brine, although if I'm going to keep them out, I like to boil the brine and leaves to kill the ferment, packing them hot into a clean jar, sealing with a metal lid, and turning the jar upside down to seal in order to prevent any pesky white kahm yeast from forming (this yeast is harmless but annoying). After opening, I usually refrigerate the jars, but again they're relatively stable in a cool dark place as long as they remain covered with brine. As an aside, using plastic lids for fermentation can be nice since they won't corrode from the acidity like metal lids will.

Stuffed Leaves with Fruit, Rice, and Nut Filling

Makes about 20 large or 30 smaller grape leaves.

These lesser-known cousins of dolmades (Greek grape leaf rolls filled with lamb and rice) are made with rice and fruit. I like to think of these as a sort of wild energy bar. They're heavily seasoned, packed with fruit, seeds, greens, and wild rice. Sour cherries are traditional in many rolls like these, but naturally sun-dried fruits such as blueberries and serviceberries are great, too. Generally I slice them into small, bite-sized rounds because they're highly seasoned.

2 large cloves garlic, finely sliced
3 tablespoons cooking oil
1 small onion, finely diced or chopped
6 ounces (170 g) cooked wild rice
¾ cup (180 ml) dried fruit of your choice; sour cherries and cranberries are good, as they're not too sweet
½ cup (70 g) toasted pine nuts or other nuts or seeds
1 packed cup (225 g) wild greens, blanched, shocked, and chopped
½ cup (30 g) fresh dill, mint, or cilantro
⅓ cup (40 g) wild rice flour or another grain flour
2 tablespoons finely diced Fermented Lemon Confit (optional, page 45)
½ teaspoon baharat spice mix, pumpkin pie spice, or a mix of cumin, ground cinnamon, ground nutmeg, and black pepper
Kosher salt and fresh-ground black pepper, to taste
20–30 Grape Leaves Fermented in Brine (page 26) or other leaves as needed

Sweat the garlic in the oil until golden, then add the onion and cook for 10 to 15 minutes or until tender. Toss the garlic and onion with the remaining ingredients except the leaves and mix well. Double-check the salt and pepper, adjusting until it tastes good to you. The mixture should be heavily seasoned. Stuff each leaf with a tablespoon or two of the stuffing and wrap tightly. Pack the rolls into a pot with a steamer insert, and cook for 30 minutes. If you have a sous vide cooker, I like to vacuum-seal these and cook at 165°F (75°C) for 4 hours, which makes for easy storage and transportation. Cut the chilled rolls into 1-inch (2.5 cm) rounds and serve as a snack or appetizer. Because these are highly seasoned, they're meant to be eaten on their own or with seasoned yogurt.

Roulades Verts (Green Rolls)

Makes about 12 larger rolls for a side dish, or up to 24 appetizer-sized rolls, depending on the size of your leaves

This is one of the hardest-working recipes in this book. Take some large edible leaves, whatever you can find, roll them up stuffed with seasoned greens mixed with a little binder, and cook. They're great hot or cold, and love to be made ahead—a fun, interactive way to switch up how you get your plant matter.

I like Roulades Verts best browned in butter or oil after steaming, which creates a slightly crisp outer layer. You can also brush them with beaten egg white after steaming and cooling, dip the brushed side in crushed nuts or seeds, and then brown them in fat, crust-side down. I eat them for a snack, and with meals as a vegetable option. These are meant to be a mild side dish, but sometimes I'll add crushed seeds, fresh herbs, chopped and cooked onions or mushrooms, or serve them with a meal that has a dipping sauce alongside, like Goddess Herb Dressing (page 43).

The best part is that there are all kinds of leaves to use. Grape leaves are a well-known wrapper, but leaves from cup-plant (*Silphium perfoliatum*), sunflower (*Helianthus* spp.), hops (*Humulus lupulus*), mallow (*Malva* spp.), horseradish, cow parsnip (*Heracleum maximum*), and dock (*Rumex* spp.) will be more tender, and come in different shades of green after cooking.

12 large leaves, such as cow parsnip, collards, chard, grape, sunflower, squash, or large mallow, for stuffing
2 packed cups (455 g) blanched and shocked wild greens
1 bunch (55 g) scallions
¼ cup (30 g) fine flour, preferably an interesting type such as wild rice or buckwheat
Kosher salt, to taste
A few scrapes of fresh nutmeg (optional)
1 large egg white, beaten with a splash of water

Bring a pot of salted water to a boil. Blanch the large leaves until just tender, then refresh them in cold water and remove to a towel to dry, removing any stem and leaving them spread open to making stuffing easier. Finely chop the blanched greens and the scallions separately, then combine with the fine flour. Taste the mixture, adjust the seasonings as needed (if you plan to serve them cool, season them a bit more heavily, as chilling mutes flavors). Put a leaf underside-up and brush with egg white, then wrap 4- to 5-tablespoon portions of the greens mixture (depending on the size of your leaves, you can make them larger or smaller) tightly in the leaves to make long, cigar-shaped packages. If your leaves are large, you may want to cut them in half to get two portions from some of them. Steam the packages for 20 minutes. The roulades can be made a day or two ahead of time, and reheated. For small servings, I may cut them into rounds and brown the cut-sides in a pan. Serve lemon wedges or a sauce alongside the roulades.

Across, Stuffed leaves are more than grape rolls. *From bottom to top:* grape, sunflower, cow parsnip, and cup-plant leaf rolls.

Campion

Historically, bladder campion (*Silene vulgaris*) seems to have been widely collected and celebrated as an edible in the Mediterranean. In Spain it's still known as collejas, and people who pick it are known as collejeros. In Italy it might be called sculpit or stridolo; in Crete, strouthoukia. I've yet to find any true bladder campion (though it does grow in the US), but I've eaten plenty of white campion (*S. latifolia*), which isn't as highly regarded as its cousin. The young leaves of white campion taste okay to me, but just okay. My favorite part of this plant is its flowers—puffed like the sleeves of a Victorian dress, they're beautiful, novel-looking flowers with a great shelf life that are also good to eat, a little sweet when young and tender.

Gazpacho Vuido

Serves 2 as an entrée, or 4 as an appetizer

A Spanish dish whose name loosely translates to "widow's soup," this is a fascinating example of a traditional dish based on wild harvested plants. The husband's absence seems to have been a common description for meatless dishes prepared in times of famine or when food was scarce, especially in Spain and Italy. Gastro-linguistic patriarchy aside, what I found most interesting was that the soup specifically calls for bladder campion greens (see the "Campion" sidebar)—an obscure edible even among knowledgeable foragers, but one that's well documented in Mediterranean ethnobotanical literature. Similar to other traditional soups made exclusively from plants, there's a starch element that gives weight to what might otherwise have been—literally and unsatisfyingly—a bowl of plants and water. In this case, the starch is a combo of starchy tubers (potato or sunchoke) and Torta Gazpacho (literally "soup bread"), a sort of dry cracker made with a touch of La Mancha saffron that gives the dough delicate yellow streaks. After warming in the soup, the dried crackers eat a bit like thick noodles.

1 recipe Torta Gazpacho (follows)
4 ounces (115 g) fresh wild greens,
  washed and dried
½ cup (14 g) green garlic, or 1 tablespoon
  sliced garlic cloves
8 ounces (225 g) sunchoke or potato,
  peeled and diced into medium-sized
  (¾-inch / 2 cm) cubes
2 tablespoons cooking oil or lard
5 cups (1.25 L) meat stock or water
Kosher salt and fresh-ground black pepper,
  to taste
Extra-virgin olive oil, or another flavorful oil,
  for serving
Fresh lemon wedge, for serving

Preferably the day before you make the soup, make the flatbread (recipe follows). The recipe will make enough dough for twice the amount of soup, since it might take a few tries to get the cooking process down in the cast-iron pan or on a griddle.

For the soup, coarsely chop the greens in a crosshatch pattern to ensure there are no long pieces of stem, then reserve. In a small saucepot or Dutch oven, sweat the green garlic and the sunchokes or potatoes in the oil for 4 to 5 minutes, season with salt and stir occasionally. Add the stock and greens, bring the mixture to a simmer, cover, and cook for 20 to 30 minutes, until the sunchokes are tender but not falling apart. Check the seasoning for salt and pepper and adjust as needed, then break a handful of flatbread sheets into pieces, add to the soup, stir to combine, and cook for a few minutes more until the pieces of bread are just tender. Serve drizzled generously with the oil and fresh lemon wedges at the table. Recipe tester Tim Vezino suggests serving extra crackers on the side for guests to add themselves.

Torta Gazpacho

Serves 2 to 4

Think of this as a tiny cracker recipe. If you want to make this in a stand mixer, double or triple the amounts; otherwise there might not be enough mass to make the dough hook catch. It will make double what you need for the soup above, but the crackers are also great on a cheese plate, baked with tomato salsa like chilaquiles, or made into a plate of nachos, as long as they're rolled thin and completely dried.

¼ cup (60 ml) water
½ teaspoon salt
Pinch of saffron threads (optional, but traditional, and adds a special flavor)
1 tablespoon melted lard or oil
Roughly ¾ cup (90 g) high-quality flour, preferably freshly ground, and made from a blend of interesting flours; equal parts spelt flour and all-purpose flour is fine, too

Heat the water, salt, saffron, and lard until hot, remove from the heat, and steep for 15 to 30 minutes, stirring it once or twice while it cools. Put the flour in a medium mixing bowl. Add the liquid and knead until a stiff dough comes together, adding more water a teaspoon at a time if needed. Form the dough into a ball, wrap in cling film, and refrigerate for 15 minutes.

To cook the flatbread, cut the dough ball into four pieces, and roll out each piece into a thin sheet, as you would pasta. (One recipe tester preferred the second thinnest setting on a pasta roller.) Cut each into large squares, roughly the size of a palm, and reserve.

To cook the dough, heat a cast-iron skillet, or other flat grill without any oil. Lay a square of dough on the hot surface and cook until the underside has a few attractive blackened spots from the pan. Cook each square well to get good color and lightly charred spots on both sides, working in small batches or one at a time, until all the dough has been cooked. Lay the finished flatbreads on a cookie sheet, trying not to overlap them too much, and dry them for 15 minutes in a 250°F (120°C) oven, or until crisp. Cool the torta, then store at room temperature in an airtight container. The torta can be made days in advance.

Minestrella (Tuscan Soup of Many Greens)

Serves 6

In the sheer amount of wild plants it uses, Minestrella is one of the most unique recipes I've uncovered while writing this book. I can't remember where I heard of it first, but what probably caught my eye was a line to the tune of: "A springtime soup from the Lucca province of Tuscany traditionally including anywhere from 15 to 40 (roughly) wild plants, served with corn bread." But from there the trail went cold, and tracking down even a single recipe to adapt involved all of my Italian linguistic power (Google Translate only goes so far), especially with the Mignecci cakes that must accompany the soup. What's clear is that Minestrella is an ancient dish born of hunger and native, edible knowledge—like eating a bowl of history. Here's the basic idea:

When the first young wild plants appeared in spring, people ritually set out to gather as many as they could find: bitter greens, aromatic greens, sweet greens. Every. Green. Possible. From there they'd cook the greens until soft, then soak them in fresh water as a way to calm any bitter, strong flavors. Most modern chefs would consider this practice insane, but it's a great example of native knowledge and nutritive wisdom, hidden in a soup.

The act of identifying and collecting such a vast variety of plants, then cooking and eating the dish, is no less a consumption of our shared human art and culture than learning from an exhibit of artifacts, or witnessing a master's brushstrokes in a landscape painting.

Just like Gazpacho Vuido (page 31), a starch element adds heft to this soup. Minestrella must include beans, specifically the fagiolo giallorino (literally "small yellow bean"). As it's nearly impossible to source the real thing, white tepary beans (*Phaseolus acutifolius*, a wild species from the American Southwest) make a fitting substitute. You can also use your favorite dried, light-colored bean, or a can of cannellini beans. By using different combinations of plants, the possible variations on this soup that you can make are infinite, and no two will be the same.

12 ounces (340 g) fresh wild greens,
  of the greatest variety possible
1 small yellow onion (4 ounces / 115 g)
2 small carrots (4 ounces / 115 g)
1 small rib celery (2 ounces / 55 g)
2 large cloves garlic, chopped
¼ cup (60 ml) olive oil, plus more for serving
4 cups (945 ml) homemade pork, chicken,
  or vegetable stock, or a combination of
  stock and cooking liquid from the beans
1 cup (240 ml) cooking liquid from the
  beans, or stock
10 ounces (285 g) cooked beans, or 3 ounces
  (85 g) dried beans, such as tepary beans,
  chickpeas, or cannellini, divided
Kosher salt, to taste

Serving
Fresh-cracked black pepper (optional)
Fresh-grated Parmesan, such as Parmigiano
  Reggiano (optional)
Mignecci (recipe follows)

Bring a gallon (4 L) of salted water to a boil and blanch the greens for 1 minute, then refresh in cold water. Allow the greens to sit in cool water for a few hours to help calm any strong or bitter flavors. If you are using milder greens, they might not need this soaking.

Remove the greens, squeeze out excess water, chop them medium-fine, and reserve. Put the onion, carrot, celery, and garlic in a food processor or blender, purée into a smooth paste, and reserve.

Heat the oil in a stockpot and cook the vegetable purée for 10 minutes or until it starts to brown around the edges. Add the stock, bean cooking liquid, and ½ cup (70 g) of the beans; heat, then purée with a hand or immersion blender or food mill until smooth.

Add the greens and remaining beans. Season with a good pinch of salt, and cook for 30 to 45 minutes, or until the greens are very tender. Double-check the seasoning, adjust as needed for salt and pepper, and, preferably, chill the soup overnight to let the flavors meld.

Reheat the soup to serve, adjusting the liquid if it's thicker than you like. Ladle 1 cup (240 ml) of soup into each bowl, garnish with plenty of olive oil, fresh-cracked pepper, Parmesan, and one of the Mignecci (recipe follows), cut in half, which is used to scoop up the greens.

Mignecci

Makes about 12 Mignecci

The recipe for this garnish—a sort of unleavened corn cake—was more difficult to translate than the soup itself. The most intriguing part is that the cakes are cooked between two hot irons. To mimic the irons, I used my great-grandmother's krumkake iron, unhinged, which gives the finished cakes the look of doubloons—a sort of currency to go with the treasure chest of greens this recipe is. Since most people don't have krumkake irons, the recipe below calls for two cast-iron skillets. To account for the learning curve most of us will experience when making the Mignecci, the proportions here make more than you need, so don't worry about burning a few.

1½ cups (195 g) fine cornmeal
1½ cups (180 g) all-purpose or
  whole wheat flour
Scant 1½ cups (375 ml) cold water
2 tablespoons lard or olive oil, plus more
  for greasing the pans, as needed
1 teaspoon kosher salt

Mix all the ingredients well and allow to rest for a few hours to allow the cornmeal to hydrate. It will be a loose dough, like a thick batter.

To make the mignecci, clean the bottom of a medium (8- to 10-inch / 20–26 cm) cast-iron skillet; you will be cooking on the bottom of the pan. Invert the skillet on a gas burner or grill, bottom up, having another pan of slightly smaller size heating, as well; this smaller pan should be preheated right-side up, as it will serve as your top press in cooking the dough. Lightly grease the undersides of both pans.

Place roughly ¼ cup (55 g) of the dough on the inverted pan, then set the other pan on top of the batter to press it down. The skillets should be placed bottom-to-bottom, with the dough pressed between them—mimicking cooking between two hot irons or stones. Just as with crepes, the first one or two might not get the correct color since it takes some time for the pans to heat to the proper temperature. The pans should be very hot, slightly smoking, and kicking off enough heat that your instincts should be warning you to be very careful, unless you're a burn-scarred kitchen troll.

Once you get going, the mignecci will cook quickly; you'll need only about 30 seconds to cook and nicely brown each one. It takes some practice. If the thought of cooking with screaming-hot pans intimidates you, just make thin patties and fry them up, like wee pancakes; they'll still taste good after they soften, soaked by the final broth.

Friulian Sautéed Greens (Pistic)

Even more obscure than the Minestrella is Pistic, a dish from Friuli Venezia Giulia in Northern Italy. As with Minestrella, many greens are used, and although the 15 to 40 plants the Minestrella recipes call for sound nearly impossible to me, every reference to Pistic I've seen calls for around 50! The preparation is simple: Just boil the greens in salted water until tender, drain, and sauté with fat and perhaps some garlic. I'd probably serve it with olive oil and lemon, too.

I think the most beautiful part of this "recipe" is that a name for something like this even exists. If I went out, collected every green I could find, simmered them with aromatics, then sautéed them in duck fat until they were rich and delicious, they would still be just a dish of cooked greens. Knowing the dish comes from a specific place, and using its name like an invocation, makes it come alive.

Spring Greens Dumpling

Makes 6 wedges to serve as a side or main course when combined with other vegetables

A very old recipe from times when a household might have had just one pot, and the sort of cooking that evokes ancient stone farmhouses with roaring fires heating a bubbling joint of game. While some meat was cooking in the pot, other ingredients might be bound with flour or meal, seasoned, tied into a bundle, and cooked in the flavorful broth. After the meat was tender, the "dumpling" would be served alongside the meat and broth. Traditionally you'd put this dumpling in a pot to serve with a large cut of meat, but it's just as good cooked without meat, in flavorful mushroom or vegetable broth. Scatter sautéed vegetables over the top after serving the dumpling pieces and broth in bowls to make it more of a complete meal. The dumpling is also good cut into cubes after cooking and chilling, warmed up and served in its broth as a first course, hopefully accompanied by servings of the cut of meat it was cooked with.

6 ounces (170 g) assorted wild greens, finely chopped
2 ounces (55 g) wild onion leaves, ramp leaves, or green onions
1 teaspoon salt
1 cup (120 g) low-gluten flour, such as barley, oat, wild rice, or buckwheat
1 large egg
1 teaspoon baking powder
1 tablespoon water

Serving

Good-tasting oil, such as extra-virgin olive oil, Smude's sunflower, or a nut oil
Freshly grated Parmesan cheese (optional)
Fresh-cracked black pepper

Wash the greens and onion leaves, then dry well. Grasp all of the greens and leaves on a large cutting board and shred them finely with a large knife, then mound the greens back together, rotate 90 degrees, and shred again. Continue to finely chop all of the greens, then combine with the remaining ingredients and allow to rest for a few minutes to let the salt draw moisture from the greens.

In a medium saucepan, bring 6 cups or so of stock to a simmer. Form the dumpling into a ball as well as you can, then wrap it in cheesecloth to help it hold its shape. Use more cheesecloth than you think you'll need, tying it around a wooden spoon or a similar utensil to suspend the dumpling in the cooking liquid. Simmer gently for up to 2 hours, or until tender, then remove the dumpling, unwrap it, slice it into wedges, and serve with the broth it cooked in, topping each bowl with a drizzle of good-tasting oil. Pass the Parmesan and pepper at the table.

Variations

Four cups of finely minced greens such as parsley, spinach, and kale can be substituted for the wild greens. You can make your own blend of greens using whatever's available to you.

Tian of Wild Greens

Serves 4 as a side dish

A study in minimalism adapted from the great Richard Olney, and one of the many variations you can make with the chiffonade technique (see Simple Chiffonade of Greens on page 17). Finely shaved and diced greens cook into a thin cake with a delicate, crisp top that cries out to be paired with fried eggs on a plate, roast chicken, sautéed mushrooms—or all by itself with a squeeze of lemon. Many leafy greens will work, but they should be greens that hold a good amount of water; greens like kale or collards are too dry and will turn into a pile of chips that won't stick together. A 10-inch (26 cm) cast-iron skillet is great, but any baking dish will work, provided you have enough greens to fill a pan to overflowing. The tian is great for lunch, dinner, or breakfast, day-old, room temperature, cool, or piping hot straight from the oven. It's a useful technique to add to your repertoire.

1 pound (455 g) mixed wild greens, preferably spinach or chard
2½ tablespoons cooking oil, divided
3 tablespoons bread crumbs
Kosher salt, to taste
Fresh-ground black pepper
A few scrapes of fresh nutmeg (optional)

Wash and dry the greens well. Preheat the oven to 450°F (230°C). Grasp a handful of greens and squeeze it into a ball, use a large knife to shave (chiffonade) the greens, then rotate each handful 90 degrees and shave again to make tiny squares. Pour half the oil in a 10-inch cast-iron skillet or similar pan. Pack the greens down, sprinkling the crumbs evenly over the top. The pan should be nearly overflowing with greens. Season the top very lightly with salt, pepper, and nutmeg—the greens lose a lot of mass here, so be careful not to overseason them. Drizzle the remaining oil over the top in a crisscross pattern and bake for 10 minutes at 450°F, then turn the heat down and bake for another 40 minutes at 375°F (190°C).

The tian is a sort of rustic French casserole of greens with a crisp dusting of bread crumbs.

Lambsquarters and Tender Greens

The recipes here are loosely based around greens that are young, tender, or mild-flavored. This could be tender young leaves you might put in a salad, or greens that cook up soft and mild tasting such as lambsquarters or mallow.

DIY Gomae

Serves 2

This is the chilled salad of cooked greens (typically spinach) that you'll find at just about any sushi restaurant. Spinach or lambsquarters are fine, but violets, Malabar spinach, or mallow leaves, with their gentle slipperiness, are an experience, and I recommend them. The first time I had gomae, I noticed the pairing of sesame oil and its seeds, so my first instinct was to switch things up by using different nuts and seeds, along with their respective oils, and maple syrup instead of white sugar. Green-orange pumpkinseed oil with a paste of pumpkin-seeds is particularly good, as are hickory nuts, sunflower seeds, and black walnuts, along with their oils. Come up with your own blend using different nuts or seeds and their respective oils, and your favorite greens.

8 ounces (225 g) fresh greens, with minimal amounts of stem
3 tablespoons nuts or seeds
1 tablespoon soy sauce or equivalent
1 tablespoon oil from the same nuts or seeds
1 tablespoon maple syrup

Blanch the greens in boiling salted water until they're tender and taste good to you, then shock in cold water and squeeze dry. Toast the nuts, then grind to a paste in a mortar and pestle, and stir in the remaining ingredients. Toss well with the greens, double-check the seasoning, adjust as you see fit for salt and sweetness, and serve, cool or chilled, with chopsticks.

Dotty's Wild Green Salad

Imagine you walk outside and make a trip around the yard, stopping here and there to clip different young greens, some sweet, some tender, choosing each leaf, stem, or flower carefully, understanding how their textures and character will dance on a plate and surprise whoever eats it with the variety of each bite. Soft, tender, or bitter greens are punctuated by intense, refreshing blasts of herbs like basil, mint, cilantro, sweet bronze fennel fronds, or tangy wood sorrel. The walk around the yard becomes a journey that whoever eats it gets to travel in each bite.

A simple salad made of pure wild greens or a combination of wild and cultivated, in my mind, is one of the highest forms the craft of foraging can take: a pinnacle of the type of intuitive, native knowledge most people will never glimpse in their life. You don't need a recipe, but here are a few tips I think are important:

- Vinegar that's slightly sweet helps cut through the earthy heartiness of salads like this. White balsamic and dark balsamic vinegars are my favorites, but quality vinegar or lemon juice seasoned with a touch of maple syrup or sugar works fine, too.
- Clusters of lambsquarters work hard in this. Sometimes I include up to 50 percent of them by volume, since they're so mild and pleasant to eat.
- One of the simplest dressings is also the greatest: a high-quality vinegar or other acid, and oil, in separate bottles on the table. I never use bottled commercial dressing.
- Add dressings judiciously. We're eating greens here, not dressing.

- Play with texture, and imagine what people will taste as they eat. Whole small leaves can be good, as can small clusters of leaves, as well as crisp things like small shoots or other parts of plants you like. A knife-and-fork salad can be fun.
- Adding thinly shaved vegetables for color and texture is good; try colorful carrots and lavender radishes (purple) or watermelon radishes (bright pink inside).
- Flowers are a crowning achievement—there isn't a more perfect place to show them off. See a list of my favorite edible flowers on page 195.

Freshly picked young greens, the largest variety you can find
Leaves of fresh herbs, to taste, especially basil, shiso, or cilantro, left whole if small or torn if large
Edible flowers, such as nasturtiums, bellflower, monarda, hosta, et cetera
Best-tasting oil available, especially extra-virgin olive, Smude's sunflower, pumpkinseed, or another nut or seed oil
Vinegar, especially a slightly sweet kind such as white or regular balsamic, or lemon juice
Kosher salt and fresh-ground black pepper, to taste

Refresh the greens in cold water and leave for 15 minutes until they perk up. Spin the greens completely dry, or wrap gently in towels. To serve, put the greens, herbs, and flowers in a salad bowl, seasoning lightly with the oil and vinegar or lemon juice (or other dressing), salt, and pepper to taste. Try to underseason the greens to avoid overwhelming them, and taste as you go. Serve on cool plates, garnishing with extra flowers and herbs as you like.

Tree Food

We get plenty of food from trees, including nuts and fruits, but there's something special about edible leaves and other tender parts. This idea was completely new to me—and felt like eating elf food. Haw (*Crataegus* spp.) shoots are nice and tender, if small. Some of my friends really enjoy young maple blossoms, which I have yet to try. My favorites, though, are Siberian elm (*Ulmus pumila*) samaras and basswood (*Tilia americana*) leaves, which bear fruit so heavily during their short season that if the trees were organized in the right way, I'd think someone could market them commercially as a new hyper-seasonal crop. At the right point, both samaras and basswood leaves are tender and delicious with a sweet green taste, but the best by far are young clusters of barely opened basswood leaves that taste like tender, ruffled layers of sweet peas.

Young, barely opened basswood leaves are one of the finest treats of spring.

Tree Salad

This is a salad made with mostly tree-food products of early spring. Basswood leaves, especially the almost translucent young ones, are delicate, so I like to serve this salad with the dressing underneath, a trick I borrowed from my friend Chef Wyatt Evans when he was running his restaurant Heirloom in St. Paul. This is a delicious salad, yes, but it's more than that, too: It's an idea for you, a suggestion about consuming basswood leaves and samaras, as both, harvested in their prime, are restaurant-quality items any chef would kill to have. A scattering of toasted nuts underlines the tree-food theme. I like to use a blend of 75 percent basswood leaves to 25 percent other greens for variety—whatever I have on hand, but especially young sprouts or leaves like parsley, chickweed, ground elder, or sorrel.

Young, tender, good-tasting basswood
  leaves and elm samaras
Other tender greens (optional) to fill out
  the salad
Dressing of your choice, especially
  Goddess Herb Dressing (recipe follows),
  a cider vinaigrette, or simply your best oil
  and vinegar
Lightly toasted nuts (a few), for serving
Spring flowers, such as lilac or mustard,
  for serving

How I assemble this depends on the dressing I want to use. A sour cream dressing (such as Goddess Herb) is thick enough to be spread on the plate, showing off the individual edible components and making you dress the salad as you eat, but simply tossing with oil and vinegar or a vinaigrette works, too. Garnish with nuts, flowers, and more samaras just before serving.

Goddess Herb Dressing

Makes about 2 cups (480 ml)

If you look in my fridge, there's probably a jar of this dressing in there right now. This is one of my favorite dressings for salads, but you'll find yourself spooning it on everything from grilled meat and fish to soups, stews, and vegetables. Tarragon makes a great Goddess, but I typically make this with whatever herb is growing at the moment. The combinations you can make here with different tender-textured herbs are infinite, and each one lends a slightly different taste. As a shortcut, or if I'm avoiding raw egg, there's nothing wrong with substituting 1 cup (220 g) of good, thick mayo for the egg and oil. For a smaller batch, cut all the ingredients in half and use one egg yolk.

½ cup (110 g) sour cream
½ cup (25 g) sliced chives

1 cup (60 g) loosely packed flavorful herbs, such as tarragon, basil, cilantro (especially green seeds), lemon balm, et cetera
1 cup (60 g) loosely packed mild herbs, such as Italian parsley, chervil, wood sorrel, et cetera
¼ teaspoon kosher salt
¼ teaspoon fresh-ground black pepper
½ cup (135 ml) fresh lemon juice
1 large egg
½ cup (135 ml) extra-virgin olive oil
½ cup (135 ml) mild cooking oil

Combine all ingredients except the oils in a blender. Mix the oils. Purée, drizzling in the oil until thick. Transfer the dressing to a container and refrigerate. The sauce should be neon green and vibrant. It's best used within a few days, but will keep a decent flavor for a while longer.

Bakoula

Serves 4–6 as an appetizer

One of the best-known recipes for wild plants in Morocco and northern Africa, bakoula (also spelled *bqula* and *baqoula*) is a dish of blanched or boiled greens cooked with garlic, a pinch of spices, olives, and preserved lemon. Typically mallow is used, often in combination with purslane, but any naturally tender, leafy green such as garlic mustard, violets, or just spinach will be fine. It's great hot or made ahead of time and served as a cooked salad.

Generous 1 pound (455 g) fresh mixed greens, preferably wild including some purslane and mallow or violets
1 large clove garlic
3 tablespoons extra-virgin olive oil
Pinch of sweet paprika
Pinch of fresh-ground cumin, or to taste
Kosher salt, to taste
2 ounces (55 g) or more of your favorite olives (I like Castelvetrano or black Moroccan oil-cured olives), with or without pits, divided
2 teaspoons Fermented Lemon Confit, finely diced or sliced (recipe follows)

Blanch the greens until wilted, then chill in cold water, squeeze dry as well as you can, and reserve; you should have roughly 2 packed cups (480 ml). Meanwhile, sweat the garlic in the oil until golden, add the paprika and cumin, stir, then add the greens, season with salt, stir to heat through, and cook gently until they're tender and taste good to you. Add half of the olives, stir, then transfer to a serving bowl. Garnish with the remaining olives and preserved lemon.

Fermented Lemon Confit

Makes 1 pint (480 ml) after salting and trimming

12 ounces (340 g) organic lemons
  (roughly 3 large lemons)
¼ ounce (7 g) kosher salt (roughly
  1 teaspoon)

Quarter the lemons, then toss with the salt and vacuum-seal (you could also ferment them in brine). Ferment the lemons for up to 2 weeks, opening the bag occasionally to burp it and release carbon dioxide, and reseal. When you're pleased with the fermentation (after 1 to 2 weeks), mash the lemons up in the bag to release their juice, strain out the juice and reserve for another purpose, and reseal the lemons. To confit the lemons, cook sous vide in a water bath at 165°F (75°C) for 2 hours, or until tender. If you don't have a sous vide cooker, you can simmer the vacuum bag in hot water for an hour, or in a slow cooker. After cooking, chill the lemons, then cut off the white pith, leaving only the tender rind. Cut the rind into tiny cubes and add to soups and stews, or anywhere you'd use pre-served lemons.

Tahini Sauce for Wilted Greens

Makes 1 cup (240 ml)

Here's another great mallow dish you might be served in the Middle East. The tahini sauce, in all its nutty, lemony glory, will make any green you choose taste new and delicious. The sauce makes enough for a few servings. Simply blanch or steam some greens until tender, then drain well and serve with the sauce on the side. *Sauce* is a bit of a misnomer here, as I like my tahini thick like whipped cream. You can thin it to be pourable, if you prefer.

1 large clove garlic (or 2 smaller cloves)
¼ cup (60 ml) lemon juice
½ teaspoon salt
¼ teaspoon cumin
½ cup (130 g) tahini
¼ cup (60 ml) cold water
2 tablespoons olive oil

Chop the garlic and toss with the lemon and salt, then allow to sit for 15 minutes to halt any fermentation. Transfer the mixture to a food processor, then add the cumin, tahini, and water; purée until very smooth, drizzle in the oil at the end, which will incorporate some oil into the mix and make it nice and fluffy. This basic sauce will last in the fridge for a week. Stir well or bring to room temperature to restore its original consistency.

Sochan

Sochan (*Rudbeckia laciniata*, also known as cutleaf coneflower) is the most abundant, delicious, leafy green that no one's talking about. Sochan is a cousin to the common, and also edible, black-eyed susan (*R. hirta*). Sam Thayer has a great account of sochan in his third book, *Incredible Wild Edibles*. It's traditionally harvested by a number of Indigenous North Americans, the best known being the Cherokee. I've also heard of sochan being sold in farmers markets in the South. It's a giving plant, allowing for multiple harvests during the growing season, my favorite being the large basal leaves that come in the fall. The flavor is special, and depending on the age, some people will want to blanch it to tame the celery-esque, aster flavor. For a special Cherokee-inspired dish, see Corn and Bean Terrine (page 230).

Sochan (*Rudbeckia laciniata*) in bloom, showing its delicious late-season leaves. At this stage the flavor is much stronger than in the spring.

Sochan Crudité

When sochan first comes up, the shoots are great raw—crisp and clean, and very different from the stronger flavor they develop as the plant ages. For the brief moment the greens are in the shoot stage, it's fun to make an appetizer out of them. Gather shoots tall enough to fit in a water glass or something similar, wash and dry them, and stand them upright in the glass. Serve the greens with a shallow bowl of your favorite dipping oil—Smude's sunflower oil and acorn oil from Forager's Harvest are two of my favorites. Gently dip the crisp leaves into the oil, with a pinch of crunchy salt on the side.

Sochan with Beans and Hominy

Serves 2–4

Inspired by Cherokee author Nancy Plemmons, who said the most essential ingredients of Cherokee cuisine were bean and cornmeal dumplings, fatback, and sochan. Here, those ingredients are all cooked together, with a good amount of lard or drippings.

8 ounces (225 g) sochan
¼ cup (70 g) cooked beans (preferably cooked from dried)
¼ cup (70 g) cooked hominy (preferably cooked from dried)
3 tablespoons bacon drippings, animal fat, or equivalent
Kosher salt and fresh-ground black pepper, to taste

Cook the sochan in simmering salted water until it's just tender and tastes good to you. Remove, drain, and cool, then chop it roughly so it can fit on a spoon and sweat with the beans, hominy, and drippings. Double-check the seasoning, adjust as needed, and serve.

Breathing life into a millennia-old tradition, Forager's Harvest cold-pressed hickory nut oil is made from hand-collected wild nuts, and is a luxury. Order in advance, as it sells out rapidly every year. It's sold under the WildWoods Orchard label.

Wood Nettle Versus Stinging Nettle

I love nettles, and I loved them even more when I learned there are multiple types. Most people know *Urtica dioica*, the common stinging nettle, but where I live there's also wood nettle or *Laportea canadensis*. Both types are delicious, but wood nettle doesn't get nearly the attention it deserves for being a great food plant, and is particularly delicious in its shoot form. Wood nettle has a milder flavor than stinging nettles, too, which have a subtle but noticeable oceanic flavor, especially when puréed. Both would love to be on your dinner plate, spread with soft butter.

Wood nettle (*Laportea canadensis*)

My Favorite Stinging Nettle Soup

Serves 4–6

This is the nettle soup I designed for restaurant service. It's similar to most nettle soups you'll see, but I add a few chopped nettles for texture after the soup is puréed to remind people of what they're eating. I also want to taste nettles more than anything, so I use rice to thicken the soup rather than potato. Young nettles will be the best; older ones may need to be cooked a bit longer to make them tender.

8 ounces (225 g) young stinging nettles
  or nettle tops
1 rib celery
1 small yellow onion
1 small leek or a few small shallots
3 tablespoons unsalted butter
¼ cup (50 g) long-grain rice
¼ cup (60 ml) dry white wine
4 cups (945 ml) chicken stock,
  preferably homemade
½ cup (135 ml) heavy cream
Kosher salt, to taste
White pepper, to taste (optional)

Serving (optional)
Chopped hard-boiled eggs, or hard-boiled
  quail eggs
Dollops of sour cream loosened with cream
Fresh dill

Bring a gallon of lightly salted water to a boil. Blanch the nettles for a few seconds, just to wilt them, then shock in cold water, squeeze dry, and chop roughly; you should have a generous cup. Remove a third of the nettles and set aside. Dice the celery, onion, and leek (you want a total of about 8 ounces / 225 g). Sweat the vegetables in the butter without coloring them, add the rice and cook for a

minute more, then add the wine and simmer until reduced by half. Add the chicken stock and bring the mixture back to a simmer, then cover and cook on medium-low until the rice is tender, about 15 to 20 minutes. Pour the soup into a blender, working in batches if needed (or use an immersion blender), and purée the soup with two-thirds of the cooked nettles until smooth. Transfer the soup to a metal pot set in a sink of cold water and stir to cool it and preserve the color if you're not serving immediately. Add the rest of the nettles to the soup as a garnish. Finally, whisk in the cream. Double-check the seasoning for salt and pepper, then transfer to a container and refrigerate until needed. I like to serve it with sour cream, chopped hard-boiled egg, and fresh dill.

Italian Nettle Soup (Zuppa di Ortiche)

Serves 4–6

Just as with Scandinavian nettle soups that might call for chopped hard-boiled eggs or fresh dill, look at a bunch of different Italian nettle soup recipes and you'll start to see some similarities. Most notable to me is that most Italian nettle soups seem to contain tomato (generally chopped) and pasta or rice. Cooked with tomatoes and stock, any greens will taste great, and it's a refreshing break from creamed, puréed soups. Pass the olive oil, crusty bread, black pepper, and Parmesan at the table.

1 tablespoon thinly sliced garlic
¼ cup (60 ml) olive oil or lard
3 ounces (85 g) diced leek (1 small leek)
1 small onion, diced small to yield about
  4 ounces (115 g)
Pinch of dried chili or red pepper flakes
1 can (15.5 ounces / 425 g) chopped
  peeled tomatoes
12 ounces (340 g) fresh nettles, or about
  8 ounces (225 ml) blanched or frozen nettles
Kosher salt and fresh-ground black pepper,
  to taste
6 cups (1.5 L) meat stock, such as chicken

Serving
1½ cups (300 g) cooked pasta or rice
Extra-virgin olive oil, lemon wedges, and
  grated high-quality Parmesan

Sweat the garlic in the oil over low heat until just light brown but not burned. Add the leeks and onion and cook for a few minutes more, until translucent. Add the chili, tomatoes, nettles, ½ teaspoon of salt, and the stock, then bring to a simmer and cook for 5 to 10 minutes. Turn off the heat and pulse the mixture with a hand blender until almost smooth. Cook the soup, covered, for another 15 to 20 minutes, or until the greens are tender. Add the pasta, taste and correct the seasoning for salt and pepper as needed, then serve with a generous pour of good olive oil, lemon, and a sprinkling of Parmesan. A spoonful of walnut pesto scented with lemon zest makes a nice garnish.

Aztec-Inspired Amaranth Stew

Serves 2–4

Inspired by Mesoamerica, this is all about using the two parts of amaranth—its leafy greens and its seeds—both long appreciated by the Aztecs and Mesoamericans who cultivated it as a food plant. Amaranth is a strange grain. As a flour, it has a strong flavor some people don't care for. As a grain, the flavor is mild and pleasant, but it will never get fluffy and will always have a porridge-like consistency. Just like okra, amaranth's gentle silkiness is great in soup as a non-flour thickener, and even better when balanced with assertive partners like tomato, chilies, cilantro, and cumin. An herby corn salsa or a relish made of fermented sweet corn makes a nice garnish for variation. Multiple recipe testers recommended doubling the batch to have leftovers.

- 1 pound (455 g) diced venison shoulder or other fatty stew meat
- 1 teaspoon salt, plus more to taste
- ¼ teaspoon fresh-ground black pepper
- 1 teaspoon fresh-ground cumin seed
- 2 ounces (55 g) dried hominy or 5 ounces (140 g) cooked
- 1 large guajillo chili or 1 tablespoon chili powder
- 1 can (14 ounces / 400 g) whole peeled tomatoes, puréed and strained, or 1¼ cups (310 ml) tomato sauce
- 3 tablespoons oil or lard
- 1 small yellow onion
- 1 small serrano pepper (or similar), seeded and chopped (optional)
- 1 tablespoon chopped garlic
- 4 ounces (115 g) red bell pepper, in 1-inch (2.5 cm) dice
- ¼ cup (60 ml) dry white wine
- 4 cups (945 ml) meat stock
- ⅓ cup (65 g) amaranth seeds
- Chopped fresh cilantro, to taste
- 2 cups (60 g) sliced amaranth leaves

Season the meat with the salt, pepper, and cumin, and allow to rest, uncovered, in the fridge. Leave it overnight, if possible, or at least for a few hours to dry out and help browning. If you're using dried hominy, cover it with boiling water and let it rest overnight, as well, or at least for a few hours.

Toast the guajillo chili lightly, allow to cool, then break it open and discard the seeds. Crumble the chili into the tomatoes, then purée in a blender.

Preheat the oven to 250°F (120°C). In a Dutch oven (or other oven-safe pot), heat the oil and brown the meat well, then add the onion, serrano pepper, garlic, and bell pepper. Sweat for a few minutes. Deglaze the pan with the wine, then add the stock, hominy, tomato-chili purée, and amaranth seeds. Bring to a simmer, then cover the pot and transfer to the oven for 1 hour, or until the meat is tender. Finally, remove the stew from the oven, add the cilantro and sliced amaranth leaves, and simmer a few minutes more until the leaves are tender, adding a little extra stock or water if it threatens to get too thick. Finally, taste and correct the seasoning, and serve.

Molohkia: A Mediterranean Mallow Soup

Serves 4–6

Plants in the mallow family (Malvaceae) are widely used in the Mediterranean, where they thrive in sandy, rocky soil. Arguably the best-known recipe is Molohkia (also spelled *mloukhiya*, *molohiya*, and *mulukhiyah*), a sort of mallow stew that sometimes includes chicken. Molohkia is rumored to be Egyptian in origin, but has been adopted by plenty of cultures in the Levant. The traditional mallow used is *Corchorus olitorius* or jute mallow—a cousin to common mallow in the United States—but I've made it with both violets and mallow and thought both were good. Whichever mallow you use, the finished product will have a velvety texture a bit like okra (the plants are relatives) after cooking. Add some shredded, cooked chicken for a more substantial, but still traditional, version.

Garlic oil
2–3 large cloves garlic, thinly sliced
¼ cup (70 ml) olive oil

Soup
8 ounces (225 g) fresh violet or common mallow greens
¼ cup (70 ml) olive oil
6 ounces (170 g) yellow onion, diced small
3 tablespoons wild rice (for thickening the soup)
5 cups (1.25 L) good meat or vegetable stock, preferably homemade
Good pinch baharat or seven-spice seasoning, or to taste (optional; pumpkin pie spice mixed 50/50 with cumin is a decent substitute)
1 ounce (28 g) cilantro
Kosher salt and fresh-ground black pepper, to taste
1 medium tomato, diced small (optional)
Lemon juice or sherry vinegar, to taste
Freshly cooked wild rice, to taste (about 2 cups / 400 g)

To make the garlic oil, sweat the garlic slices in the oil on low until lightly browned and aromatic, then turn the heat off and cool—it should brown lightly, but be careful not to burn it. Reserve.

To make the soup, blanch and shock the greens, or freeze until wilted and thaw, then chop coarse. Heat the oil in a stockpot and add the onion and raw wild rice. Cook for 5 minutes to sweat the onion, season with salt and pepper then add the stock; bring to a gentle simmer and cook covered on low for 20 minutes, or until the rice is tender. Add the chopped greens, baharat, and cilantro, and cook for a minute or two, then use an immersion blender or transfer to a blender and purée carefully, working in batches if needed, starting on low power and moving up to high, blending the soup until very smooth. Double-check the seasoning and correct as needed.

Mix the tomato with the lemon juice and season with a pinch of salt and pepper. Ladle the hot soup over, or on the side of, portions of hot wild rice. Finally, spoon some of the garlic slices and oil over each serving, along with a spoonful of tomato, and serve.

Erbazzone

Serves 6–8 as a lunch or entrée

A famous Italian double-crusted pie of greens flavored with a little Parmesan cheese, and bacon or pancetta, if you like. Most recipes call for Swiss chard now, which makes me think the original greens used may have been wild beet greens. I like to use a blend of cooked greens and whatever's available fresh, and no two versions I've made have been the same. You can pack the crust into a pie dish and cut wedges, or make it into a square (my personal favorite). It travels very well and holds heat like a dream—great for picnics. Some of the recipe testers recommended making it into hand pies for more portable portions.

Pastry crust

8 ounces (225 g) unsalted butter, chilled
2 cups (240 g) flour (I like to use a blend of whole wheat and pastry flour, but you could use all-purpose if you like)
½ teaspoon kosher salt
Cold water, as needed to bring the dough together

Filling

2 ounces (55 g) slab or thick-cut bacon, in ¼-inch (6 mm) dice
3 ounces (85 g) green onions or ramp leaves, in ½-inch (1.25 cm) slices
1½ pounds (680 g) mixed wild greens, washed and dried
Kosher salt, to taste
½ cup (50 g) grated Pecorino Romano cheese
3 egg yolks
¼ teaspoon baharat spice mix, pumpkin pie spice, ground nutmeg, or equivalent
1 beaten egg, for brushing the top

To make the pastry crust, cut the butter into small pieces, then mix with the flour and salt using a pastry blender, knives, or your hands until the mixture looks like coarse meal. Gradually add water, little by little, just until the dough can be gathered into a ball. Separate the dough into two equal pieces, flatten into disks, wrap in plastic, and refrigerate to hydrate the flour until the disks become firm (at least an hour, or overnight). The dough can be made days ahead of time and kept refrigerated.

To make the filling, sweat the bacon on medium heat until the fat renders, about 5 minutes; the bacon should be tender, but not crisp or hard. Add the onions to the pan and cook for a minute or two. Meanwhile, coarsely chop the greens, add to the pan with the bacon, season with salt and cover to help steam the greens, and cook, stirring occasionally, adding a tablespoon or two of water if the pan threatens to dry out. Cook the greens until they're tender and taste good to you (about 10 minutes for me), then transfer to a mixing bowl and cool for a few minutes. Press on the greens with a towel to remove any remaining liquid, cool for a few minutes more, then mix in the cheese and egg yolks, along with the spices. Double-check the seasoning for salt and adjust until it tastes good to you.

Meanwhile, roll out the bottom pastry crust and use it to line a pie pan—or alternatively, roll out the dough into a square about 10 to 11 inches (26–28 cm) on a side. Preheat the oven to 400°F (200°C). Pack the greens mixture into the crust, pressing down to remove air, then roll out the top crust, lay it over the top, crimp the edges, brush with beaten egg, cut a few slices in the top to let air escape, and bake for 15 minutes. Then turn down the heat to 350°F (180°C) and bake for about 30 minutes more, or until the top is nicely browned and attractive. Cool for a few minutes before slicing into individual servings. The Erbazzone holds heat well, travels like a dream, and is good at room temperature, too.

Beets with Their Stems and Leaves

For years I avoided buying beets with their attached greens, since I thought the stems were too tough, and if for some reason I had to buy them with their leaves attached, I'd probably instruct the cooks to toss them after they stripped the leaves, as I knew after cooking they'd never amount to much. I was wrong, and wasteful. During the summer, beets can be mostly stem, often vastly so. The plant is related to amaranth, and the leaves of both are interchangeable for most recipes. The tricky part is that beet roots, stems, and leaves all have different cooking times ranging from long to short, respectively. Here's the best way I know to cook beets—stems, leaves, and all.

Remove the leaves and stems from a few beets and wash everything well. Wrap each beet tightly in foil, then put in a dish and bake at 325°F (160°C) until just barely tender when pierced, about 1 hour depending on your oven and the size of the beets (small beets will cook much faster). Cool the beets in cold water to make peeling easy; cut each peeled beet in half, then into wedges, depending on their size.

Remove the leaves from the stem. Cut the stems on the diagonal into ½-inch (1.25 cm) pieces, then blanch them in boiling water for a minute or two until they're tender and taste good to you (also a good technique for chard, celery, and cardoon stems). Cut or tear the leaves into 1-inch (2.5 cm) pieces. Heat a good knob of butter in a wide pan, then add the beet wedges and warm them through on medium-low. Add the stems and cook for a minute more. When the beets are hot, add the leaves, season to taste with salt and pepper, then cover the pan just to wilt the leaves with the steam. Remove the lid, check the seasoning and adjust, toss a few times, then finish with a dash of red wine vinegar to taste, and serve.

Creamed Greens with Spinach and Jalapeño

Serves 2–4

This dish was inspired by Chef Alex Robert's casual restaurant, Brasa, which serves a simple creamed spinach my girlfriend and I always order. Creamed greens tend to really turn me off if they're thick, gooey, and heavy with cream. *These are not those greens.* They're not even as much creamed greens as they are stewed greens with a splash of cream. Served in a cup or ramekin, they're a perfect complement alongside something starchy to soak up the pan juices, such as rice, a slice of crusty bread, or a piece of fried chicken.

Jalapeños can vary in heat, so add them to taste or substitute a tiny knife-tip of cayenne. You want greens that lose volume and get soft and tender here—think spinach, violets, waterleaf, lambsquarters, chard, or mustards, rather than heavier greens like kale or collards.

1 pound (455 g) tender young greens, especially lambsquarters, violets, garlic mustard, spinach, or chard
¼ cup (60 ml) finely diced white onion
1 teaspoon minced or pressed garlic
1 small jalapeño pepper, seeds removed, finely chopped
2 tablespoons unsalted butter
¼ cup (60 ml) heavy cream
1¼ cups (300 ml) chicken stock or water
¼ teaspoon kosher salt, plus more to taste

Wash, clean, and dry the greens. If the stems are long, cut them into 1-inch (2.5 cm) pieces, but try to keep the leaves whole if you can. Gently sweat the onion, garlic, and jalapeño with the butter for 2 to 3 minutes in a saucepan large enough to accommodate the greens, then add the greens, cream, stock, and salt. Cover and simmer over low heat for 20 minutes, or until the greens are tender and taste good to you. The greens should be wet, and the cream should not thicken the sauce. If the mixture cooks down too much, refresh it with a splash of water to loosen it. Correct the seasoning for salt and serve.

Dandelions and Bitter Greens

The recipes that follow call for greens with some bitterness or stronger flavors—mustards, mature sochan, dandelions, or other strong-tasting plants. Where possible, I've tried to note examples of specific greens that are used, or that I prefer for one reason or another, but if there are none available near you, or if you want to use milder-tasting greens, you can mix and match plants however you like.

Greens with Olive Oil and Lemon (Horta)

Serves 2–4

The Horta of Greek fame is nothing more than greens cooked in salted water until tender, anointed with the best-tasting olive oil you have and fresh lemon juice. There are many traditional recipes for wild greens, and they're often interchangeable, but one thing I see over and over again with Horta and its Lebanese cousin Hindbeh (page 66) is the omnipresence of dandelions or other asters, such as chicories. My recipe is no exception.

Kosher salt, to taste
8 ounces (225 g) fresh wild greens,
  preferably a blend including dandelions
Highest-quality extra-virgin olive oil, acorn
  oil, or Smude's sunflower oil, for serving
  (optional)
Fresh lemon wedges, for serving (optional)

Bring a pot of salted water to a boil. Add the greens and simmer until they're tender and taste good to you; remove them, drain well, and transfer to a serving plate. Drizzle with plenty of olive oil and serve with lemon wedges and extra salt on the side.

Barely Cooked Watercress Soup with Lemon Cream

Serves 2–4

Watercress soup is a classic. This version uses rice as a thickener instead of the more common potato, because I prefer the neutral flavor. I never serve puréed soup without some sort of textural garnish—in this case a "salad" of chopped watercress mixed with toasted seeds. Unlike the process for most watercress soups, I add finely sliced watercress at the very end, then purée and quickly chill it to keep some of its fresh character.

Soup
1 small leek, tender white and
   green parts only
2 tablespoons lard or cooking oil
5 tablespoons white rice
4 cups (945 ml) chicken or other meat stock
   or vegetable broth (preferably homemade)
4 ounces (115 g) fresh watercress
Kosher salt and fresh-cracked black pepper,
   to taste

Lemon cream
3 tablespoons sour cream
3 tablespoons half-and-half or whole
   (full-fat) milk
Fresh lemon zest, to taste
Dash of fresh lemon juice
Kosher salt, to taste

Watercress salad (optional)
1 tablespoon sunflower seeds,
   freshly toasted
½ tablespoon Smude's sunflower oil or
   another high-quality salad oil
Perfect, small watercress leaves, for garnish

To make the soup, dice, wash, and dry the leek, then sweat it in the oil for a few minutes. Add the rice and stock to the pan, cover, and bring to a simmer. Turn the heat to low and cook about 20 to 25 minutes, or until the rice is tender. Meanwhile, rough-chop the watercress and its stems, reserving a quarter of them for the salad garnish. Fill a sink one-quarter of the way full of cold water to chill the soup.

Transfer the rice mixture to a blender, add the chopped watercress, and purée until very smooth, then immediately transfer the soup to a metal mixing bowl and place the bowl in the sink of cold water, whisking gently to help decrease the temperature of the soup and keep the vibrant green color and flavor of the cress. Season the soup to taste with salt and pepper, chill completely, and set aside. The soup can be made a day or two ahead of time up to this point.

To make the lemon cream, mix the sour cream, half-and-half, lemon zest, and lemon juice. Season to taste with salt.

To make the watercress salad, chop the sunflower seeds, then mix with the reserved, chopped watercress and the oil. Season the mixture to taste with salt and pepper, and set aside.

To serve, preheat small soup bowls, then heat the soup, taste and adjust the seasoning as needed, and ladle 1-cup (240 ml) portions into the preheated bowls. Garnish each with a dollop of the lemon cream and a bit of the watercress salad.

Steaming and Steam-Wilting Greens

Steaming is one of the easiest and most efficient ways to cook greens, and since they aren't immersed in boiling water, they'll retain more of their natural flavor. A steamer basket inserted into a pot is probably the most common method, and it's one I use often, but a hybrid technique I like is what I call steam-wilting, which allows me to quickly drain the greens and add fat to the pan right before serving, ensuring the greens are seasoned and delicious before anyone takes a bite, whereas steamed greens need to be seasoned at the table.

To steam-wilt, I put about half a finger's width of water in the bottom of a deep pot, fill it with greens, cover it and turn the heat to high, and cook until the greens are just tender and wilted. Then I drain any excess water, season to taste, and mix with a fat (generally oil or butter) while the greens are still in the pan. It's a great way to cook tender, mild-tasting greens such as watercress that cook quickly.

Steam-wilting is much like steaming, but there's no steamer basket, and I'm less likely to overcook the greens. It's perfect for greens that take up a lot of space but cook down, such as watercress.

Rustic Watercress Soup with Carrots and Ramp Leaves

Serves 4

Watercress has a natural affinity for carrots and things with carotene, highlighted here in a simple soup that's left with a bit of texture, instead of being completely smooth. Violets, spinach, or other tender greens are a good substitute.

4 ounces (115 g) yellow onion, chopped (1 small onion)

8 ounces (225 g) russet potato, peeled and chopped (1 large potato)

4 ounces (115 g) carrots, grated, divided (2 small carrots)

4 tablespoons unsalted butter

¼ cup (60 ml) dry white wine

4 cups (945 ml) chicken stock or vegetable broth

1 teaspoon kosher salt

Pinch of sugar

4 ounces (115 g) fresh watercress, chopped

½ ounce (14 g) ramp leaves (optional)

Serving

Fresh watercress leaves

Fresh-cracked black pepper

Extra-virgin olive oil

Sweat the onion, potato, and half of the carrots in the butter for a few minutes until just tender, then add the wine and cook until evaporated. Don't let the bottom of the pan darken. Add the stock, salt, and sugar; bring the mixture to a boil, then turn the heat down to low and cook for 20 minutes. Add the watercress, and the ramp leaves if you're using them; purée with an immersion blender, leaving the mixture a bit coarse. Add the remaining carrots and pulse with the blender a few times to break it up. There should be visible pieces of carrot and watercress in the soup. Put the soup back on the heat for a moment so the carrots become tender. Adjust the seasoning as needed, and top with a few sprigs of watercress, cracked black pepper, and drizzles of extra-virgin olive oil before serving.

What's a Raab?

In my world, *raab* was always kitchen shorthand for broccoli raab. But over the years, I noticed that chefs would borrow the term to fill a hole in our lexicon of edibles, since, at least to my knowledge, there isn't a culinary name for edible flower buds. But as in so many cases, an Italian pet name rolls easily off the tongue and looks better on a menu than a descriptive phrase like *unripe flower bud*. I now use the term *raab* to refer to the young buds of mustards and other brassicas, but also other plants such as the common milkweed—and probably more than a few others I haven't discovered yet.

Garlic mustard (*Alliaria petiolata*)

Dame's rocket (*Hesperis matronalis*)

Garden yellow rocket (*Barbarea vulgaris*)

Common milkweed (*Asclepias syriaca*)

Orrechiette alla Barese with Sausage and Wild Raabs

Serves 4 as a light entrée

Once I learned what a brassica flower looked like, the whole outside world seemed to turn into a grocery store filled with cousins of broccoli and mustard greens. From there, as I watched the plants grow, I noted that many resembled broccoli raab or rapini before they flowered. As it turned out, the plants are cousins and taste eerily similar. The first thing that came to mind (and made my mouth water) was orrechiette with broccoli raab—one of the most classic dishes in the Southern Italian canon, and likely the pasta course of my last meal. Just about everyone has a different take on it, but most agree on the anchovies, bitter rapini, and ear-shaped pasta. Cheese is debatable. Variations abound, but the best, by far, is this version I learned from Chef William Salvadore, a Milan native who trained in the Michelin three-star restaurant La Gavroche. He made the dish without sauce or cheese, and I can still remember his voice bellowing through the kitchen, saying, "Is this not the best freaking pasta you have ever had?" It's definitely one of them. The combination of crispy bread crumbs, olive oil, spicy sausage, and bitter greens is a roller coaster of umami, and the perfect foil for any of your favorite strong-tasting bitter greens.

6 ounces (170 g) wild mustard raabs, or a similar substitute
½ cup (120 ml) oil, divided (I like to use a 50/50 blend of extra-virgin olive oil and grapeseed oil)
12 ounces (340 g) Italian sausage, preferably a variety flavored with fennel seed
12 anchovy fillets preserved in oil
1 cup (50 g) panko bread crumbs
8 ounces (225 g) dried orrechiette pasta
Red pepper flakes, to taste
Kosher salt, to taste

Bring a pot of salted water to a boil. Blanch the raabs for 30 seconds, then refresh in cold water. Squeeze the raabs dry as thoroughly as possible, chop roughly, and set aside.

For the pasta, heat a tablespoon of the oil in a large sauté pan and sweat the sausage on medium heat, breaking it into small clumps with a wooden spoon. Remove the sausage from the pan when cooked through and reserve. In the same pan, cook the anchovy on low heat, mashing them up a bit. Add the rest of the oil and cook until the anchovies are golden, aromatic, and dispersed in the oil. Add the bread crumbs to the oil and stir to coat, cooking on medium heat until the bread crumbs are golden brown, adding a glug of oil if the pan gets dry. Add the sausage back to the pan, leaving behind any juices it gave off.

Bring a pot of salted water to a rolling boil, then add the orrechiette. Stir the pasta vigorously during cooking, since it's notorious for sticking together.

When the pasta is cooked, drain it thoroughly, tossing in the colander repeatedly to remove excess water, then add to the pan with the sausage and crumbs. Add the chopped raabs, chili flakes and salt to taste, and extra olive oil if needed. Heat the mixture through, then serve immediately. If this pasta isn't eaten quickly, trapped steam will destroy the crunch, which is the best part. Taste and believe.

Scurdijata

Serves 6

Along with orrechiette and broccoli raab, Scurdijata is one of the hallmarks of Apulian food in Southern Italy, which relies on wild greens and starch to make a meal. There are similar modern recipes that use potatoes hiding under names like *verdure trovata* or "found vegetables," but the oldest recipes wouldn't have used potatoes—they're a New World crop. It's the sort of fiendishly resourceful, Italian-grandma-leftover wizardry I love, and after you taste it, you might find yourself cooking greens and beans just to have leftovers around to make it.

1 small onion, chopped
1–2 large cloves garlic, thinly sliced
½ cup (135 ml) mild olive oil, or extra-virgin oil mixed 50/50 with a flavorless oil, divided, plus extra for serving
Good pinch of red pepper flakes
15 ounces (425 g) leftover cooked beans
2 packed cups (455 g) leftover cooked greens, especially mustard greens or bitter broccoli raab
1 cup (240 ml) cooking liquid from beans, or meat stock
Kosher salt, to taste
1½ ounces (40 g) stale bread, cut into diamonds or cubed (about 1 generous cup / 240 ml)
Fresh lemon wedges, for serving (optional)

Sweat the onion and garlic in ¼ cup (60 ml) of the oil, then add the red pepper flakes. Add the beans and greens and sweat them for a few minutes more. Add the bean cooking liquid and a good pinch of salt, then simmer, mashing some of the beans with a spatula as you go. Continue until the pan is nearly dry. Meanwhile, fry the bread chunks in the rest of the oil until golden. Toss half of the fried croutons into the bean mix, and double-check the seasoning. It should be well seasoned, and everything should be soft and tender—the beans lending their flavor to the greens. Put into a serving dish, garnish with the remaining croutons, and serve with lemon and oil at the table.

Fava Bean Purée with Wild Chicory (Fave e Cicoria)

Serves 4 as an appetizer or side

This is another well-known Southern Italian dish, and a creative example of cuisine that relies on wild plants and a simple starch—a good example of the famous cucina povera, or "poverty cuisine." Typically, wild chicory (*Cichorium intybus*) or dandelions are used, but the rich, silky fava bean purée will be a perfect counterpoint to any of your favorite bitter or strong-tasting greens. Check your local Middle Eastern or Asian market for dried, shelled fava beans, or order online.

8 ounces (225 g) dried, shelled fava beans
1 dried bay leaf
½ small yellow onion
Kosher salt
2 tablespoons high-quality salad oil
  (such as extra-virgin olive oil, acorn oil,
  or Smude's sunflower oil), plus extra
  for serving
1 large clove garlic, thinly sliced
2 tablespoons cooking oil
1 small hot chili, preferably Calabrian
  pepper or cherry bomb, sliced
4 ounces (115 g) fresh, bitter wild greens,
  such as dandelions or garlic mustard, cut
  into 1-inch (2.5 cm) pieces
Good rustic bread, such as sourdough,
  for serving (optional)
Fresh lemon wedges, for serving (optional)

Cover the fava beans, bay leaf, and onion with 3 cups (720 ml) of water, bring to a simmer, cover, and cook for about an hour or until tender. Keep the beans warm. Bring a few quarts of salted water to a simmer. Remove the onion and bay from the beans and discard, then drain the favas well and transfer to a food processor. Purée the favas, season with salt, and drizzle in the salad oil until thick, fluffy, and smooth. Meanwhile, sweat the garlic in the cooking oil until aromatic, then add the chili and cook for a minute more. Cook the greens in the simmering water until just tender (a few minutes), then drain them and add to the pan with the garlic and chili. Stir to combine, and season to taste. Spoon the bean purée into a shallow serving dish, garnishing with the greens on one side. Serve with crusty bread, lemon wedges, and extra olive oil.

Fava Bean Purée with Wild Chicory is a classic Apulian dish.

Lebanese Greens with Caramelized Onions (Hindbeh)

Serves 2–4

Similar to Horta (page 57), this is a traditional Lebanese dish typically made using dandelions or wild chicory, but just about any greens can be used. It's really nothing more than wilted greens with caramelized onions, and those simple, pure flavors are a study in less being more. Adding pine nuts, tossing in a good pinch of cumin, or using lamb tallow instead of olive oil are other variations worth trying. Dandelions are traditional, but other plants in the family with stronger flavors like sochan or wild lettuces would be fine, too.

1 large yellow onion
2 tablespoons olive oil, cooking oil, or animal fat, especially lamb
Kosher salt and fresh-ground black pepper
8 ounces (225 g) fresh dandelion greens or other strong-tasting (not necessarily bitter) wild greens

Fresh lemon wedges, for serving (optional)

Cut the top and bottom from the onion, remove the skin, and halve it top-to-bottom. Set the halves cut-sides down on a cutting board, and halve them through the equator. Slice the onion into 1-inch (2.5 cm) julienne, as thin as you can. In a 10-inch (26 cm) skillet or similar wide pan, heat the oil until very hot, then add the onion and turn the heat down to medium. Season with a pinch of salt and pepper, and cook for 20 to 30 minutes, stirring occasionally, until the onion is deeply browned and aromatic, deglazing with a tablespoon of water as needed if the pan threatens to dry out (I like my onion quite dark). Remove half of the onion and reserve. Meanwhile, cook the greens in salted water until they're tender and taste good to you, then shock in cold water, drain, squeeze out excess water, and coarsely chop. Add the greens to the pan with the onion and warm them through, adding a little water if needed to moisten. Taste and correct the seasoning for salt and pepper, then top with the reserved onion and serve hot (with lemon wedges, if you like).

Simple Carrots with Watercress

Serves 2–4

This is another fun way to play with watercress and with the appetizing combination of orange and green. It's really nothing more than some glazed carrots with a few handfuls of greens thrown in. Many other greens will be good here, too, especially bitter greens like wintercress or dandelions that play off the carrots' subtle sweetness.

10 ounces (285 g) carrots (about 3 medium carrots)
1 cup (240 ml) chicken stock or water
1-inch (2.5 cm) piece of fresh ginger, finely grated
3 tablespoons unsalted butter
½ teaspoon kosher salt, plus more to taste
1 tablespoon pure maple syrup, or a couple pinches of sugar
4 ounces (115 g) watercress—preferably in small young clusters or roughly chopped (approximately 2 very generous handfuls)
1 ounce (28 g) ramp leaves, chopped, or a few sliced green onions

Peel the carrots and cut them on the diagonal into ¼-inch (6 mm) thick coins. If your carrots are large, cut them in half the long way, then cut on the diagonal into half-moons.

Put the carrots, stock, ginger, butter, salt, and maple syrup in a 12-inch (30 cm) skillet; cover and bring to a boil. Remove the lid and continue cooking.

When the liquid gets thick and syrupy and the carrots are tender, reduce the heat, making sure the pan doesn't dry out.

Double-check the seasoning and adjust as needed. Add the watercress and ramp greens, cover the pan for a few minutes to wilt them, then toss, adjust the seasoning, and serve.

CHAPTER 2

Abundant

Vegetables,
Wild and Tame

Most of this book focuses on how my culinary training has helped me navigate cooking with wild food. What I didn't expect was that hunting wild plants would change how I think about the vegetables I'd been cooking my whole life.

The hunter's eye I developed watching plants new and old grow, searching not necessarily for what would be edible in the future but what I could eat in the moment, became instinct, and before I knew it I was using my hunter's eye with every vegetable I saw. Those paradigm-shifting gifts of nature, in a nutshell, are what this chapter is all about, with a few veggie favorites thrown in along the way.

Many of the vegetables we see in the grocery store have far more gifts to give than what we generally consider. Broccoli is sold as a large bunch of unopened flowers, but the leaves, young and old, are also delicious, as is the "marrow" or tender inner portion of the stem. There are similar parallels for other brassicas (a plant family that includes cabbages and turnips, among others), as well as nightshades (including tomatoes and eggplant), members of the carrot family (parsley, fennel, lovage, et al.), cucurbits (pumpkins and squash), and other commonly cultivated vegetables. Plant shoots are another example, asparagus being just one of many you might see in a garden in spring. I originally called this chapter "The Garden" because, unlike many of the wild plants and herbs in the book, many of the recipes here are derived from these conventional vegetables. However, while some of the more unfamiliar plants can be harvested wild—including purslane, angelica, milkweed, parsnip leaves, and wild fennel—they can also be grown in a garden or found nearby. Seeing the more unfamiliar plants alongside more common vegetables, I think, makes it easier to recognize them as the foods they are, rather than some alien, foreign thing, hence the chapter subtitle, "Vegetables, Wild and Tame."

The first recipe, CSA Fermented Giardiniera, is a fitting introduction you could put your whole garden into, so to speak. It's an intuitive (and delicious) way to explore using possibly random combinations of vegetables you might find in your CSA box, like a small head of Romanesco, a turnip, and a lone winter radish. Once you get the method down, it can also be a springboard for making your own combinations, like a wild blend of blanched burdock flower stalks and roots with chopped wild onions, or just a traditional cauliflower-celery-carrot-pepper blend.

CSA Fermented Giardiniera

Makes 2 quarts (2 L)

When I ran Lucia's restaurant, having farmers come in to drop off CSA boxes for people to claim was good for business, and for the community, but inevitably some people missed their pickup. When that happened, I'd take the boxes, each basically filled with one each of the same vegetables, and make them into fermented giardiniera. It's a fun way to use random blends of vegetables, and it's never found a pizza, burger, or cured meat sandwich it didn't like. Feel free to cut the recipe in half to test it out. Because fermentation is more precise when things are measured, I strongly suggest using a scale to weigh the ingredients here. There's just about no wrong way to make this, but you wouldn't want to use all vegetables that have high amounts of sugar, like carrots, squash, or beets, since they can develop a slimy brine— I'd keep any of those to under 25 percent of the total weight of vegetables and peppers. Giardinierra should be salty, but if you want to tame it a bit, rinse the vegetables after the fermentation is complete.

950 grams (scant 2¼ pounds) mixed trimmed fresh vegetables, in ½-inch (1.25 cm) dice
225 grams (about 8 ounces) jalapeños or other hot fresh peppers, in ¼-inch (6 mm) slices
15 grams (about 1½ tablespoons) minced garlic (about 2 cloves)
60 grams (2 ounces) pickling or kosher salt
Good-tasting oil, such as Smude's sunflower oil or a medium-bodied olive oil, as needed for topping off the jars

Combine the vegetables with the peppers, garlic, and salt, mix well, then pack into a vacuum bag, seal, and store in a cool dark place for 2 weeks to ferment, following the instructions for dry fermenting (page 26). After 2 weeks, remove the fermented vegetables and drain any juice, then pack tightly in quart (945 ml) or pint (480 ml) jars and top off with oil, leaving ½ inch of headspace. Wiggle a wooden skewer around in the jar to remove air pockets, then top with a lid and process in a water bath for 10 minutes for pints and 15 minutes for quarts.

The Botany of the Garden

A couple of questions I get asked from time to time are: "Sure, Alan, I guess it's kind of interesting to know plant families and a little bit about the edible uses of them, but can I, a chef (or home cook), actually use or apply any of this knowledge?" Along with, "I live in town and don't have the time or knowledge to go outside and hunt ingredients—are you crazy?" And the answers to these questions are: yes and no. Yes, you can apply botany to a restaurant or home kitchen in an easy, practical way, and no, you don't have to put a toe outside, if you don't want to. Mirepoix, the classic French soup combination of carrot, onion, and celery, is a good starting point for understanding how you can use botany in a practical way to tweak the different flavors of plant families.

Here's the basic idea: Carrots, celery, and onion are three different plants, from two different plant families. Carrots and celery are both in the Apiaceae or carrot family; onions are in the Allium or lily family, and covered more in the next chapter, "Aromatic." The practical application is this: Plug different vegetables into your basic soup according to the plant family they're in. You can get creative, but try to keep mostly to onion and carrot plants since brassicas, especially things like turnips, can overtake subtle flavors. For example, if I want to keep a soup white, I might add celery root (a common soup vegetable in Europe) instead of orange carrots, still keeping with the "two carrots, one onion" template of the classic mirepoix. Another version might involve starting a rich tomato stew with large pieces of fennel, celery, and pearl onions—again, two carrots, one onion. Two carrots, one onion is only one of many versions you could apply here using the basic idea. Let's look at some others.

There's another versatile soup base I call white mirepoix: typically leeks and onions, and celery or fennel. Viewed through our plant family lens, this is: two onions and one carrot. White mirepoix is perfect when I don't want the orange color of a carrot; more important, white mirepoix doesn't add extra sugar to a soup. You might not think of carrots as very sweet, but compared with other vegetables, they are. I like to use white mirepoix with savory puréed soups when I want to control both the color and the sugar content, such as when creating a good bowl of lobster bisque; creamy, light-colored mushroom soup; dark, savory gumbo; or a pearl-white potato soup. To switch up the white mirepoix blend and keep in the "two onions, one carrot" template, I might use diced fennel, pearl onions, and leeks in a stew, or (gasp!) break the rule of three and use fennel, celery, carrots, and onions, or three carrots and one onion.

Finally, let's look at another trinity. I'm tiptoeing on food heresy here, but with good intention. The trinity—chopped celery, onion, and bell peppers—is a Creole base for many different dishes, most famously étouffée, jambalaya, and gumbo. Different from our two previous mirepoix, this trinity includes a third family: the nightshades, giving us the template of "one onion, one carrot, one nightshade." But instead of switching out all the plants for another, I would swap out only onion and carrot family members here, since it's hard to find a texture and taste reminiscent of peppers. For example, I might make a Creole-inspired stew starting with diced onion, fennel, and bell pepper, or a rice pilaf with finely chopped green garlic, chives, and bell peppers. Whatever combinations you choose, whatever formulas you make, it's a completely different way of thinking about flavor pairings, and how to build a new dish to call your own, as well as being a great way to introduce people to how and why botanical families can be useful. The recipe for Carrot Family Soup in this chapter is an example of how I use this basic idea to make a soup using mostly members of the carrot family along with some alliums, and a garnish that incorporates the aromatic seeds of carrot plants like dill, caraway, coriander, or cumin.

In addition to the carrot and nightshade families, this section also includes recipes featuring brassicas and cucurbits (squash). Among the earliest vegetables cultivated by humans, pumpkins and squash are probably my favorite example of how studying wild plants changed the way I cook and think about vegetables. For as long as I can remember— at least until a few years ago—anytime I thought about pumpkin or zucchini, I thought of pumpkin pie or a mundane vegetable side. They're all of that, and so much more, but I didn't start to understand how *much* more until I watched them grow in a garden myself, before I knew what they were. Taking a good look at them morphing and evolving throughout the growing season reveals plants that give not just a final end product or seasonal decoration, as most people think of them, but a veritable cascade of different edible products throughout the

growing season, if we're willing to pay attention. As any gardener knows, young zucchini will be the most tender, but another secret is that green, unripe pumpkins, squash like butternut, and storage gourds like kabocha are also traditionally harvested green and "unripe"—as in Nepal, where they might be made into curries or pickles (achaar). At the green stage, the seeds, tender-crisp, juicy, and hull-less, make an interesting addition to soup or salad.

Next come the ripe gourds we know and love, that give us everything from pie to baked zucchini boats. Finally, the seeds of the gourds and other cucurbits, shell and all, have long been used in many West African countries, where the seeds are known as egusi and are dried, ground (shells and all), and used to thicken dishes instead of flour.

Last come vegetables of the mustard family, also known as brassicas. These include vegetables such as turnips and broccoli that many grocery shoppers don't even know are related. I've tried to include recipes for them that I find interesting or novel, along with tried-and-true favorites I can't live without.

Apiaceae (Carrot Family)

Familiar Carrot Family Ingredients

- Angelica
- Anise
- Caraway
- Carrot
- Celery
- Chervil
- Coriander
- Cumin
- Dill
- Fennel
- Lovage
- Parsley
- Parsnip

Fennel Frond Cakes

**Makes about 12 small cakes
(two bites each)**

Have you ever walked through the grocery store, looked at the giant fronds of a fennel bulb, and thought: *I love fennel, but I hate throwing away all the fronds*? I have, and I've instructed cooks to throw away truckloads of the fronds when we ran out of stockpots to put them in, which is just a different way to throw them away. No more! Not since I discovered a genius method, courtesy of Angelo Garro, the California forager of *The Omnivore's Dilemma* fame.

After slow cooking, fennel fronds (or greens) turn tender and pleasant, but more important they reveal their anise lineage once they're exposed to heat. Cooked tender and mixed with a few other ingredients, then fried into crisp cakes, they're dreamy served next to fish, pork, chicken, or on their own as an appetizer, anointed with lemon. Serve them piping hot with a crisp shaved fennel salad to celebrate the entire plant. Fennel's cousins with tough, leafy tops—such as caraway and garden carrots—can be cooked similarly.

8 ounces (225 g) fennel fronds from
    wild fennel, or the leafy green stalks of
    2 cultivated fennel bulbs
1 egg
½ cup (50 g) finely grated Parmesan
½ teaspoon kosher salt
½ teaspoon toasted ground wild or
    cultivated fennel seeds
1 scrape of lemon zest
½ cup (55 g) bread crumbs
2 tablespoons heavy cream
Fresh-ground black pepper, to taste
Cooking oil, as needed

Bring a gallon of salted water to a boil and cook the fennel fronds, whole, for 15 minutes at a steady simmer. Taste a piece of the fennel fronds at this point to gauge the texture; if it's soft enough for you, remove them, and if not, cook them a few minutes more. When you're pleased with the texture (they will get tender), remove the fronds to a colander to drain and cool to room temperature. Squeeze the fronds dry, then chop them finely. Combine with all the remaining ingredients except the cooking oil.

Heat a bit of the oil in a pan while you take a small portion of the fennel mixture, mold it into a test patty, and cook to try out the seasoning and set. If the sample cake falls apart when flipping, add some extra bread crumbs; if it tastes mild, add a pinch of salt. When you're ready to cook the cakes, take 2 tablespoons at a time and form into a patty, then brown gently in oil on both sides.

Carrot Cakes with a Salad of Carrot Leaves

Makes 12 cakes

Just like fennel fronds, carrot leaves have a terrible reputation, and I always wondered why companies sold carrots with their leaves attached at all. I mean, what a waste of space, right? No human wants to eat stringy, tough carrot leaves. Wrong. Carrot greens take up a lot of space raw, but not cooked. They also get tender after cooking, and make a great, herby salad. In repentance for how many carrot greens I threw away via the stockpot or the compost, I wanted to make a whole-carrot dish. Look for carrot juice in your local co-op.

1 pound (455 g) carrots
2 tablespoons cooking oil, such as grape-seed, plus more for cooking the cakes, as needed
½ tablespoon finely minced ginger

½ cup (135 ml) carrot juice (or water, in a pinch)
½ teaspoon kosher salt
1 tablespoon maple syrup
½ cup (30 g) roughly chopped Italian parsley
1–2 tablespoons aromatic herbs of your choice (try mint, marigold leaves, cilantro, dill, or whatever you like)
¼ cup (30 g) flour or flour equivalent
¼ cup (28 g) breadcrumbs
Pinch of curry powder
2 large eggs
2 ounces (55 g) sliced green onion
Carrot Leaf Salad (recipe follows)

Gently scrub and wash the carrots, then grate on a box grater; you should have about 4 cups. In a wide pan, such as a 12-inch (30 cm) sauté pan or cast-iron skillet, warm the oil and ginger and cook for 3 to 4 minutes without browning. Add the carrots, carrot juice, and salt, then cover the pan and cook on medium for 2 to 3 minutes. Remove the cover and stir, then increase the heat to high and cook rapidly until the pan is nearly dry and the liquid has evaporated. The carrots should be tender but not mushy. Transfer the carrots to a bowl to cool. Mix the cooked carrots with the remaining ingredients, taste and correct the salt (sample before adding the eggs if that weirds you out). Ideally, you'll let the batter rest for an hour or two here, but the fritters can be cooked straightaway if you have to. If your batter seems wet, add another table-spoon of flour to tighten it up.

To cook the cakes, oil a large cast-iron skillet or other large pan, and heat to medium-high. Take heaping spoonfuls (about 2 tablespoons) of the batter and form them into small cakes. Cook the cakes until they're well browned on each side to ensure a good set, then serve with Carrot (or Parsnip) Leaf Salad and maybe a sauce made from yogurt, lemon wedges, or Dried Ramp Ranch Dressing (page 168).

Carrot (or Parsnip) Leaf Salad

Serves 4

A great way to try carrot or parsnip leaves, if you haven't had them. (If you want to try parsnip greens, make sure to avoid getting the sap of parsnip leaves on your skin by using gloves and by being mindful of how you handle them.) I first learned about this use of carrot leaves in *Cooking South of the Clouds* by Georgia Freedman, which featured a dressing with soy sauce, hot chilies, black vinegar, and garlic, but the simple, tried-and-true combination of lemon juice and olive oil is also delicious. Feel free to experiment. I guarantee you won't toss out carrot leaves again.

1 pound (455 g) carrot leaves
Fresh lemon juice
Kosher salt
Good-tasting salad oil, such as extra-virgin olive or Smude's sunflower

Strip the carrot leaves from the hardy inner stems (the leaves can be cooked and served whole, too, but I prefer the leaves without the inner rib, and so will first-time picky eaters). Bring a large pot of salted water to a boil. Add the leaves and cook until they're tender and taste good to you—a couple of minutes. It's okay to taste them once or twice and keep cooking. Remove the leaves and chill in cool water, then drain and squeeze out as much water as you can. Pull the ball of greens apart a bit and fluff them on a cutting board, then chop roughly a few times in a crosshatch pattern—just enough to cut them into pieces that are easy to pick up with a fork. Remove to a bowl, season to taste with the lemon juice, salt, and oil, and serve.

Carrot Family Salad

Serves 4–6

One of the most addictive slaws I know, this was inspired by a shaved fennel and celery root salad I ate with Sam Thayer and his family, and is a great way to taste and appreciate different plants in the carrot family without going into the woods. The most basic version uses fennel and celery root, but other carrot plants can be added, too—try finely julienned carrots, parsnips, or herbs like mitsuba, cilantro, parsley, dill, or lovage, as well as any of their seeds, especially in the green stage. Adding slices of your favorite peeled, tart baking apple or thin slices of Fermented Lemon Confit (page 45) also makes for a good dish. To make it like Sam does, you'll want to use hickory nut oil.

6–8 ounces (170–225 g) fennel bulb, cut into 1-inch × ¼-inch (2.5 × 0.6 cm) thick strips
1 celery root (12-ounce / 340 g), peeled and grated
3 tablespoons highest-quality salad oil, such as hickory nut or Smude's sunflower oil
¼ teaspoon kosher salt, plus more to taste
2 teaspoons apple cider vinegar, or to taste
Fennel fronds, finely chopped, for serving (optional)

Mix the fennel and celery root well with the oil, salt, and vinegar. Double-check the seasoning, adjust as needed, and serve, garnished with chopped fennel fronds. The salad can be made a few hours ahead and will be good for a few days. It will use a little more oil than you'd expect.

Carrot Family Soup

Serves 4–6 as a light entrée

The flavor here comes across a bit like chicken soup. Consider adding some sausages in place of the chicken, for variation.

4 ounces (115 g) diced leek, tender white and green parts only, rinsed (1 small leek)
4 ounces (115 g) diced yellow onion (1 small onion)
1 tablespoon chopped garlic (2–3 cloves)
3 tablespoons cooking oil
Pinch of kosher salt, plus more to taste
¼ cup (60 ml) dry white wine
8 ounces (225 g) peeled, diced celery root (1 small celery root)
4 ounces (115 g) diced celery (2 small stalks)
8 ounces (225 g) diced fennel (1 medium bulb)
4 ounces (115 g) peeled, diced carrot (2 small carrots)
8 cups (2 L) good chicken or vegetable broth
¼ cup (15 g) chopped cilantro or lovage, (1 whole bunch)
1 cup (200 g) cooked natural/hand-harvested wild rice, or other rice, to taste (optional)
8 ounces (225 g) diced, cooked chicken, or other meat (optional)
Chopped fresh parsley, for serving (optional)

Aromatic sour cream
½ cup (110 g) sour cream
1 tablespoon lemon juice
Zest of ½ small lemon
¼ teaspoon fresh-ground celery seed, or ground cumin, caraway, or coriander
¼ teaspoon salt

Sweat the leek, onion, and garlic in the oil with a pinch of salt. Add the wine, then the remaining ingredients except the chicken and parsley and simmer until the vegetables are soft, about 30 minutes. Add the chicken, taste, and adjust the seasoning until the soup tastes good—soups usually take a lot more salt than you think. It'll taste a lot better the next day.

To make the sour cream, combine all ingredients, stir thoroughly to combine, and store, covered in the fridge, until needed. Garnish the soup with parsley and serve with dollops of the sour cream; have people stir them in before eating.

Parsley-Family Tabouleh, with Toasted Barley

Serves 4–6 as a side dish

A great way to show off useful parsley cousins I harvest like mitsuba or ground elder is a "parsley and friends" themed tabouleh—that classic Middle Eastern salad that uses handfuls of parsley. Since the greens are finely chopped, it's also a great dish to make later in the season when plants have lost their early tenderness. I use toasted barley here, but you can substitute any grain you like; bulgur is traditional. This is also intentionally light on the grains—feel free to increase the quantity if you like.

4 ounces (115 g) ground elder, mitsuba, Italian parsley, or another carrot family green you like

3 tablespoons raw hulled barley

2 ounces (55 g) sweet red onion, in ¼-inch (6 mm) dice

¼ cup (60 ml) lemon juice

¼ cup (60 ml) extra-virgin olive oil

Kosher salt, to taste

4 ounces (115 g) peeled, seeded cucumbers, in ¼-inch (6 mm) dice

6 ounces (170 g) ripe tomatoes, in ¼-inch (6 mm) dice

Up to a day or two beforehand, refresh the greens in cold water, spin dry, and refrigerate. The greens will perk up and gain volume, creating a fresh, crisp salad.

When you want to make the salad, toast the barley at 375°F (190°C) for 20 minutes, or until it's rich smelling and golden, stirring occasionally. Cook the barley in lightly salted water just until tender, then drain, rinse, and reserve. Soak the diced onion in cold water for 30 minutes to mellow its flavor, then drain and reserve.

Remove any tough stems from the greens. Working in batches if needed, grasp small bunches of greens, compress them a bit on a cutting board, and shave them as thinly as you can into a chiffonade. Carefully rotate the mass of greens and cut perpendicular to your first cuts, to dice them very small. The age of your greens will dictate how small they'd like to be diced; the tougher the greens, the finer the dice. I've made this dish using greens harvested from feral patches all the way up to when the plants were making seed heads; it was still pleasant as long as I cut the greens very small.

Toss the greens with the remaining ingredients. Double-check the seasoning, adjusting as needed. Serve or refrigerate for up to 2 days, tossing occasionally to distribute the juices.

Carrots (or Beets) Glazed in Their Juice

Serves 4 as a side dish

Glazing or cooking vegetables in their own juice has been a chef's secret for years, and carrots are probably my favorite, with beets coming in a close second. The method for both is easy.

1 pound (455 g) carrots (or beets)
1 cup (240 ml) carrot (or beet) juice
2 tablespoons unsalted butter
Pinch of salt
Pinch of sugar
Chives or parsley, for serving (optional)

Gently scrub the carrots clean, then cut on the diagonal into ¼-inch (6 mm) ovals. Beets should be roasted beforehand and then cut into wedges or cubes. Heat the cut vegetables in a wide pan with the carrot or beet juice (look for both at your local co-op, or juice your own with a juicer) and reduce rapidly on high heat until most of the liquid is gone, adding a little extra liquid and covering the pan if the carrots need more time and the pan threatens to dry out. When half the liquid still remains, add the butter, salt, and sugar, and swirl the pan occasionally to help the butter emulsify into a thick glaze. When the sauce is thick and coats the vegetables, double-check the seasoning, toss in some chives or parsley, and serve.

Lovage Sauce

Makes 2 cups (480 ml)

If I had to pick one herb for you to sample out of everything in this book, lovage would be a strong contender. Lovage and its cousins, like smallage (also good, but more like celery leaf), are ancient herbs; I read about it first in Apicius, the old Roman "cookbook" from the first century AD, along with other archaic-sounding aromatics like silphium and asafetida. Silphium is believed to be extinct, but asafetida is still used in India under the name *hing*.

Here and there you might see an intrepid grower at the farmers market selling lovage, but they rarely stick with it, because people just don't know what to do with it. Raw, the flavor is strong—too strong for most. The best way I can describe it is like celery on steroids. Just like celery, it will turn a sausage pink if added to the meat mix, from the high concentration of natural nitrates.

Lovage and its friends are fantastic in soups, broths, and meat mixtures like sausages, but far and away the greatest thing I've ever tasted made with lovage is this sauce I learned and adapted from Brett Weber, former sous chef to Chef Dan Barber and a veteran of the award-winning restaurant Charlie Trotter's in Chicago.

The texture of this sauce is like a thin mayonnaise. Adding a bit more oil will thicken the sauce, making it a terrific dip for anything from french fries to fingers. To me, it might just be the ultimate condiment. When I served it at an event, one person pulled me aside to tell me it was "God's own creation!" It's hard to convey in words how it tastes, a sort of celery flavor so potent it's like green electricity. If you have a garden, have access to a garden, or just want to get creative "guerilla gardening" a sunny spot in your neighborhood park, find a way to plant it, for no other reason than to taste this sauce.

2 ounces (55 g) fresh lovage leaves
1 large egg yolk
¼ cup (60 ml) water
¼ cup (60 ml) fresh lemon juice
½ teaspoon kosher salt
1 tablespoon Dijon mustard (optional)
1½ cups (375 ml) mild salad oil

Blanch the lovage in boiling salted water just until wilted (a few seconds), then refresh in cold water and squeeze dry. Chop the lovage, then combine with all ingredients except the oil in a blender or food processor. Drizzle in the oil and process until a thick sauce forms. Pour the sauce into a jar with a tight-fitting lid, and store in the refrigerator for up to a few days.

Brassicaceae (Mustard Family)

Familiar Mustard Family Ingredients

- Arugula
- Bok choy
- Brown mustard
- Broccoli
- Brussels sprouts
- Cabbage
- Cauliflower
- Collard
- Horseradish
- Kale
- Kohlrabi
- Radish
- Rutabaga
- Turnip
- Wasabi

The Whole Broccoli Frittata

Serves 4–6 as a light entrée

The first time I walked through a garden growing broccoli, I noticed straightaway the large, collard-like leaves—something you never see in the store. Broccoli is more than just florets. The leaves are one of my favorite fall greens. Cousins like Italian spigariello or leaf broccoli are grown specifically for their sweet, robust leaves. The leaves are great added to any dish with broccoli, or just cooked by themselves, but enjoying the leaves, stem, and florets in a dish like this simple frittata is a great way to use the whole plant. Feel free to use other leafy greens, especially nettles, instead of the broccoli. For a smaller version, use 4 eggs, slightly less broccoli and other ingredients, and an 8-inch (20 cm) pan, with slightly less broccoli or greens.

½ ounce (14 g) attractive broccoli leaf, stem removed (1 large leaf)
5 ounces (140 g) broccoli, trimmed into 1-inch (2.5 cm) pieces, stem peeled down to the tender core (1 small head)

6 large eggs, at room temperature
¼ cup (60 ml) heavy cream
2 tablespoons unsalted butter
Kosher salt and fresh-ground black pepper
2 ounces (55 g) fresh chèvre

Preheat the oven to 250°F (120°C). Bring a pot of salted water to a boil, then add the broccoli leaf and cook for 30 seconds or so. Next, add the florets and stem and cook for another 30 seconds. Remove the vegetables to cold water to halt the cooking, drain well, dice the broccoli leaf into 1-inch squares, and reserve. Combine the eggs and cream in a bowl, whisking until mixed. Melt the unsalted butter in a 10-inch (26 cm) cast-iron skillet or other 10-inch non-stick oven-safe pan. Add the broccoli leaves, florets, and stems. Season to taste with salt and pepper, then add the egg mix, cook for a minute or two, and stir a few times, as if you're making a folded omelet. Crumble in the fresh chèvre and stir to incorporate. Bake for 10 minutes or until the top is just barely set, being careful not to overcook the frittata. I also like to turn the oven off and allow the frittata to cook very slowly if I'm waiting for other dishes to cook or guests to arrive. Accompanied by a green salad, this makes a great brunch or lunch dish.

Raw Turnips with Really Good Oil and Salt

I unearthed this gem from *The Little House Cookbook: Frontier Foods from Laura Ingalls Wilder's Classic Stories* by Barbara M. Walker and Garth Williams. During the long winter, when the Ingalls family almost died of starvation, a snack they had was simply raw turnips with salt. With their thick skins and cold-hardiness, turnips are a perfect storage vegetable, but they're also delicious raw or as part of a modern, seasonal crudité platter, and they make a great vehicle for oils such as Sam Thayer's acorn or hickory nut oil or whatever good-tasting oil you have—olive, Smude's sunflower, pumpkinseed, or other nut oils like walnut and pecan.

Instead of today's widely available Hakurei salad turnips, reach for the non-waxed storage varieties the Ingalls family would have had access to, preferably from a local co-op. Pink scarlet turnips will be the sweetest, followed by gold turnips, and finally the common purple-top variety. The key is to peel the turnip twice, once through the outer, tough skin, and second through the finer, inner lining to reveal the juicy, tender heart. From there, cut the turnips into quarters if they're large, slice them ¼ inch (6 mm) thick, dip them in a shallow bowl of the oil of your choice, and sprinkle with crunchy salt, preferably something like Falksalt or Maldon. They make a good, rustic appetizer.

Brussels Sprout Slaw

Serves 4–6 as a side dish

After you taste this, you'll wonder why you've never made sprout slaw before.

12 ounces (340 g) Brussels sprouts
¼ teaspoon kosher salt
2 tablespoons very good salad, nut, or olive oil
1 tablespoon lemon juice, to taste
A few cracks of black pepper
Chopped parsley, chives, or dill, to taste

Hold each sprout by the stem and shave as finely as possible on a mandoline. Keep shaving until you have a good bowlful—about 10 ounces (285 g). Toss the shaved sprouts with the remaining ingredients to combine. Taste, adjust the seasoning until you like it, and serve.

Restaurant Brussels Sprouts

A perfectly cooked bowl of Brussels sprouts is probably the best-selling side dish I've ever run on a menu. I'm particular about how I like them cooked, and here are some key points I used to drill into my line cooks. Adding the leaves from trimming at the end is key, as it helps bulk them out and make small side dishes look full. The fresh leaves add a splash of neon green too, which is nice, just in case during the heat of service someone forgets about a pan in the oven. Cooked perfectly like this, there's no need for bacon, although I won't turn it away. It works best with large sprouts, like those from a store.

Here's what I do. Preheat the oven to 350°F (180°C). Gather the Brussels sprouts and trim the ends; you want to make sure a few leaves fall off each sprout while you trim—save every single leaf. Next, make a shallow cut into the base of each sprout, then cut each sprout in half perpendicular to the first cut as if you're making an X on the stem. Drizzle a glug of oil, butter, or lard into a cold 10- or 12-inch (26–30 cm) skillet. Place the sprouts facedown to promote even browning, then season with a pinch of salt. Heat the sprouts for a few minutes on high, until they start to take on color (flip one to check if you need). Put the pan in the oven to cook a few minutes more. When the sprouts are almost tender, take the pan out and put it back on the burner, tossing in the leaves you saved. Cover the pan and heat on medium-high for a few additional minutes, stirring once or twice until the leaves are just wilted, then serve.

Braised Cabbage with Bacon and Caraway

Serves 4 as a side dish

Probably the most popular cabbage side dish I've ever put on a menu. This can turn cabbage haters around, but it's important to have a mandoline or cabbage slicer to shave the cabbage as thin as possible. It's also the perfect place to use other wild seeds you might have—caraway is my favorite, but green mitsuba (*Cryptotaenia canadensis*) seeds are a good match here, too. I use homemade slab bacon from venison, mutton, or goat, but use whatever you have available. Pancetta is a good substitute if slab bacon isn't available.

3 ounces (85 g) slab bacon or regular bacon
¼ teaspoon wild or cultivated caraway seeds
Green cabbage, cut into wedges and shred-
    ded as thin as possible on a mandoline, to
    yield 1 pound (455 g)
Kosher salt, to taste
1 tablespoon chopped fresh dill, or 2 table-
    spoons chopped fresh parsley or cilantro
    (optional)

In a wide pan, such as a 12-inch (30 cm) cast-iron skillet, render the bacon on medium-high until it's crisp and the fat has released. Add the caraway seeds and a pinch of salt to the pan and cook for a minute or two, until aromatic. Add the cabbage to the pan, turn the heat down to medium, cover, and cook for 5 minutes. Remove the lid, stir, cover again. Cook 10 to 15 minutes more, stirring and turning the cabbage occasionally to coat with the fat, cooking until the cabbage is tender, translucent, and tastes good to you. Check the seasoning for salt, adjust as needed, add the herbs, then serve. The cabbage can also be cooked in advance and reheated, but wait to add the herbs until just before serving.

50/50 Cabbage (Braised Cabbage and Kraut)

A recipe for serving sauerkraut to the young, jaded, or both. I originally prepared this with three or four types of cured pork as a riff on the classic Alsatian choucroute garnie, but it's also delicious by itself as a side. It's easy to make. Take some sauerkraut and add a little water or stock—not too much, just enough so that the cabbage steams a bit and doesn't burn—cover, cook until it's tender, then add twice the volume of finely shredded, fresh savory or napa cabbage (green cabbage will take longer to cook but is a fine substitute) and a pinch of toasted caraway seeds, and cover again. Cook on low for a few minutes until the fresh cabbage just wilts and tastes good to you, then adjust the flavor with salt and a good knob of butter. Continue cooking, stirring, and tasting until it's all tender and irresistible, then eat with a knife-tip of butter at the table. It's a great complement to a Sunday roast.

Braised Red Cabbage with Dark Fruit, Apples, and Dill

Serves 8–10 as a side dish

The Germanic heritage of the Midwest is heavy here, and versions of this are still served at a number of restaurants in my region, my two favorites being the Winzer Stube (in Hudson, Wisconsin) and the Gasthaus Bavarian Hunter (in Stillwater, Minnesota). Made with the darkest fruit you can find—especially tangy blackcurrant preserves, syrup made from aronia, or elderberries—it's one of the best partners out there for wild game.

2 tablespoons unsalted butter, divided
⅓ cup (80 ml) dark fruit preserves, preferably seedless (try blackcurrant, aronia, chokecherry, blackberry, or elderberry)
1 teaspoon minced or grated fresh ginger

⅓ cup (80 ml) vinegar, preferably red wine, wild berry, or high-quality raspberry vinegar
Red cabbage, quartered and shaved on a mandoline as thin as possible, to yield 1¼ pounds (570 g), cores discarded
Kosher salt, to taste
1–2 tablespoons maple syrup, to taste (optional)
1 fresh baking apple, for serving
1 tablespoon chopped fresh dill, for serving (optional)

In a very wide pan, such as a 12-inch (30 cm) cast-iron skillet, heat 1 tablespoon of the butter with the preserves, ginger, and vinegar. Add the cabbage, turn the heat to medium-high, cover, and cook for 5 to 10 minutes. Remove the lid and stir the cabbage, then cover again and cook for another 20 to 25 minutes.

Taste the cabbage, adjust for salt and sweetness, adding a touch of maple syrup or a bit of sugar if you think it needs it. The cabbage should be slightly sweet in order to balance the brightness of the vinegar, and as the juices cook down and the cabbage wilts, the flavors will concentrate, so if it tastes odd, overly tart, or weakly flavored to you, don't worry—just keep cooking it down until most of the liquid is evaporated.

When the pan is nearly dry (keep an eye on it so it doesn't brown), turn off the heat, leave the cabbage in the pan, and allow it to cool and continue cooking with the pan's residual heat. After the cabbage has cooled, pack it into a container and refrigerate if you won't be serving right away.

To serve, peel the apple and dice it into ½-inch (1.25 cm) squares, discarding the core. Sweat the apple chunks in the remaining tablespoon of butter until just tender, then add the cabbage to reheat, adjust the seasoning if needed. Add the dill, mix well, and serve hot or at room temperature.

Fermented Radish Spread

Makes about 2½ cups (280 g)

This Ashkenazi Jewish preserve is known colloquially as schmaltz, after the rendered poultry fat that makes the spread so delicious. Modern versions are probably marinated and served fresh, but the original versions were likely fermented and bracingly aromatic, like this one. It's traditionally a deli condiment, and it shines when spread on hot toast or as a sandwich spread, or even as an all-purpose condiment. Any winter radish can be used, but Spanish black radishes are most traditional. Daikon radishes—especially rich, colored ones like green meat, watermelon, or lavender radishes—are beautiful, too. Store this spread in a jar to prevent having to defend or explain its smell to others. You'll get some variation in flavor and aroma between radishes, but after fermenting with garlic and onions, rest assured that you're going to end up with a delicacy. Less adventurous eaters will probably find the smell offensive. But if you like blue cheese, if you like garlic, if you like rich fermented things, you'll love this. It's great spread on sandwiches or grilled bread, or eaten with crackers and cheese.

1½ pounds (680 g) winter radishes, peeled and grated
2½ tablespoons kosher salt
1 tablespoon minced garlic
¼ cup (55 g) chopped sweet yellow onion
¾ cup (180 ml) rendered poultry lard (schmaltz) or a light-flavored oil such as Smude's sunflower oil that won't firm when chilled

Combine everything but the poultry lard and mix well, then vacuum-seal, label, date, and allow to ferment for 2 weeks. After 2 weeks, squeeze the radish mixture dry, then blend it in a food processor, drizzling in the schmaltz until the mix becomes spreadable. Transfer to a jar with a very tight lid and refrigerate.

Variation: Sour Onion Spread

Using all onions instead of radishes would make a condiment with an even more spreadable consistency.

Variation: Aromatic Seeds

Just as with sauerkraut—but even more so—adding some aromatic seeds to the initial ferment is really good, especially toasted caraway. I'd start with a teaspoon or two.

Solanaceae (Nightshade Family)

Familiar Nightshade Family Ingredients

- Eggplant
- Ground cherries
- Peppers
- Potatoes (not including sweet potatoes)
- Tomatoes
- Tomatillos

Simple Tomato Sauce Scented with Leaves

Makes 3 cups (720 ml)

The theory that tomato leaves are poisonous, toxic tendrils infected with deadly nightshade juju just isn't true, as food author and *New York Times* columnist Harold McGee has written. The leaves do, however, have a strong tomato flavor, so a good way to use them as a green is in small amounts in a blend—say, 1 part tomato leaves to 3 parts basil for making pesto. You can also use them to infuse tomato sauce, which is probably my favorite.

Try adding a bouquet of tomato leaves tied together to a simple pot of tomato sauce, allowing it to infuse as you would basil. Discard the leaves after cooking. Inspired by Paul Bertolli and Harold McGee, both of whom have similar recipes.

Small handful of tomato leaves, 4–5
  (6-inch / 15 cm) lengths
1 can (32 ounces / 900 g) whole, peeled
  tomatoes (or fresh tomatoes, blanched,
  peeled, seeded, and chopped to yield
  3 cups / 720 ml)
1 large clove garlic, trimmed and lightly
  crushed with the back of a knife
1 ounce (28 g) each carrot, onion, and
  celery, finely chopped
2 tablespoons unsalted butter
¼ cup (60 ml) dry white wine
Kosher salt, to taste

Wash and dry the tomato leaves, then tie into a bouquet with butcher's twine and reserve. Working over a sink, or a bowl in a sink, squeeze the seeds out of the tomatoes. Discard the seeds. Transfer the tomatoes to a bowl with their juice. Sweat the garlic, carrot, onion, and celery in the butter until the onion is translucent, about 5 minutes. Add the wine and cook for a minute, then add the tomatoes and their juice, bring to a simmer. Then reduce the heat, cover, and cook for 20 minutes on medium heat, adding the bouquet of tomato leaves about halfway through. Remove and discard the leaves, then purée the mixture using an immersion blender or a high-speed blender for 3 to 4 minutes or until very smooth, then cool and refrigerate. Be very careful puréeing hot sauces in a blender, as they will build up pressure in the blender bowl if air isn't allowed to circulate.

Eggplant Baked with Wild Herbs and Tomato

Serves 4–6

A sort of Italian eggplant casserole you can build in advance and throw in the oven, guaranteed to convert people who might pass on eggplant (as with marinated eggplant, the secret is blanching to improve the texture). Tomato sauce and cheese never made anything taste bad, either. For a rustic version, or if you just don't want to use the blender, chop the vegetables small and leave them in the tomato sauce. The wild herbs are optional; dried oregano or thyme are great substitutes. Depending on the occasion, I might serve this dish with grilled bread as a first course, or as a side dish to chicken or pork. The picture shows the dish topped with puffed wild rice after baking, which I did for a gluten-free option, but I've listed breadcrumbs in the recipe as they're more readily available.

1 medium-sized globe eggplant, skin on
1 medium leek, tender parts only, in 1-inch (2.5 cm) dice
1 large clove garlic, about a tablespoon roughly chopped
2 tablespoons unsalted butter, divided
¼ cup (60 ml) dry white wine

1 can (14 ounces / 400 g) whole peeled tomatoes, puréed and strained to remove seeds
Kosher salt and fresh-ground black pepper
4 ounces (115 g) medium-diced fresh mozzarella, or fresh mozzarella balls
A few leaves of fresh basil, torn
1 tablespoon crushed, dried bergamot (*Monarda fistulosa*), stems removed (or 1 teaspoon crushed, dried oregano)
Pinch of chili flakes
¼ cup (15 g) toasted panko bread crumbs, or as needed

Dice the eggplant into 1-inch (2.5 cm) cubes. Bring 2 quarts (2 L) lightly salted water to a boil, then add the eggplant, return the mixture to a boil, and cook for 1 to 2 minutes, until the eggplant is translucent. Remove the eggplant, cool, then gently squeeze out the water in a towel and reserve. Sweat the leek and garlic in 1 tablespoon of the butter for 5 to 10 minutes until tender. Add the wine, cook down by half, then add the tomato purée and cook for 10 minutes on medium heat to evaporate some liquid. Combine the tomato-leek sauce with the eggplant in a bowl, season the mixture to taste with salt and pepper, then add the mozzarella, basil, bergamot, and chili flakes. Pack the mixture into a casserole dish, top with the bread crumbs, dot with the remaining tablespoon of butter, and bake at 375°F (190°C) until hot throughout, browned, and bubbly. Allow to cool for 5 minutes, then serve.

My Favorite Marinated Eggplant

Makes about 3 cups (720 ml)

A tangy, spicy, punchy preserve for sand-wiches, for crackers, or on a platter with dips like hummus and tapenade, olives, sliced meats, and charcuterie. Besides baked with tomatoes, it's the best way I know to prepare eggplant. If you've never liked egg-plant, or have a loved one who doesn't, try this, and prepare to put it on everything. The secret is blanching the eggplant to wilt it first, a trick I borrowed from my old sous chef from Argentina, Katriel Menendez (who went on to start his own spice company, Argentine Chef, argentinechef.com). Shav-ing or grating the eggplant is best for spreading on things, but ¼-inch (6 mm) coins are great too, especially put on a sand-wich as you would pickles. Consider all of

the proportions here as suggestions, not mandates—for example, adding extra oil will make this nearly spreadable at room temperature. Large eggplants are usually too seedy for this, so look for the slender Japanese variety.

1½ pounds (680 g) Japanese eggplant
 (4 large eggplants)
1–2 tablespoons maple syrup, to taste
¼ cup (60 ml) flavorful oil, such as
 extra-virgin olive oil
3–4 tablespoons good-quality red wine
 vinegar
Red pepper flakes, or 1 minced fresh hot
 chili such as serrano or jalapeño, with or
 without seeds
1 cup (60 g) loosely packed torn mint or
 cilantro leaves
Fresh-grated lemon zest, to taste
1 large clove garlic, finely grated or very
 finely minced
Kosher salt and fresh-ground black pepper,
 to taste

Wash and clean the eggplant, then shred on the largest holes of a box grater or cut into long ¼-inch (6 mm) slices and julienne, or cut into coins ¼ inch thick. Meanwhile, bring 3 quarts (3 L) of lightly salted water to a boil, then blanch the eggplant for 30 to 60 seconds, working in batches if necessary. When the eggplant is tender, remove it and drain in a colander. When it's cool, gently squeeze out the water, transfer to a bowl, and combine with the remaining ingredients. Keep season-ing the eggplant until it tastes good to you; since I use it as a condiment, I like it aggres-sively seasoned, spicy, herby, and a little sharp from the vinegar. It will improve the day after it's made and can be kept, pressed down in a jar, with a layer of oil over it, for months. Bring it to room temperature to allow the oil to soften before serving.

Cucurbitaceae (Gourd Family)

Familiar Gourd Family Ingredients

- Cucumbers
- Gourds
- Melons
- Pumpkins
- Squash (including winter, butternut, and so on)
- Zucchini

Oaxacan Squash Vine Soup with Masa Dumplings

Serves 4 as an entrée

A fascinating recipe related to me by a dish-washer from Oaxaca (*Sopa de Guías con Chochoyotes*). On the street in his neighbor-hood, women would hawk small bundles of squash vines, leaves, flowers, small squash, and little bags of masa together—most of the ingredients you need for making the soup, which, in its original form, is just another example of historical vegetarian (poverty) cuisine. Just like the Minestrella (page 33) it's nothing more than a simple broth bolstered with starch—in this case, tiny masa dumplings called *chochoyotes*—to make it more filling.

Most recipes say to cook the masa dump-lings directly in the soup, but getting the water temperature and simmering consis-tency just right is a trick: If the soup is rapidly boiling, the dumplings will disinte-grate, and if the soup isn't simmering quickly enough, the dumplings can disinte-grate. With that in mind, I treat them here like gnocchi, blanching them separately so you can get the hang of cooking the dump-lings without worrying about them dissolving in the finished soup. After a reheating or two (like many soups and stews, it's better the second day), the dump-lings can and should break down a bit, which thickens the soup.

Masa Dumplings
½ cup (120 ml) boiling water
½ cup (60 g) masa flour
¼ teaspoon salt
2 tablespoons lard or oil
Generous pinch each ground cumin
 and coriander (optional)

Soup
3 packed cups (85 g) tender squash shoots
 and leaves
10 ounces (285 g) zucchini, preferably very
 small and young
3 large cloves garlic (½ ounce)
1 medium yellow onion (6 ounces),
 finely diced
2 tablespoons lard or oil
3 large ears of sweet corn, kernels cut
 from the cob (1½ cups)
Kosher salt, to taste
6 cups (1.5 L) chicken stock, water,
 or a combination
15 squash blossoms, halved, pistils removed
Fresh chopped cilantro, or culantro,
 for serving (optional)
Fresh lime wedges, for serving (optional)

To make the dumpling dough, combine the water, flour, salt, lard, and spices, stirring to form a soft dough. Cover the dough and allow to hydrate while you prepare the soup.

To make the soup, cut the squash shoots into ½-inch pieces and dice the leaves to avoid long pieces in the soup. Reserve the cut leaves and shoots. Quarter the zucchini the long way, then dice, or cut into rounds if very small. Mash the garlic to a paste in a mortar (tradi-tional) or mince, then in a stock pot sweat the garlic and onion in the lard. Add the zucchini, squash shoots and leaves, and sweet corn, and cook for 5 minutes. Salt to taste, add the stock, bring to a simmer, and turn off the heat.

Bring 2 quarts of lightly salted water to a simmer. While the water is coming up to temp, roll teaspoon sized clumps of masa dough into balls and lightly indent with a finger to form a small cavity. Simmer the dumplings just until they float, then transfer to the soup. Turn the heat back on for the soup, add the squash blossoms just to heat through, double check the seasoning and adjust as needed. Serve immediately, garnished with the cilantro, with lime wedges on the side.

Squash Spoonbread

Serves 6–8

This rich side dish made from squash lies in the realm of a soufflé, but is less fussy. It's very versatile; I used to serve it for breakfast, brunch, lunch, or dinner, or spooned individually into ramekins as the base of a vegetarian entrée, depending on what part of my menu needed attention. Consider garnishing with things like maple syrup, toasted nuts, or fried sage, depending on when you'd like to serve it.

1 pound (450 g) mashed, cooked kabocha or another starchy squash, such as acorn or butternut
4 ounces (115 g) butter
½ teaspoon baking powder
¼ teaspoon baking soda
3 large eggs, separated
2½ cups (625 ml) whole (full-fat) milk
¾ teaspoon salt
½ teaspoon fresh-grated nutmeg

2 tablespoons chopped sage (optional)
½ cup (65 g) plus 2 tablespoons fine cornmeal
2 tablespoons maple syrup

Preheat the oven to 325°F (160°C). In a food processor, purée the squash, butter, baking powder, baking soda, and egg yolks until very smooth. In a pot large enough to accommodate the milk and squash purée, warm the milk with the salt, nutmeg, and sage, then turn off the heat and allow to infuse for 15 minutes. Strain out the sage. Heat the milk again until it begins to steam, then whisk in the cornmeal until cooked and thickened, about 5 to 10 minutes. Remove from the heat, cool for 10 minutes, then carefully mix in the squash purée a few spoonfuls at a time. Meanwhile, whisk the egg whites to soft peaks with the maple syrup, then gently fold in the squash mixture. Pour the batter into a liberally greased 10-inch (26 cm) cast-iron skillet or baking pan and bake at 325°F until just set, about 45 to 50 minutes.

Curried Squash Soup

Makes 14 cups (3.5 L)

Everyone loves an orange squash soup, and this one, gently sweet and spiced, with richness from coconut milk, is the holy grail of them for me and is the exact recipe I developed for serving each fall in my restaurants. You can make it with any orange-fleshed squash, but the best, by far, will be from starchy, sweet kabocha (or a similar variety like buttercup) from a seasonal farmers market (or look for them year-round in Asian markets). Sometimes I make this soup with the relish, sometimes without, but it

adds some good texture and flavor contrast. It's just fine sipped out of a mug while wearing mittens, too. This will serve a family of six with leftovers, or eight people as a lunch.

Pepper relish (optional)

1 small shallot, in ¼-inch (6 mm) dice
2 tablespoons cider vinegar
Pinch of kosher salt
2 orange, yellow, or red sweet peppers
2 small, hard baking apples, such as
  Granny Smith
2 tablespoons blended olive oil, or
  flavorless oil

Soup

6–7 pounds (2.7–3.2 kg) squash, whole,
  or 8 cups (1 kg) packed cooked squash
3 tablespoons coconut oil, lard, or flavorless
  cooking oil, plus a bit more to lightly coat
  the squash
1½ teaspoons kosher salt, plus more
  to taste
3 tablespoons roughly chopped garlic
  (4–5 large cloves)
1 medium yellow onion, in ½-inch
  (1.25 cm) dice
3 tablespoons peeled and roughly chopped
  fresh ginger
1 tablespoon finely chopped lemongrass
2 tablespoons sweet curry powder
¼ teaspoon ground cinnamon, cloves, or allspice (your choice)
½ teaspoon grated nutmeg
4 cans (each 14 ounces / 400 ml)
  coconut milk
½ cup (135 ml) maple syrup
2 cups (480 ml) chicken stock or water

Serving (optional)

Greek yogurt or coconut cream
Torn fresh basil or mint
Chopped, toasted walnuts

To make the optional relish, in a mixing bowl combine the shallot with the vinegar and a pinch of salt. Char the peppers over a flame all over, then put in a plastic bag and allow to cool. Peel the peppers, rinsing with water lightly if needed to clean them. Dice the peppers small and combine with the shallots. Peel the apple, then dice the same size you diced the peppers. Sweat the apples in a tablespoon of oil—with a bit of water added so they don't take on any color—for a few minutes until just tender. Combine the apples with the peppers and shallots, double-check the seasoning, and reserve. The relish can be made days in advance.

To roast the squash and build the soup, preheat the oven to 350°F (180°C). Cut the squash into large, manageable pieces, or cut in half if you're using small squash such as acorn. Remove the seeds and discard. Toss the squash with a bit of oil and salt, then roast cut-side up for 45 minutes or until just tender. Allow the squash pieces to cool until you can handle them, then scoop out the flesh. Meanwhile, in a stockpot, sweat the garlic, onion, and ginger in 3 tablespoons coconut oil, then add the spices and cook for a minute or two, stirring occasionally. Add the coconut milk, maple syrup, stock, and roasted squash and cook for 15 minutes, or until everything has started to break down and become amalgamated, and the onion and garlic are soft. Purée the mixture with a hand or immersion blender or transfer to a blender and purée carefully until very smooth.

Double-check the seasoning, adjust as needed, then cool the soup. (If it's fall, I put a lid on the pot and stick it outside, then transfer it to the fridge when cool.) The soup will last for 5 days in the fridge; it can be frozen but should be puréed to re-emulsify before heating and serving.

To serve the soup, ladle into warmed bowls, then garnish with a dollop of the relish, yogurt, basil, and walnuts. When I serve soups like this at home, it's convenient to set up a small buffet to let guests garnish their soup individually, or pass the garnishes in separate bowls at the table.

Green Pumpkin or Squash Agrodolce

Serves 4 as a side

This quick marinade is based on one for zucchini my friend and mentor Chef Andy Lilja taught me to make. We used to serve it as a side to wood-fired chicken, but it's also great with pork and white fish, or tucked under a salad of fresh greens with a serving of fresh goat cheese and grilled bread. Sometimes I dice the squash, sometimes I slice it, depending on how it will be served. Golden raisins plumped in wine, or baking apples cut into the same shape as the squash, are a nice variation.

1½ ounces (40 g) shallot, cut in ¼-inch (6 mm) dice or minced
1 tablespoon cooking oil
1 pound (455 g) green squash or pumpkin, cut in ½-inch (1.25 cm) dice
Kosher salt, to taste

½ cup (135 ml) vegetable stock or water
1 tablespoon maple syrup
3 tablespoons apple cider vinegar
1 teaspoon chopped fresh tarragon, dill, or your favorite herbs, to taste

In a pan wide enough to accommodate the squash in one layer, sweat the shallot in the oil for 2 to 3 minutes on medium heat, then add the squash, season to taste with salt, and add the stock, maple syrup, and vinegar. Bring to a simmer, and press a piece of parchment onto the surface to hold in some moisture while the squash simmers. Alternatively, you can cover the pan with a lid for a few minutes, then remove it and proceed.

Simmer gently until the squash is tender and translucent, adding a little extra liquid if necessary, depending on the size of your pan. When the squash is tender, toss in the dill or tarragon and serve. It's also fine served at room temperature, garnished with toasted walnuts or sunflower seeds.

Green Pumpkin Pie

Makes 1 double-crust 9-inch (22 cm) pie

In *The Long Winter*, Laura Ingalls Wilder describes Ma preparing an apple pie from green pumpkin when they feel the strong winter coming. Of course I had to try it. Sure enough, green unripe pumpkin (and many others, including butternut squash) can be cooked in place of apples, and the two have an affinity for each other. In the green stage their flavor is very neutral; they take on the flavor of whatever they're seasoned with, in this case, pumpkin pie spices. Plenty of accounts of people making green pumpkin pie exist online, but they see the pie as a sort of experiment—they start out assuming it won't taste good, so they don't put much thought into the mechanics, such as needing a good amount of starch or flour to avoid a wet pie from the vinegar necessary to lend the pumpkin pieces some tang. Done right, though, it's a great pie, and an even better conversation starter.

Double piecrust

2 cups (240 g) all-purpose flour
1 teaspoon salt
1 teaspoon sugar
8 ounces (225 g) unsalted butter, cold
½ cup (110 g) full-fat sour cream
1 teaspoon Galium Vanilla Extract
   (page 190) or vanilla extract (optional)

Filling

1 small green pumpkin, about 6 pounds
   (2.6 kg)
1½ cups (300 g) maple sugar or
   brown sugar
½ cup (135 ml) apple cider vinegar
4 tablespoons cornstarch
¾ teaspoon ground cinnamon
⅛ teaspoon ground cloves or allspice
½ teaspoon ground nutmeg
½ teaspoon ground ginger
¼ teaspoon salt
Beaten egg white, for the crust
Coarse sugar, for the crust (optional)

To make the crust, combine the flour, salt, and sugar in a mixing bowl. Cut the butter into ½-inch (1.25 cm) pieces, then add to the flour and mix to a coarse meal. Add the sour cream and the extract, and combine just until the ingredients come together into a dough. Divide the dough to create two flat disks; wrap these in cling film or fit in a tightly sealed container and let them rest for at least 15 minutes in the fridge, or until needed.

To make the filling, cut the pumpkin into quarters, then peel. It will take about four to five strokes with a vegetable peeler to get past the multiple skins and sinew of the pumpkin. Completely remove any foamy portions attached to the unripe seeds. Cut the quarters in half, then cut into ¼-inch-thick (6 mm) slices to resemble apple slices, and reserve 2½ pounds (1.1 kg) (a scant half) of them. Toss the remaining squash with the sugar, vinegar, cornstarch, spices, and salt, and allow to macerate for 20 minutes, tossing occasionally. Transfer the macerated pumpkin and the liquid, scraping out the bowl, to a 12-inch (30 cm) cast-iron skillet (or similar). Heat to a brisk simmer, stirring occasionally, then turn off the heat and cool for 15 minutes to evaporate some water. It should look like prepared pie filling.

Preheat the oven to 350°F (180°C). Roll out the bottom piecrust and set in an ungreased pie pan. Transfer the filling to the lined pan. Roll out the top crust and gently place it on top of the filling, folding the top crust under the bottom crust's edges. Crimp the edges, brush liberally with the egg white, sprinkle with the sugar, cut a few slits in the top to allow air to escape, then bake 45 to 55 minutes. Allow the pie to cool to room temperature, then serve.

Shoots: Expanding on Asparagus

Almost everyone likes asparagus, and to a lot of people it is the archetypal spring vegetable. For the vast majority of the growing season, though, asparagus isn't the tender green stalk we know and love—it's more of a feathery-green bush that makes little red seeds, as any person who has a patch in their garden can tell you. It's the young meristem, stalk, or shoot that we value, and it's only one of many different edible and similarly delicious things nature has made that we can find and eat, if we know what they look like and when to harvest them. Some of them look eerily similar to asparagus, like hosta shoots, which are in the same family (Asparagaceae), poke sallet, and Japanese knotweed. Some are much smaller,

including tender hop shoots and tips—long appreciated in Northern Italy and written about by food writers Elizabeth David and Patience Gray. The plants in this book all make good shoots to eat. A lot of other plants, caught in the right moment, can be called shoots, too, but these are the beefiest, shootiest ones I know of.

For better flavor and for safety, many of these plants should be blanched before eating—including milkweed (*Asclepias syriaca*), all fiddleheads, and staghorn sumac (*Rhus typhina*). Daylily (*Hemerocallis fulva*) shoots should not be served raw, and poke sallet especially should be boiled—not just blanched—and drained.

Shoot vegetables are a lot more than asparagus. Hostas, caught at the right stage, can be just as good.

Selected Plants with Edible Shoots

- Cattails (*Typha latifolia*)
- Common milkweed (*Asclepias syriaca*)
- Daylily (*Hemerocallis fulva*)
- Goldenrod (*Solidago* spp.)
- Hops (*Humulus lupulus*)
- Hosta (*Hosta* spp.)
- Japanese knotweed (*Reynoutria japonica*)
- Lady fern (*Athyrium filix-femina*)
- Ostrich fern (*Matteuccia struthiopteris*)
- Smilax shoots (*Smilax* spp.)
- Solomon's seal (*Polygonatum biflorum*)
- Staghorn sumac (*Rhus typhina*)
- Vetch (*Vicia americana*)
- Wood nettles (*Laportea canadensis*)

Asparagus-End Bisque

**Makes 7 cups (1.75 L),
or 6–8 appetizer portions**

My favorite asparagus soup uses only the woody ends. Chefs are always trying to figure out how to make something from nothing, and how to stretch food—especially expensive, locally harvested asparagus. Once you try it, you might start hoarding your asparagus ends instead of composting them.

1½ pounds (680 g) asparagus ends,
    roughly chopped
5 cups (1.25 L) chicken or vegetable stock
4 ounces (115 g) diced onion (1 small onion)
3 ounces (85 g) leek or fennel, washed,
    cleaned, and chopped
3 ounces (85 g) celery, chopped
2 tablespoons plus ½ cup (135 ml)
    flavorless oil
5 tablespoons white rice
½ cup (135 ml) dry white wine
½ cup (135 ml) heavy cream
Kosher salt, to taste
½ bunch Italian parsley, blanched,
    shocked in cold water, and chopped
    (optional, for color)
Sour cream thinned with a splash of
    cream, flavored with lightly toasted
celery seeds and grated lemon zest,
    for serving (optional)
Small blanched vegetables, such as
    asparagus tips, fava beans, peas, or
    chopped nettles, for serving (optional)

Chop the asparagus ends into pieces, then purée in a blender with the stock, working in batches if needed, then reserve the asparagus slurry. Sweat the onion, leek, and celery in the 2 tablespoons of oil, then add the rice, deglaze with the wine, and reduce by half. Add the asparagus slurry, bring to a simmer, and cook for 30 to 45 minutes on low heat. Add the cream. With an immersion blender, or working carefully in batches with a countertop blender, purée the soup, gradually pouring in the remaining oil to reduce the friction of the blades and make a velvety-smooth purée. Pass the soup through a fine strainer, season to taste with salt, then transfer to a container and chill. When it's cool, purée a few cups of the soup with the parsley, straining it back into the soup to refresh the color. To serve, reheat gently over low heat, stirring frequently. Pour into prewarmed bowls and garnish each serving with a drizzle of sour cream and a decorative sprinkle of freshly blanched vegetables.

Goldenrod Shoots Gomae

Serves 2

This recipe expands on the basic gomae idea (see DIY Gomae, page 39) by using various ingredients from the Asteraceae plant family (sunflower oil, seeds, and goldenrod). Canada goldenrod shoots (*Solidago canadensis*) have a strong flavor, so I like them paired with other strong flavors, such as fish sauce. To accentuate the feel of "shoots," remove all the leaves but some on the top, or leave them on, which will have more of a feel of eating a leafy green.

8 ounces (225 g) goldenrod shoots,
  or another green (a few handfuls)
¼ cup (30 g) raw sunflower seeds
1 tablespoon fish sauce
½ tablespoon apple cider vinegar or
  rice wine vinegar
1 tablespoon Smude's sunflower oil
1 tablespoon maple syrup
Sliced hot chili, to taste, for serving

Blanch the goldenrod shoots in boiling salted water until they're just tender, then shock in cold water and squeeze dry. Toast the seeds, cool, then grind to a paste in a mortar and pestle, and stir in the remaining ingredients except the chili. Toss well with the greens, double-check the seasoning, adjust as you see fit for salt and sugar, and serve cool or at room temperature, garnishing with the hot chili to taste before serving. Drizzle any remaining sauce over the top, if you like.

Glazed Hop Shoots

Long enjoyed in Italy and Belgium, hop shoots make a great addition to the spring shoot repertoire. They're a luxury, too— a seasonal delicacy that can reportedly sell for upward of $400 a pound! The simplest way I know to cook them is quickly: Cover the bottom of a lidded sauté pan with a thin film of water, bring it to a simmer, add a knob of butter and a pinch of salt, then add a handful of hop shoots, cover the pan, and cook for a few moments, just until they're tender and taste good to you. By this time the water should have evaporated and glazed them lightly in delicious, buttery juices.

Hop shoots can be gathered in a good quantity when you find the right patch.

Garden Peas with Vetch and Pea Shoots

Most farmers local to me know vetch (*Vicia americana*) as a common weed. It's a weed with a superpower, though, since it's in the Fabaceae (bean) family, and with that comes the power to fix and restore nitrogen in the soil from the atmosphere, the same function that makes soybeans a valuable crop to plant in a field after a year of growing corn. Historically, Native Americans ate the young growing tips of vetch, which, if you look closely, resemble the delicious creeping tendrils of peas, and have a similar taste. If you look online, various sites might say the plant is poisonous, but that should refer to grazing animals, and only if they eat large quantities.

Walking through the garden with creeping, twirling pea shoots wet with the morning dew one day inspired me to make a little study of peas and vetch. Take a few young peas, cook them quickly in a dash of oil over high heat, then toss in a handful of tender flowering pea shoots, cover the pan for a moment, and cook until just starting to wilt. Season them well with a little oil, salt, and pepper, and toss in some fresh torn mint leaves at the end. Garnish the plate with vetch tendrils.

Hosta Shoots

Hosta shoots were probably the first shoots I noticed growing in a garden that prompted me to think, *That looks like something I want to eat.* Indeed, hostas are edible, and a delicious example of edible landscaping. In Japan they're known as urui and fall under the catchall term *sansai* (mountain vegetable), along with other plants like Japanese knotweed and the angelica tree (*Aralia elata*). Not all hostas are created equal, though. The best hostas for eating will be the largest plants you can find; I think smaller shoots are barely worth the trouble.

Seared Hosta Shoots

Serves 2–4

My favorite way to cook hosta shoots is hot and fast, seared in a cast-iron skillet, although they make a great addition to stir-fries, too. A good seasonal accompaniment is a knob of Ramp or Wild Onion Leaf Butter (page 172).

Cooking oil, as needed
8 ounces (225 g) hosta shoots
  (2–3 shoots per person)
Kosher salt and fresh-ground black pepper,
  to taste

1–2 tablespoons Ramp or Wild Onion
  Leaf Butter (optional)
Fresh lemon wedges, for serving (optional)

Heat the oil in a cast-iron skillet (or other heavy pan) over high heat. When the oil just begins to smoke, add the hosta shoots and let them cook for a minute or two, until caramelized on one side and just wilted. Season to taste with salt and pepper, and remove from heat before adding the butter and stirring just to melt. Arrange the shoots on a plate with lemon wedges, drizzling with any butter remaining in the pan.

Hosta Kimchi

Makes a 1-quart (945 ml) jar

Hostas are a bit like rolled-up lettuce, and they take really well to the kimchi treatment. That being said, the basic measurements here will work with just about any plant, and would be especially good with aromatic plants like blanched cow parsnip or angelica blossoms, or even napa cabbage. Purslane makes a great addition, too. Use ¼ cup (30 g) of gochugaru flakes for a mildly spicy kimchi, or ½ cup (60 g) for a spicier version.

1 pound (455 g) hosta shoots, napa cabbage, or other vegetable (roughly 6 loosely packed cups)
3 ounces (85 g) daikon radish, sliced into ¼-inch (6 mm) half-moons (about ½ cup)
3 ounces (85 g) ramp leaves, or green onions, sliced into 1-inch / 2.5 cm lengths
Scant ¾ ounce (20 grams / 3 teaspoons) kosher salt

Chili paste

½ cup (135 ml) water
1 tablespoon maple syrup
3 tablespoons fish sauce
1 tablespoon white rice flour (or grind white rice as finely as possible in a coffee grinder)
¼ cup (30 g) Korean gochugaru chili flakes (coarse)
3 large cloves garlic, minced
1-inch (2.5 cm) cube fresh ginger, minced

Cut the hostas into 1-inch (2.5 cm) pieces and combine in a bowl with the radish, ramp leaves, and salt, mix very well, and allow to sit for an hour or two.

Bring the water, maple syrup, and fish sauce to a simmer with the rice flour until thickened, cool to room temperature, then mix with the chili flakes, garlic, and ginger. Rinse the salted hosta mixture well, drain, and pat dry with a towel if needed to remove excess moisture. Toss the hosta mixture with the chili paste, then pack into a quart (945 ml) jar. Screw on the lid and leave out for 2 to 5 days (depending on how sour you want the kimchi to be), removing the lid occasionally to let carbon dioxide escape, then refrigerate. The kimchi will last for a month or longer if regularly pressed under its liquid.

Crisp Fiddlehead Pickles

Makes 4 jars, each 1 pint (480 ml)

Fiddleheads make great pickles, but over-cooking can make them soft. Once upon a time, a chef showed me how to pickle asparagus tips to keep them crisp by pouring boiling pickle liquid into the jar and turning them upside down to seal. As far as fiddleheads go, I would use only ostrich fern (*Matteuccia struthiopteris*) or lady fern (*Athyrium filix-femina*) fiddleheads for this, but plenty of other tender vegetables will work, too. Think of the spices as a suggestion.

½ tablespoon black peppercorns
½ tablespoon coriander seeds
½ tablespoon fennel seeds
4 cups (945 ml) water
2 cups (480 ml) vinegar (apple cider, white, white wine, or champagne vinegar)
¼ cup kosher salt
Zest of 1 lemon, peeled in strips
4–5 small cloves garlic, finely chopped
4–5 sprigs thyme
2½ pounds (1.1 kg) fiddlehead ferns
  (the youngest, tightest ones you can find)

Toast the spices until fragrant, then combine with the water, vinegar, salt, lemon zest, garlic, and thyme, and bring to a boil. Allow to infuse while you prepare the rest of the ingredients.

Bring a large pot of water to a boil. Add the fiddlehead ferns to the pot, cover to bring the pot back to a boil, and cook for 1½ minutes, stirring occasionally to ensure even blanching. Drain the fiddleheads and remove to a tray lined with a towel to absorb water.

Working quickly, pack each pint jar three-quarters of the way full of fiddleheads, placing a piece of lemon zest, a clove of garlic, and a sprig of thyme from the boiled pickle liquid in each. Reheat the pickle liquid to a rolling boil, then pour the liquid into the jars, covering all of the fiddleheads, leaving ⅛ inch (3 mm) headspace. Allow the liquid to settle for a moment, wiggle a chopstick in each jar to remove air pockets, adding a little more liquid to cover if needed, then screw on the lids and turn the jars upside down. Leave the jars undisturbed until they're cool.

Once the jars cool, they should have sealed just as if you were to use a water bath, but without the excess cooking time that would make the fiddleheads soft. Voilà! Crisp pickled fiddleheads. Look over the jars carefully to make sure they've all formed seals. Refrigerate any that haven't sealed, and consume these within a month.

Eating the Whole Fiddlehead

Fiddleheads, even though they're wild, suffer from the same mistreatment that a lot of vegetables do when they're sold in stores during their short season: Suppliers and foragers deem only a certain part of the plants "fit to be eaten." The prized part of a fiddlehead fern is the tightly coiled crozier, with the stem being an afterthought. In fact, the entire tender stem is edible and delicious, even though it's long and awkward (nothing a quick chop can't fix). After I blanch the stems to keep their color (again, never eat them raw), I'll add them to all kinds of things, like Hosta Kimchi (page 111) or a quick sauté of spring vegetables.

Across, fiddleheads can be mostly stem, and that stem is still great to eat.

Lacto Knotweed Pickles

One of the strangest wild edibles I know, Japanese knotweed resembles bamboo in shape and size, and is something like swampy rhubarb in flavor. It's an acquired taste, to be certain, but in the right places it can be very good, especially lacto-fermented. It's well known in the foraging community, but I learned about it from French chef Jacques Chibois, who grew it in his culinary garden at his restaurant La Bastide Saint-Antoine. Speaking of gardens, do not plant it in yours. Knotweed is the most invasive plant I've ever seen. Scraps and trim from the plant can't be composted raw, and should be baked, boiled, or hurled into the depths of Mount Doom since clippings can potentially create new colonies. On a bright note, it's great for pollinators!

Knotweed is mucilaginous, slimy, sticky, and weird when it gets cooked, but *cooked* is the operative word here. Vinegar (as in pickling) also activates the mucilage slightly, but if you don't use heat or vinegar, the mucilage is hardly noticeable. Enter fermentation, and a tip of the hat to my friend Jacqui Shykoff, a forager who supplies restaurants in France with wild goods. To make this dish, gather fat, tender knotweed shoots and peel them, then cut into 3-inch (7.5 cm) pieces and fit into a quart (945 ml) jar. Follow the directions for Grape Leaves Fermented in Brine (page 26), then screw on a lid and allow to sit at room temperature. As it sits, the knotweed will gradually, gently take on sour qualities, but will remain crisp—without mucilage. It can be refrigerated or kept at room temperature, but I refrigerate the jars after I've opened them a few times to prevent the growth of kahm yeast. These pickles are great added to dishes with fish or shrimp as a final garnish, tucked into spring rolls, or added to a bowl of ramen at the end (in lieu of sour bamboo). These are also wonderful prepared with a few hot chilies, garlic cloves, and dill sprigs as you would sour kosher dills.

Knotweed shoots, just emerging.

Milkweed

I have a dream where lawns, instead of being filled with the same monoculture-evoking green grass, are filled with plants native to the area, many of them food plants.

In the summer, when the wildflowers are at their peak, the yard is a mini game preserve, a vision of what the land was like before human touch. The air is thick with birdsong, a chorus of buzzing insects pollinating plants on their journey for nectar, and the whirring blur of hummingbirds. Nearby a gray squirrel nibbles the cap of a mushroom, a bolete bonded to the oak tree in the yard where he'll be harvesting nuts in the fall. Around the corner a rabbit munches wild carrot greens, trying to stay out of sight of the hawk perched in the same oak tree.

Towering above it all—above the big bluestem grass and wild onion flowers, above the ferns grown tall in the shady areas near the spring—are beautiful, tall milkweeds showing their purple flowers. After a monarch butterfly pauses on one to nibble a leaf, a human hand reaches in for a few young seedpods, taken inside quickly to meet a hot pot of water, a pat of butter, a squeeze of lemon.

I learned about milkweed first from my father, who told me he learned to eat the young buds, which look a bit like broccoli, when he was in the Boy Scouts; the rest I learned from reading Sam Thayer's first book, *The Forager's Harvest*. Some people say cattails are the grocery store of the woods, and while that's a nice idea, with milkweed I think it's actually true. Milkweed continuously offers different, great-tasting edible parts throughout the growing season—more than nearly any plant I know. Unfortunately, a lot of people don't think milkweed should be harvested, and every year I prepare to defend my use of the plant against the chorus of people admonishing me: "Stop! Just stop telling people to harvest milkweed! You're killing the monarchs,

and you, *you* will be personally responsible when they're extinct, you irresponsible, gluttonous forager! Go pick dandelions, nettles, and weeds—at least those are sustainable!"

I appreciate the sentiment of milkweed's defenders: Protecting butterflies is a righteous cause. But we're thinking about the plant all wrong if we scold people who would harvest it as a food. Foragers, and people who appreciate milkweed, can be the saviors of the monarchs, not their destroyers. How? First, we need to stop calling milkweed a weed, and start considering it for what it can be: a food plant (a vegetable, even!) for humans and insects alike, one that can and should be planted, instead of unnecessarily safeguarded as some dwindling natural resource. (I'll add that it's always good to find large colonies to harvest from, so that you can leave plenty of food for other creatures that rely on the plant in the area.)

Common milkweed (*Asclepias syriaca*) has a wealth of edible parts that are effortless to harvest—the entire aboveground plant as long as it's young and tender. They're also delicious, lacking the bitterness stereotypically associated with many wild foods. (If your milkweed shoots taste bitter, you probably harvested the look-alike dogbane instead, which you should discard.) Common milkweed boasts a sweet, green flavor somewhere between green beans, peas, and nature.

As I see it, over the course of the growing season, the plant provides eight unique, edible stages of growth and harvestable parts for the cook. In spring there are the young, tender shoots. Later, what I call the clouche or complete top of the stalk, including immature buds and leaves, constitutes another small vegetable, followed by the more fully formed and better-known green flower buds, which, harvested when still firm and then steamed or gently treated, cook up a bit like broccoli florets.

Through the whole growing season, milkweed leaves, although tougher and dry in the later stages of growth, can be blanched and eaten, or made into colorful, chlorophyll-rich purées for coloring doughs, breads, or soups.

Milkweed reaches the height of its beauty during the growing season, with edible flowers of the deepest mauve to purple, heavily scented with perfume as rich as, if not richer than that of any rose. The flowers' aroma makes them perfect for scenting drinks, infusing into sorbet bases or syrups to be mixed with soda, sprinkling whole on salads sweet and savory, or strewing over hot or cold plates as a garnish. As a finale, the plant makes pods I like to call wild okra for their shape when they're young and tender, as well as to disguise them a bit and add some romance.

I've never had a problem eating any part of milkweed, but some people do. If it's your first time eating the plant, it's a good idea to blanch it in salted, boiling water until tender, then try eating a small amount to see if it agrees with you. I'll also add that I don't eat milkweed raw, with the exception of the flowers in small amounts as a garnish, and I don't eat entire plates of it; my typical portion is just 2 to 4 ounces (55–115 g) at a time. However, once you try Cornmeal-Fried Milkweed Pods, you might find it hard not to gorge yourself on them.

Lastly, while the window for harvesting is short, even after the pods are too tough to eat, the inner silk with its almost cheesy consistency when cooked (before the seeds are developed) is the final edible part the plant gives us.

All of that food, from a "weed" that will be perfectly at home around your garden. Imagine if even 0.01 percent of every garden that could support it included milkweed as a food plant. Just think how much food humans and butterflies could share!

A few edible parts of milkweed: *from left to right*, shoots, buds, pods.

Steamed Milkweed Buds

Milkweed shoots are great, but the brilliant green flower buds, still tight like miniature broccoli, are even better. They can get oily when sautéed in lots of fat, so I often prefer to steam them, napping them with a little butter or whatever I feel like after they're cooked.

To steam the shoots, put a steamer basket in a pot with a scant inch (2.5 cm) of water. Cover the pot and bring it to a rolling boil, then add a couple of handfuls of buds—don't overcrowd the pan. Replace the cover and set a timer for 5 minutes, then resist the temptation to remove the lid. When the timer goes off, the buds should be cooked through, hot and tender, but not mushy.

One of the best ways to enjoy them is with just a bit of butter and a sprinkle of salt and pepper, but you don't have to stop there. Hands down, my favorite way to eat milkweed shoots is drizzled with warm butter and a few spoonfuls of Ramp Steak Sauce (page 174), but you can also treat them like the seasonal luxury they are—like little artichokes. Try dipping them in a little aioli or Lemon Jam Aioli (page 154), or drizzle with melted Ramp or Wild Onion Leaf Butter (page 172). Instead of butter, oils are good, too—especially ones like Sam Thayer's hickory nut or acorn oil, or just your favorite olive oil. Keep some crunchy salt handy for sprinkling. The flavor is delicate, so just a few simple herbs can be all they need. Try tossing freshly steamed buds in a bowl with melted butter and some chopped chives, wild onion tops, tarragon, or parsley. Just like other green vegetables, milkweed buds pair well with mushrooms—serving a few small, whole golden chanterelles or shiitakes steamed alongside them and dressed with butter is a treat.

Dried Milkweed Buds or Fiddleheads

These two wild vegetables are both delicious dehydrated for cooking in the off season, a trick I learned from my friend, Native American ethnobotanist Linda Black Elk. Milkweed buds can be dried from raw, but fiddleheads will keep a better color if they're blanched for a few minutes, dried, and then set to dry. After they're completely cracker-dry, they can be stored in jars at room temperature, and rehydrated in water to bring them back. They're both tasty tossed into soups and stews at the end of cooking. Fiddleheads, especially, get a concentrated flavor that's almost oceanic from drying.

Cornmeal-Fried Milkweed Pods

Makes 3–4 milkweed pods per serving

Here wild okra gets the fried okra treatment, but just between you and me, these are better. The secret is in the texture of the pods themselves. Liquid naturally clings to them, so instead of having to use a flour-egg-crumb breading that could get heavy, all the wee pods need is a soak in some beaten egg or buttermilk, followed by a dredge in some cornmeal, before their date with a bit of oil in a hot pan.

Fine cornmeal, as needed for dredging
A generous dash each: salt, pepper,
  cayenne, and paprika (also worth trying:
  ground dried ramp leaves or similar, or
  curry powder)
Small, young milkweed pods (no larger
  than 2 inches / 5 cm)
Buttermilk, or beaten egg, as needed for
  dredging the pods
Condiments, for serving: hot sauce, lemon
  wedges, hot sauce mixed with mayonnaise,
  garlic aioli, or Goddess Herb Dressing
  (page 43)

Season the cornmeal with a good pinch *each* of salt, pepper, cayenne, and paprika. Blanch the pods in boiling water for 1 to 2 minutes, then remove and drain completely. Put the blanched pods in a bowl and cover with buttermilk, then toss the individual pods in the cornmeal. Heat a pan with a layer of oil (or prepare a deep fryer) and cook the pods until golden all over, then cool on a paper towel to drain excess oil. The pods hold heat very well, so allow them to cool for a few minutes before digging in.

Milkweed Shoots Milanese

Asparagus Milanese is asparagus served with a fried egg and Parmesan. Making a similar dish with milkweed is a great way to treat the first milkweed shoots of the year, and it's as easy to make as it is delicious.

Just take a handful of milkweed shoots, about 2 or 3 ounces (55–85 g) per person, remove all the leaves up to the top, and trim any firm stem at the bottom, as with asparagus. Bring a pot of salted water to a boil and blanch the shoots for a minute or two, or until just tender. Meanwhile, fry 1 egg per person, sunny-side up in a knob of butter, nice and slow so they don't brown. Add a splash of water to the pan and cover it for a moment or two to remove the rawness from around the yolk. Drain the shoots well, blotting on a towel, then serve the shoots with the egg on top, drizzled with some good-tasting oil, plenty of cracked pepper, and a grate or two of good Parmesan.

Milkweed Bud Fettuccine

Serves 4

This pasta dish is one of the first things I made with milkweed, and a good example of how even the tough leaves can be put to work. Here the leaves are used to color the pasta dough, while the buds are tossed in at the end with a few scrapes of lemon zest and a good knob of butter. It's a great way to enjoy the buds by themselves and celebrate the season.

2–3 ounces (55–85 g) small, firm
  milkweed buds
5 tablespoons unsalted butter, divided
4 tablespoons shallots, in ¼-inch (6 mm) dice
Kosher salt, to taste
½ cup (135 ml) chicken or vegetable stock
1 recipe Milkweed Leaf Pasta Dough (follows)
⅛ cup (30 ml) water from the pasta pot
2 teaspoons fresh-grated lemon zest
4 tablespoons Parmigiano Reggiano, or other
  domestic Parmesan, plus more for serving

Bring a pot of lightly salted water to a boil. Blanch the milkweed buds in the boiling water for a minute, then refresh in cold water. Drain the milkweed buds thoroughly and reserve.

In a large sauté pan, melt half of the butter and add the diced shallots. Cook the shallots on medium until they are translucent and soft, about 2 to 3 minutes, then season with a good pinch of salt. Add the stock and cook until reduced by half, then turn off the heat.

Make the pasta, then add half the recipe (8 ounces / 225 g) of it to the boiling water and cook until done, about 1 minute. Drain, reserving ⅛ cup of the cooking liquid. Add the cooked pasta to the pan with the stock and shallots, then add the cooking liquid, the reserved milkweed buds, the remaining butter, and the lemon zest. Cook for another minute or two, swirling the pan until the liquid is thickened slightly and creamy. Add 4 tablespoons of Parmesan and toss to coat, then divide the pasta among four heated bowls and serve immediately. Pass additional Parmesan at the table.

Milkweed Leaf Pasta Dough

**Makes about 1 pound / 455 g
(4 generous servings)**

2 ounces (55 g) fresh milkweed leaves
4 large egg yolks
1½ cups (180 g) all-purpose flour
¾ teaspoon kosher salt
1–2 tablespoons water, as needed to help
  bring the dough together
Semolina flour or fine cornmeal, for dusting
  the work surface (optional)

Blanch the milkweed leaves for 30 seconds in boiling salted water, then refresh in cold water and drain well. Chop the leaves fine, then purée in a blender or food processor with the egg yolks until smooth.

In the bowl of a stand mixer (or by hand), combine the flour, salt, and milkweed purée, mix with a paddle attachment until the dough just comes together, then switch to the dough hook and knead to a smooth dough, adding a little water if needed to help the dough come together. Allow the dough to rest for 30 minutes before rolling out.

Cut off a quarter of the dough at a time and roll out thinly with a rolling pin. Roll out the pasta to the second or last setting on a pasta machine, then cut ½-inch (1.25 cm) fettuccine noodles, either with a knife by hand or with an attachment. Toss the cut fettuccine in semolina flour to prevent sticking. Freeze the pasta, or store in the refrigerator for up to 3 days, tossing occasionally with more semolina flour if needed to prevent sticking.

Milkweed Flower Shrub

Makes 1 generous cup (240 ml)

A sweet-and-sour syrup made from milkweed flowers that I add to drinks. In this basic recipe, you can see that all the parts are at a 2:1:1 ratio, so it's easy to multiply and scale as needed. It's great used to mix in drinks, and makes things taste a bit like watermelon Jolly Ranchers. Excellent with vodka and sparkling water or tonic, or added to something like white sangria.

1 cup (240 ml) champagne or white
  wine vinegar
1 cup (200 g) sugar
2 ounces (55 g) milkweed flowers, or
  enough flowers so the vinegar and
  sugar can barely cover them

Stir the vinegar and sugar until melted, then add the milkweed flowers and allow to sit in a container, covered, at room temperature. Strain after a week and store in the fridge for the best flavor.

Creole Milkweed Pod Stew

Serves 4–6 as an entrée

A southern-inspired stew featuring the trinity (peppers, onion, and celery) with milkweed pods standing in for okra. For a gumbo-type dish, use 5 cups (1.25 L) of meat or vegetable stock, add a spoonful or two of tomato paste, and thicken it with browned roux.

8 ounces (225 g) bacon, preferably in slab form, diced (½–1 pound / 225–455 g of your favorite sausage makes a good substitute)
3 large cloves garlic
2 teaspoons smoked paprika
1 medium yellow onion, in ½-inch (1.25 cm) dice
1 rib celery, in ½-inch (1.25 cm) dice
1 large bell pepper, any color but green, in ½-inch (1.25 cm) dice
Kosher salt, to taste
2 cups (480 ml) canned tomato sauce (or puréed peeled, seeded tomatoes)
3 cups (720 ml) meat or vegetable stock
7 ounces (200 g) young milkweed pods, 1–2 inches (2.5–5 cm) in size, trimmed, cleaned, and cut into ½-inch (1.25 cm) rounds
1 tablespoon crumbled bergamot, or 1 teaspoon dried thyme
Tabasco, or a chili sauce of your choice, to taste
Cooked wild rice, or white rice, for serving (optional)

In a soup pot, render the bacon to give up fat until crisp. Meanwhile, crush the garlic cloves with the back of a knife, remove the skin, and chop roughly. Add the garlic to the pan, stir, and cook on medium until browned but not burned. Add the paprika, stir, and cook 1 minute more. Add the diced onion, celery, and pepper, season with a good pinch of salt, and cook until translucent. Keep an eye on the bottom of the pan so it doesn't get too dark, adding a splash of water if needed. Add the tomato sauce, stock, milkweed pods, bergamot, and a couple of shots of Tabasco; cover and cook for 20 minutes or until the pods are tender. Check the seasoning for salt and spiciness, adjust as needed, then serve with cooked wild rice, steamed white rice, or alone as a stew.

Purslane and Stonecrop

Purslane (*Portulaca oleracea*) is one of the best examples of our dichotomous relationship with plants, and how perception is everything. Across Central and South America, verdolagas, as they're known, are beloved edible plants and sold in markets. Contrastingly, in American weed control manuals, purslane is described as a nuisance, a blemish in a perfect lawn, and the only recommended preparation is a dose of herbicide, like Roundup. Whatever you call it, it's an edible succulent with juicy, slightly tart leaves and an impressive nutrient profile. Purslane's flavor is mildly tart fresh, and delicious raw, fermented, or blanched if it's older. If you don't have access to a garden, try your local Asian market.

If you're like me, you've probably walked by stonecrop (*Sedum/Hyphotelium* spp.) plenty of times without thinking twice, as it's commonly planted in gardens, although now that I've started harvesting it, I see wild escapees here and there, especially near old, abandoned farms. I didn't notice it until I read it was edible in my friend Ellen Zachos's book *Backyard Foraging*. The stonecrop I've eaten has a stronger flavor that I'd describe as very green and earthy, although I've read that there are variations among species, and that plants growing in full sun can have a stronger flavor. The leaves have a crisp, juicy texture and are great in salads. I like them paired with Mediterranean flavors, especially tomatoes and salty, briny things like capers, anchovies, and olives.

Stonecrop Salad with Tomatoes and Olives

This has been my favorite way to enjoy stonecrop so far. Take some cherry tomatoes, preferably really good, in-season ones in a variety of colors. Cut them in half or leave them whole, depending on their size. Add some orpine leaves about the same size as the tomatoes, along with some halved olives you like (Castelvetrano, dry black, and kalamata are all great here), a few slices of hot pepper (pickled Calabrian chilies are great if you can find them) or pepper flakes, sliced herbs such as parsley or basil, olive oil, and salt and pepper to taste. Let the salad sit at room temperature for a bit so the flavors can marry before eating.

Purslane in Salsa Verde with Carnitas

Serves 6 as an entrée

A classic preparation from south of the border, this is purslane in salsa verde with carnitas, as opposed to carnitas with purslane in salsa verde. The meat is more of an accent here, and the finished serving size of meat to juicy purslane is about equal. It's a great way to enjoy the plant, especially if the people eating it are skeptics, since tart tomatillos and crispy pork make anything delicious.

Carnitas
2 pounds (910 g) pork shoulder, cut into
   pieces (each 1½–2 ounces / 40–55 g)
1 teaspoon kosher salt
1 teaspoon ground cumin
1 large onion
Small handful garlic cloves
4 cups (945 ml) water
1 dried bay leaf

Salsa verde
1½ pounds (680 g) tomatillos, peeled
   and rinsed
1 medium yellow onion, quartered
1 large jalapeño*
4 medium cloves garlic, in the skin
2 cups (120 g) (loosely packed) chopped
   cilantro, divided
Kosher salt and fresh-ground black pepper
1 large lime

---

* If you can handle some heat, char the jalapeño whole and add to the blender. If you are at all heat-sensitive, halve the jalapeño and remove the seeds, then season the sauce to taste for spiciness afterward.

1 pound (455 g) fresh purslane (or more
  if you like)
2 tablespoons oil or lard, plus more for
  searing the pork

Serving
Steamed rice
Fresh lime wedges
Fresh sprigs of purslane
Fresh cilantro

To make the carnitas, combine all the ingredients in a heavy pot (such as a Dutch oven). Bring to a simmer, reduce the heat to low, and cook for 1½ hours or until fork-tender. Cool and reserve.

To make the salsa verde, preheat the oven to 350°F (180°C). Heat a heavy skillet, preferably cast iron, without adding oil. Add the tomatillos, onion, jalapeño, and garlic and cook on high until charred lightly all over, turning occasionally. Transfer the pan to the oven and bake until the tomatillos are just tender, about 15 minutes. Transfer the mixture to a blender with 1 cup (240 ml) of the pork cooking liquid and 1 cup (60 g) of the cilantro, then purée until smooth but not obliterated. (If you have a high-speed blender, don't purée on high—this can break the seeds and make the sauce bitter.) Season to taste with salt, pepper, and a generous squeeze of the lime. Sweat the purslane in 2 tablespoons of the oil, then, when it's wilted, pour in the tomatillo sauce and simmer until it thickens to your liking. Toss in the rest of the cilantro at the end.

Just before serving, heat a generous amount of oil, pat the pork pieces dry, then fry them until crisp, seasoning with salt and pepper. You'll have extra pork stock left over, which you can use to make soup. To serve, put some of the salsa verde on a plate with freshly steamed rice, top with a few crispy pork chunks, and garnish with lime, purslane sprigs, and cilantro. It's also good served with warm corn tortillas.

Purslane and Sweet Corn Salad

Serves 4 as a side dish

In this marriage of some of my favorite summer produce, purslane pairs well with corn and tomatoes. If your purslane is older or large, blanch it to tenderize. Crumbled queso fresco or another mild cheese makes a good addition.

4 ounces (115 g) tender purslane,
  plus extra sprigs for garnish
3–4 ears sweet corn, in the husk, to yield
  1½ cups (8 ounces / 225 g) kernels
A few handfuls fresh cherry tomatoes
A few garlic scapes or scallions, to taste
½ teaspoon freshly toasted, ground
  cumin seeds
Extra-virgin olive oil, to taste
Fresh lime juice, to taste
Kosher salt and fresh-ground black pepper,
  to taste
Chopped fresh cilantro, to taste
Chopped fresh mint, to taste (optional)

Wash and dry the purslane, removing any tough stem portions, and cut into 1-inch (2.5 cm) segments. Roast the ears of corn, still in their husks, for 15 minutes at 350°F (180°C); cool, then cut the kernels off the cobs. In the meantime, char the tomatoes: Heat a cast-iron skillet on high until smoking (turn on an air vent or fan) then add the tomatoes to the skillet dry. Cook the tomatoes until they develop black char spots and are hot throughout, about 5 to 10 minutes. Remove the tomatoes and reserve, then rinse and oil the skillet. Char the scapes dry until cooked and lightly blackened like the tomatoes, then cool, cut in ¼-inch (6 mm) slices, and reserve.

  Mix all the ingredients together, season aggressively, then garnish with a few extra purslane sprigs and serve.

Carmelita's Purslane with Tomato and Jalapeño

Mention the word *verdolagas* to someone from Latin America, and I can just about guarantee their eyes will get a romantic glaze as they talk about their family preparations for it. I loved discussing food with my employees from Latin America to get to know them, and just about everyone I asked had a certain way they thought verdolagas should be prepared. My favorite recipe came from Carmelita, an Ecuadorian, and one of the most hardworking dishwasher / prep cooks I've had the pleasure of working with. Here's how Carmelita told me to make it.

Finely chop a small onion, a clove or two of garlic, and a small jalapeño (seeds removed or not) and sweat in lard or oil. Take a few generous handfuls of washed, chopped purslane (feel free to mix it with other greens and quelites such as lambsquarters) and add to the pan, along with some chopped, peeled, and seeded tomato, then cook until the purslane is tender and tastes good to you. Finally, add some chopped cilantro, season to taste with salt, and serve as a side dish, preferably alongside rice and beans. If you find the flavor of purslane like this too strong or tart, blanch it first and give the dish another shot.

Heirloom Tomato and Purslane Panzanella

Serves 6–8 as a side dish

To me this is summer on a plate, and putting this salad on a menu was a yearly tradition for me. Tomatoes and purslane comprise a natural pairing, at least to me, since they often grow very close to each other. It's a great way to introduce people to purslane, and a useful example of how you can incorporate the plant into different dishes—just toss in a handful!

3 slices (each ½ inch / 1.25 cm thick) good bread, preferably sourdough (such as Wild Herb Brioche, page 148)

2 ounces (55 g) red onion, in ¼-inch (6 mm) dice

1½ pounds (680 g) heirloom tomatoes, or the best fresh tomatoes you can find

6 ounces (170 g) cucumber (about half a large English cucumber)

1 large clove garlic

Kosher salt and fresh-ground black pepper, to taste

⅓ cup (80 ml) extra-virgin olive oil or Smude's sunflower oil

Torn fresh basil leaves, to taste

5 ounces (140 g) purslane tips, washed and cleaned

Champagne vinegar, or another high-quality vinegar, to taste

Edible flowers, for serving (optional; pictured are white campion and touch-me-not)

The night before, leave the bread slices out, uncovered, to dry out. When you're ready to cook, soak the diced red onion in water to cover. Core the tomatoes, then dice into rough pieces about ½ inch square. Peel the cucumber, scrape out the seeds if mature, and cut in ½-inch dice. Meanwhile, toast the slices of bread in an oven, toaster, or hot pan until crisp, then remove, cool until you can handle them, and rub lightly with the garlic clove so that it dissolves into each side of the bread (don't feel you need to use all the garlic). Tear the bread into pieces the same size as the tomato and cucumber. Combine all the ingredients except the edible flowers, and allow the panzanella to rest for a few minutes. Toss before serving to distribute the natural vinaigrette that forms, taste and adjust the seasoning, then spoon into a bowl and serve, garnishing with the flowers.

Lilium and Hyacinth Bulbs

Lilium and hyacinth bulbs are two great examples of flowers that do triple duty: They're beautiful, they attract pollinators, and their underground bulbs are a food source. In Asia, *Lilium brownii* bulbs are known as yurine and used in savory dishes like soup, as well as sweet dishes. Tassel hyacinth bulbs (*Leopoldia comosa*) have a long history of being used in Italy, where they're known as *lampascioni*, and musk and grape hyacinths (*Muscari* spp.) are also said to be consumed. So far I've eaten *L. comosa* and common, or garden hyacinth (*Hyacinthus orientalis*), which I haven't been able to find a mention of people consuming. The tassel hyacinths I've eaten were intensely bitter even after prolonged boiling, which turned off most people I served them to; the garden hyacinth bulbs on the other hand were very mild tasting, and I prefer them. You can find hyacinth bulbs growing wild, or just order them from a flower shop if you'd like to try them. You can't order by the pound (they're not considered food!) so 30 to 40 bulbs is a good place to start.

Note: Because hyacinths contain calcium oxalate crystals, like taro root, they must be boiled before eating and shouldn't be consumed raw. People who need to be on an oxalate-reduced diet, such as those with kidney stones, should probably avoid them, as well as other oxalate-rich foods like spinach, rhubarb, and almonds.

Preserved Hyacinth Bulbs (Lampascioni)

Makes 1 pint (480 ml)

This is about as good of an approximation of the traditional lampascioni pickle as I can find (if you're curious, look on YouTube—a number of charming Italian ladies share their methods). It's basically a simple pickle with garlic and herbs. The finished product is usually eaten as an antipasto, alongside things like olives, cheese, and cured meat, but I've also seen them folded into mashed potatoes, served alongside lamb, and mixed into stuffings.

1 pound (455 g) common/garden or other hyacinth bulbs (about 9)

Cooking
4 cups (945 ml) water
1 tablespoon kosher salt

Pickling
1 large clove garlic, grated or finely chopped
½ teaspoon toasted, cracked peppercorns
1 tablespoon chopped Italian parsley
1 tablespoon chopped fresh oregano
¼ teaspoon red pepper flakes
½ cup (135 ml) cider vinegar
½ teaspoon sugar
1 teaspoon salt
1 cup (240 ml) water

Cut the top and bottom off each hyacinth bulb, then cut a shallow X in the root end of each. Bring the cooking water and 1 tablespoon salt to a boil with the hyacinth bulbs and cook for 15 minutes, or until tender when pierced. Drain the bulbs, discard the water, and cool, then cut each bulb into quarters. Toss with the garlic, pepper, chopped herbs, and red pepper flakes and pack into a pint (480 ml) jar. Meanwhile, bring the vinegar, sugar, salt, and water to a vigorous boil and pour into the jar, agitating the bulbs with a skewer to remove any air pockets so the jar can be filled to the brim. Screw on the lid, turn the jar upside down to seal, and cool. Store the pickles in a pantry until opened, then refrigerate.

Hyacinth Bulbs in Red Sauce (Lampascioni en Salsa Rosa)

Makes 1 pint (480 ml)

I developed this preserve while I was translating an Italian book on cooking with wild plants. The original was a sweet-and-sour preserve with tomato, but mine skips the sugar and adds hot chili, made into a paste in the blender and thinned with white wine or apple cider vinegar. Small onion bulbs can be preserved the same way.

1 pound (455 g) Oriental hyacinth bulbs (about 9)

Cooking
4 cups (945 ml) water
1 tablespoon kosher salt
1 tablespoon chopped fresh basil, or oregano

Pickling
½ cup (10 g) dried guajillo chilies (about 2)

1 large clove garlic, grated or
  finely chopped
⅓ cup (80 ml) white wine vinegar
1 teaspoon salt
1 cup (240 ml) tomato juice, or pulsed
  tomatoes from the garden, strained

Cut the top and bottom off of each hyacinth bulb, then cut a shallow X in the root end of each. Bring the cooking water and tablespoon of salt to a boil with the hyacinth bulbs and cook for 15 minutes, or until tender when pierced. Drain the bulbs, discard the water, and cool, then cut each bulb into quarters. Toss with the basil and reserve. For the sauce, toast the chilies, then crush and remove the seeds. Purée the chilies, garlic, vinegar, salt, and tomato juice in a blender until smooth, then pack the hot bulbs in a 1-pint (480 ml) canning jar, cover with the sauce, jiggle the jar around to remove air pockets, and leave ½ inch (1.25 cm) of headspace at the top. Screw the lids on, then process the jar in a water bath for 10 minutes.

The Whole Sunflower

Sunflowers are more than a seed crop. Drive down country roads in the summer where I live, and you'll see giant sunflowers towering over gardens, telling you summer is at its peak. If you look at the plants while they're growing, at the stage before the flowers bloom you might notice that they resemble an artichoke, and you'd be right.

An artichoke, is, after all, just an unopened flower caught at the right stage. The process of cooking sunflowers is slightly different from that for cooking artichokes, with the result being a unique vegetable with the texture of an artichoke and a strong sunflower flavor.

There are a few chefs who know this trick. I learned it by watching Daniel Humm of Eleven Madison Park, but I was also reminded of it by my friend Sean Sherman, who says there was a long history of Indigenous use of sunflower heads. He describes a method for cooking them in his book, *The Sioux Chef's Indigenous Kitchen*.

In addition to their unripe flowers, sunflowers have other edible parts most chefs I know rarely think to use. The leaves, although a bit too intensely flavored to serve as cooked greens, are great blanched and used for things like Roulades Verts (page 28) or wrapping a delicate fish such as a walleye before it hits the grill. At the same time you cut the unripe flower, the top 6 to 12 inches (15–30 cm) of the stem can be tender and delicious, peeled and cooked into what I would call sunflower marrow, in a nod to Chef Dan Barber who does the same with kale, broccoli, and cauliflower stems. If you miss the period of growth for sunflower artichokes, the seeds that form afterward, still white and immature, are tender, mild, and delicious in soups, in risotti, as a sprinkle, or tossed into pilafs. Finally, the tubers or sunchokes / Jerusalem artichokes, although from a cousin plant, are delicious and have a beautiful, otherworldly shape. Harvesting them is like digging for buried treasure in the fall.

Unripe sundlower seeds.

Sunflower Artichokes

Serves 2 as an appetizer

This recipe is easily scaled, depending on how many heads you have. When choosing sunflowers to harvest, look for the largest ones you can find. Small sunflower chokes might look appealing, but there isn't much food left after trimming. I think the most interesting thing to consider, though, is what other unopened flowers are still out there for us to discover—and eat?

1 large green sunflower
5 cups (1.25 L) unsalted water or
  vegetable stock, divided
Kosher salt, to taste
Olive or Smude's sunflower oil, for serving
  (optional)

Bring 4 cups (945 ml) of the water to a simmer in a tall saucepot, then cook the sunflower head for 3 to 4 minutes. Remove the sunflower from the pot, then transfer it to a sauté pan with the remaining water and a good pinch of salt. Cover the pan, then simmer, turning occasionally, until the sunflower bud is tender when pierced with a knife, about 3 to 4 minutes, depending on size. Make sure the buds are tender, as you won't be able to clean them properly otherwise. Allow the sunflower to cool, then transfer it to a cutting board and trim with a paring knife, first removing the outer leaves, then scraping out any flower petals from the inner portion of the bud, just as you would with an artichoke.

Do not remove the base of the stem. It's delicious—almost the best part of the plant, just like an artichoke. If you won't be using the buds immediately, transfer them to a lidded container and refrigerate until needed. I like to serve them cut into pieces, warmed, drizzled with Smude's oil and lemon, and crowned with a sprinkle of sunflower seeds.

Sunflower Artichokes with galinsoga, sunflower seeds, and Smude's sunflower oil.

Smude's Sunflower Oil

Similarly to how some different fruits in the genus *Prunus* can taste like almond, different plants in the Asteraceae family—including artichokes, dandelions, and many others—can share a similar flavor. Plum kernel oil tastes of almond, and high-quality, freshly pressed sunflower oil shares the artichokey-aster flavor of its cousin plants. The only sunflower oil I've tasted that captures the flavor is from Smude's in Pierz, Minnesota. The oil is good, and strong tasting, and I like to call it the olive oil of the Midwest, as it's a great substitute anywhere extra-virgin olive oil could be used. Tasting is believing, and I highly recommend picking some up for yourself. It's easy to order through their website, which will also get you the freshest product. Store it in the fridge to keep the flavor the longest.

Marinated Sunflower Artichokes

Inspired by a dish I used to make with artichokes for the antipasti station at one of the Italian restaurants I worked at, this is delicious—old and new at the same time.

Take a sunflower and the tender portion of the stalk, about 6 inches (15 cm) or so. Cut the stalk into manageable pieces (a few inches long), peel, and simmer in water with a good pinch of salt until just tender when pierced. Trim the sunflower head, cut it into ½-inch (1.25 cm) triangles, then cut the stem into ½-inch coins. Season aggressively with lemon juice, virgin sunflower oil or extra-virgin olive oil, and salt. Add a few paper-thin slices of red onion cut into 1-inch (2.5 cm) julienne and roasted, peeled bell pepper (any color but green) cut into ½-inch dice. Season to taste with chopped fresh oregano or another herb to taste, mix, and let sit for 30 minutes or so before eating. This is an excellent cold salad, and if you don't have sunflowers to cook, it's good with artichoke tops or bottoms, too.

Glazed Sunchokes

Serves 2 as a side dish

This is one of my favorite ways to serve sunchokes, the roots of a particular sunflower known as Jerusalem artichoke (*Helianthus tuberosus*). It takes a little practice (as some of my former line cooks will tell you), but after a few tries you'll understand how to caramelize a vegetable with its natural sugars through repeated deglazing—a technique you can apply to all kinds of things. Once you get the hang of making these, you can do bigger batches and cook them in advance. If you overcook or burn them on your first try or two, don't give up.

8 ounces (225 g) sunchokes (choose slender, evenly shaped ones, as they will be peeled)
1 tablespoon lard or cooking oil
Kosher salt, to taste
Water, as needed for deglazing
1 tablespoon birch or maple syrup (optional)

Serving (optional)
Chopped soft herbs such as parsley, tarragon, chives, celery leaf, or chervil
Fresh orange zest, a few scrapes to taste
Toasted nuts, for garnish

Peel the sunchokes, then cut into even-sized pieces, about 1 to 2 inches (2.5–5 cm). (After you get comfortable with the process, you can leave peeled sunchokes whole, or nearly whole, for a more dramatic look.)

Heat the oil in a pot to medium, add the sunchokes, stir to coat with the oil, season with a pinch of salt, and cook, stirring occasionally, for a few minutes, until they begin to lightly caramelize. Deglaze the pan with a tablespoon or two of water, put the lid on, and cook until the liquid is evaporated. Shake the sunchokes around in the pan a bit; the pan should have brown residue starting to build up. Add the birch syrup and more water, and cook again. Continue adding small amounts of water, covering the pan to steam the sunchokes, until they're tender when pierced, about 15 minutes. The sunchokes should be deeply brown and glazed. Toss with the fresh herbs, orange zest, and toasted nuts, and serve.

Sunflower Satay Sauce

Makes about 1¾ cups (425 ml)

Sunflower seeds have a terrific flavor, and they're inexpensive. The best part, though, is that compared with other seeds they're rather soft, making them a good, cheap substitute for pine nuts. That tenderness means they make great, velvety butters and sauces, too. I call this satay sauce, since the flavors are similar to what you'll get with Southeast Asian peanut sauces, but toasted sunflower seeds are a version all their own. Try this delicious sauce as a garnish for grilled meat, spring rolls, or cooked bitter greens, or as a dip for Roulades Verts (page 28). For the smoothest texture, toast the sunflower seeds and cool completely, then grind to a powder in a coffee or spice grinder.

¾ cup (90 g) raw, unsalted sunflower seeds
1 tablespoon fish sauce
2 tablespoons maple syrup
1 small chili, such as a serrano, or
   ¼ teaspoon cayenne pepper
2 tablespoons soy sauce
¼ cup (60 ml) fresh lime juice
1 teaspoon chopped ginger
1 large clove garlic
½ cup (135 ml) coconut milk or water
¼ cup (60 ml) Smude's sunflower oil,
   or another mild oil

Spread the sunflower seeds in a single layer on a tray and toast in a 350°F (180°C) oven until light brown and aromatic, about 15 minutes, then cool. Purée all the ingredients except the oil in a high-speed blender, starting out slow and gradually increasing the speed to break up the nuts. Once the mixture is smooth, start slowly drizzling in the oil. The sauce should be slightly looser than peanut butter. Double-check the seasoning, adjust for lime and spiciness, then refrigerate until needed. Warm the sauce to thin it to its original consistency.

Green Sunflower Sauce

Makes about 1½ cups (375 ml)

Inspired by spicy green herb sauces made with tahini, think of this as a more herbaceous version of Sunflower Satay Sauce, with a vibrant green color. Because the herbs will eventually darken, this is best made in small batches for quick use. It's equally at home on fish, pork, or chicken as it is with roasted or raw vegetables.

1 teaspoon chopped garlic
¼ cup (60 ml) fresh lemon juice
1 generous cup (60 g) roughly chopped
   fresh herbs such as parsley, mint, cilantro,
   dill, and chives
¾ cup (90 g) sunflower seeds
¾ cup (80 ml) water
1 small chili, such as a serrano, or ½ jalapeño
   (depending on how much heat you like)
Kosher salt, to taste, about ½ teaspoon

Put the garlic in the lemon juice and allow it to sit for 10 minutes in order to tame it and prevent fermentation, then combine all ingredients in a high-speed blender and purée until very smooth. Transfer to a glass container, refrigerate, and reserve until needed.

Burdock

Burdock root is delicious, and a widely available plant you can harvest over an extended period during the growing season. I cook with two types of burdock root: common burdock (*Arctium minus*) and greater burdock (*A. lappa*) —which is the species you'll see sold as gobo in Asian markets. Both roots are fine, but digging your own burdock will require a large spade, and, hopefully, some soft earth after a rain. It can be a task, especially since common burdock has wilder, more unruly roots than greater burdock. But the second-year flower stalks of common burdock are one of the largest and easiest-to-harvest wild vegetables I know of— in just an hour or two, I can harvest over 80 pounds (36 kg) of them. I like to harvest the stalks when they're about knee- to waist-high, as long as they can be easily cut through with a knife to make sure they're tender. They make an excellent vegetable. If you don't want to dig your own, or don't have access, I think it's fine to buy them (they're cheap, too!).

Simple Blanched Burdock Flower Stalks

A very basic recipe. These are delicious sautéed with vegetable medleys or added to soups.

Bring a pot of salted water to a boil. Meanwhile, peel burdock flower stalks, first removing the outer "armor" with a paring knife, then using a vegetable peeler to remove the inner fibers. Cut the hearts into 3-inch (7.5 cm) sections, blanch for 5 minutes, remove, and cool to room temperature without shocking in ice or cold water, which could cause them to discolor. From here, the stalks can be roasted, seared, or fried. Sometimes I serve them simply par-cooked like this, with aioli or a dip, or I might brown them lightly, dredge in flour, and fry crisp. If you want to serve them cool as part of an appetizer platter alongside an aioli, make sure they're tender and taste good enough for you to eat them straight-up.

Braised Burdock and Mushrooms

Serves 2–4 as a side dish

Like Kinpira Gobo, this recipe uses the julienne technique to get the most from the burdock. Instead of going the sweet-and-salty route, this one is strictly savory, with your choice of mushrooms (pheasant backs were in season when I was making this, but any that could be julienned will work) taking the place of the carrots.

8 ounces (225 g) cleaned, peeled
  burdock root
8 ounces (225 g) fresh mushrooms,
  such as pheasant backs, or another
  mushroom you could julienne
2 tablespoons ghee, lard, or cooking oil
1 large clove garlic, crushed with the
  back of a knife and finely chopped
2 tablespoons soy sauce
Good pinch of red pepper flakes (optional)
2 tablespoons apple cider or
  rice wine vinegar
1 ounce (28 g) sliced spring onions,
  green garlic, or similar
1 small handful sliced fresh herbs,
  such as cilantro, culantro, mint, or basil,
  to taste

Cut the burdock on the diagonal into ¼-inch (6 mm) rounds, then stack the rounds up and cut them into ¼-inch matchsticks. Cut the mushrooms into ¼-inch-thick slices. Put the julienned burdock into a pot, cover with water, bring to a boil, and cook for 5 minutes, then drain completely and reserve. In a 12-inch (30 cm) cast-iron skillet (or similar), heat the fat, then add the burdock and mushrooms and cook until the mushrooms are wilted. Add the garlic and sauté for a few minutes more, then add the soy sauce, red pepper flakes, and vinegar. Cook down, tossing to distribute the flavors. Taste, adjust the seasoning as needed, then toss in the onions and herbs and serve hot or at room temperature.

Vegetable Soup with Burdock Flower Stalks

Serves 2–4

Burdock flower stalks shine in soup, but especially simple, brothy soups where they mingle with other familiar vegetables. Think of this recipe as a simple template you can make your own. A dollop of pesto makes a nice substitute for the herbs if you have some.

1 cup (225g) burdock flower stalks, peeled and diced for soup
½ cup (115 g) each carrots, onion, celery, diced for soup
3 tablespoons flavorless cooking oil
1 cup (140 g) leftover cooked meat or mushrooms, cut into ½-inch (1.25 cm) pieces (pictured are chicken of the woods mushrooms)
4 cups (945 ml) really good stock, preferably made from roasted meat scraps
1 or 2 dried or fresh bay leaves
Kosher salt, to taste
Dash of fresh lemon juice, to taste, plus additional for the lemon water
Fresh herbs, such as chives, parsley, or equivalent, for serving

Put the burdock flower stalks in acidulated (lemon) water until needed.

Sweat the vegetables in the oil (if you add mushrooms instead of meat, add them now and sweat), then add the stock and bay leaves and simmer until tender, about 20 minutes. Add the meat if you're using it and warm through, adjust the seasoning for salt, add the lemon juice and herbs, and serve.

Burdock Flower Stalk Noodles

Serves 2 as a side dish

Shaving burdock flower stalks with a vegetable peeler creates slightly tender-crisp "noodles" that make for an interesting meal. Choose the largest flower stalks you can find for the widest noodles.

4 thick sections of burdock flower stalks or shoots, about 6 inches (15 cm) long, outer skin removed, then peeled
4 cups (945 ml) water
Kosher salt, to taste
Cooking oil, as needed
¼ fresh lemon

Using a vegetable peeler (the professional kitchen standard is Kuhn Rikon) or a mandoline on a very thin setting, shave the burdock flower stalks or shoots as thin as possible into long noodles, refreshing them in water seasoned with the lemon. It's okay if you can't shave the whole thing—they were free, after all. Gently simmer the noodles in the water with a good pinch of salt until just tender, about 15 or 20 minutes. Drain the noodles and reserve.

To finish the noodles, warm some oil or fat in a pan, then add the noodles and gently cook on medium-low until very lightly browned. From here, you can do whatever you want. They make an excellent noodle substitute garnished with toasted sesame oil, sesame seeds, some sort of onion (ramp flowers are pictured), and hot chilies. Adding shrimp or other ingredients you'd like in a stir-fry is great, too.

Burdock Root Mashed Potatoes

Serves 4–8 as a side dish

A great way to serve burdock to people who may not have had it (namely, most midwesterners), I came up with this as a contribution to my friend Tom Thulen and Betsy Nelson's book *Tasting Minnesota*. The earthy flavor of the roots marries well with creamy potatoes and, along with the classic Japanese kinpira treatment, it's a good introduction to cooking with burdock roots and their unique flavor. It makes a very interesting shepherd's pie.

1 lemon
6 ounces (170 g) gobo burdock root
  (*Arctium lappa*)
2 cups (480 ml) heavy cream
Kosher salt and white pepper, to taste
2 pounds (910 g) russet potatoes
2 tablespoons unsalted butter, plus more
  for serving
Sliced chives, for serving (optional)

Fill a container with some water seasoned to taste with lemon juice. Peel the roots and place them in the water to keep their color bright.

Preheat the oven to 250°F (120°C). Remove the roots from the water and slice as thinly as you can. Put the burdock and cream into a small, nonreactive, oven-safe saucepot and bring the mixture to a simmer, seasoning lightly to taste with salt and white pepper. Transfer the pot to the oven and bake, covered, until the burdock is softened (it will never become truly "tender"), about 30 to 45 minutes. Working in small batches, purée the cooked burdock and cream in a blender, adding a little water if necessary to thin the mixture and obtain a smooth purée. Pass the burdock cream through a strainer and reserve until needed.

Peel and dice the potatoes, cover with water, bring to a simmer, turn down the heat to low, and cook until tender, then pass through a ricer or food mill while still warm. Add the reserved burdock cream and 2 tablespoons of butter to the potatoes and stir to combine, then taste and adjust the seasoning and reserve until needed. Serve the potatoes topped with a little additional butter and the sliced chives.

Kinpira Gobo

Serves 4 as a side dish

Tender-crisp, slightly sweet, and deeply savory, Kinpira Gobo, along with gomae (DIY Gomae, page 39), is one of the cornerstone side dishes you'll find at many sushi houses, and probably makes up the vast majority of how the burdock in the United States is cooked by weight. It's a versatile dish that comes together in a few minutes (after some knife work), travels like a dream, and—because roots are tough creatures—stays just fine in the fridge for a few days if you want to double the recipe and have leftovers. Parsnips, if available, make an interesting, slightly wilder (if less colorful) substitute for the carrots.

8 ounces (225 g) gobo burdock root
  (1 medium root)
8 ounces (225 g) carrot (2 medium carrots)
1¼ cups (300 ml) dashi or water, divided
1 tablespoon maple syrup or sugar
1 tablespoon apple cider vinegar
1 teaspoon fish sauce, such as Red Boat brand
2 tablespoons soy sauce
2 tablespoons toasted sesame oil, divided

Serving (optional)
2 teaspoons toasted sesame seeds

Sliced scallions, for garnish
Sliced fresh herbs, such as cilantro or mint

Have a bowl of cold water ready. Wash the gobo root well to remove dirt, trim off the ends, then cut into manageable lengths, about 6 inches (15 cm) long. Peel the lengths one at a time, then cut on the diagonal into ¼-inch (6 mm) thick, long ovals. Stack the ovals on one another a few at a time, then cut into ¼-inch matchsticks. Repeat with the rest of the gobo, putting the cut sticks into the water as you go. Repeat the process with the carrots, reserving them separately from the gobo (they don't need to sit in water).

In a heavy, 10-inch (26 cm) pan, such as a cast-iron skillet, bring the gobo and 1 cup (240 ml) of the dashi to a boil and cook for 5 minutes, covered. Pour off the dashi. Add the carrots, maple syrup, vinegar, fish sauce, soy sauce, half the sesame oil, and the remaining ¼ cup (60 ml) of dashi. Cook rapidly on high heat until the pan is nearly dry, then sauté for a minute or two. Turn off the heat, stir in the remaining sesame oil, transfer to a serving bowl, garnish with the sesame seeds, scallions, and sliced herbs, and serve warm, cool, or at room temperature.

CHAPTER 3

Aromatic

Herbs, Flowers, and Alliums

This chapter features ingredients I work with that have strong flavors and aromas. Some of the herbs (I use the term loosely here) are what you'd expect: strong-tasting, aromatic leaves reminiscent of oregano, citrus, or celery. Others possess flavors so potent they're hard to describe, like angelica or the seeds of cow parsnip or prickly ash. Some are a little different, like the young tips of conifer trees, cedar, and pinecones. I've included coniferous and other unfamiliar aromatics because, while not herbs in the typical sense, they're used to lend flavor as opposed to texture in a dish. The exception to this is angelica. Parts of this plant (such as the flowers)—although harvested from a plant that's an herb—function more as a vegetable when caught at the right moment. Wild leeks or ramps, with their woodsy, garlicky aroma, are also included in this chapter, and there's a lot of exciting things you can

Across, various dried herbs: cedar leaves and cones, meadowsweet, galium, monarda, Szechuan peppercorns, and blanched, dried immature pinecones.

explore with them, or apply to similar wild onions wherever you live, like *Allium triquetrum* (also known as three-cornered garlic or leeks on the West Coast of the US) or *A. ursinum* (also known as ramsons or wild garlic in Europe). I'm known for my creative condiments, so many of the recipes here are savory sauces and similar concoctions that capture the flavor of certain ingredients, like Ramp Leaf Salsa Verde or Wild Oregano Salmoriglio Sauce—they're a great way to save and bottle up flavors for perking up dishes at a moment's notice. Most of the recipes here are savory, but there's also a carefully selected collection of sweet things and desserts near the end that this book wouldn't be complete without.

Bergamot

When I became interested in foraging, one of the first things I'd do to teach myself about plants was to rub leaves I thought looked interesting and smell them as I walked. Wild bergamot (*Monarda fistulosa*) was the first herb (well, maybe besides skunky catmint) that I found this way. Wild bergamot, also known as wild bee balm or wild oregano, is unrelated to the bergamot oil commonly used to flavor Earl Grey tea. It's one of the most versatile of the wild herbs I've harvested in the Midwest; unlike some others, it is easy to substitute for things already in your spice cabinet, and it doesn't require a lick of ethnobotanical research to divine how it could taste good or to help navigate its additional flavors—bitterness, astringency, and so on.

Its aroma and taste are similar to a cross between thyme and oregano, which makes sense since bergamot is a source of thymol, a naturally occurring, aromatic compound that smells, not surprisingly, like thyme. Calling it the "pizza spice" herb is another useful way I describe it to people.

There are many types of bee balm (*Monarda* spp.). All of the varieties I've tried have the underlying scent of thymol (that tastes of thyme), but some also have interesting combinations of thyme and spearmint—not surprising, since this is a genus of flowering plants in the mint family. Cultivated varieties such as scarlet bee balm (*M. didyma*) have a fruity aroma that is especially concentrated in their flowers, making them a great addition to fruit salads or other dishes with raspberries.

Young bergamot leaves at a good stage for drying.

Wild Herb Brioche

**Makes 1 loaf, or approximately
18 bite-sized rolls**

A simple, soft dough that uses bergamot and a few other herbs as flavorings—mix and match your favorite herbs however you like. Each herb will add a different character, but I always add some kind of dried wild onion, usually dried ramp leaves. Sometimes I make this brioche as a loaf, sometimes as very small buns. Either way, everyone who tastes it loves how the combination of dried ramp leaves and bergamot makes it taste like garlic breadsticks. The recipe is worth making for the aroma that creeps through the kitchen as it bakes alone. You'll want a stand mixer to make this.

7 ounces (200 g) Pâte Fermentée (recipe follows), preferably a few days old, brought to room temperature from chilled

½ cup (135 ml) buttermilk, at room temperature

1 egg plus 3 egg yolks (reserve the whites for an egg wash)

½ teaspoon instant yeast

2¼ cups (270 g) all-purpose flour

1 tablespoon sugar

1½ teaspoons fine salt

Dried wild herbs: 1 tablespoon crushed bergamot leaves and 2 tablespoons *each* crushed ramp and nettle leaves

6 tablespoons unsalted butter, at room temperature

In the bowl of a stand mixer, add the Pâte Fermentée in pieces to the milk, followed by the remaining ingredients except the butter. Using the dough hook, mix to combine.

Begin adding the cold butter 1 tablespoon at a time until incorporated, mixing until the dough cleans the bowl and absorbs the butter. The dough will seem wet and sticky.

Transfer the dough to an oiled bowl, cover, and allow to rise until it has more than doubled in size. Liberally grease a loaf pan and place a sheet of parchment cut to fit the bottom inside to ensure a smooth release. Gently shape the dough into a loaf, trying not to deflate it too much. Set the shaped dough in the loaf pan, cover, and allow to rest overnight in the refrigerator.

The next day, preheat the oven to 350°F (180°C), brush the loaf with a little of your reserved egg white, and transfer it straight from the fridge to the oven. Bake for approximately 45 minutes, or until a thermometer reads 200°F (95°C) and the kitchen is filled with the smell of herbs. Gently slide a knife around the edge of the pan to loosen the loaf if needed, then remove to a cooling rack and allow to come to room temperature before slicing (if you can).

Pâte Fermentée

Makes a little over 1 pound (455 g), enough to add to 3 loaves of bread

This is the "old dough" often mentioned in old bread recipes. Somewhere along the line, someone saved unbaked bread dough and added it to a new batch of dough, then discovered that the resulting loaf had longer staying power and resiliency, as well as added depth of flavor. Think of it as a shortcut for making great bread at home if you don't have the patience to make sourdough starter. It's essentially pizza dough, and it makes great, quick pizzas—just roll the dough into ovals (any size), grill or brown in a pan to hold their shape, then top with pizza fixings and bake.

¾ cup (180 ml) plus 2 tablespoons warm but not hot water
¾ teaspoon fine salt
2¼ cups (270 g) all-purpose flour
1 teaspoon instant yeast
Flavorless oil, for greasing the bowl

Add the water and the salt to the bowl of a stand mixer. Next, add the flour and yeast, and mix with the paddle attachment until a very soft dough forms and pulls away from the sides of the bowl, about 10 minutes. Remove the dough to a lightly oiled mixing bowl, cover, and allow to double in size, then punch down and refrigerate. When kept covered in the fridge, Pâte Fermentée keeps for a week, or it can also be frozen.

Wild Oregano Salmoriglio Sauce

Makes about 1½ cups (375 ml)

This is an old recipe of mine, and probably the biggest reader favorite I have using wild oregano. The word *salmoriglio* is similar to *salmura* ("brine," in Italian), but shouldn't be confused with *salmorejo* ("tomato soup," in Spanish). *Salmoriglio* basically refers to a condiment from Sicily made with oregano or other herbs, lemon, and seawater. My version is a purée (others are chunky with strips of zest) similar to chimichurri, but without any heat. Fish, poultry, grilled vegetables, fresh, soft cheese—salmoriglio is good on all kinds of things.

½ cup (135 ml) mild oil, such as grapeseed or canola
¼ cup (60 ml) virgin sunflower or olive oil
1 ounce (28 g) flat-leaf parsley, leaves only
1 ounce (28 g) bergamot, leaves only (fresh oregano can be substituted)
1 large clove garlic
¼ cup (60 ml) water
¼ cup (60 ml) fresh lemon juice
Grated zest of 1 large lemon
½ teaspoon salt
Pinch of red pepper flakes

Mix the two oils together. Blanch the parsley and bergamot in boiling water for 5 seconds, then remove the herbs with a strainer or slotted spoon and place in cold water to refresh. Drain the refreshed herbs and squeeze out any residual water, then chop coarse.

Put all the ingredients except the oils in a blender. Begin puréeing the mixture, drizzling in the oils until the sauce is puréed and very smooth.

Double-check the seasoning for salt and pepper, adjust as needed, then transfer to a container and refrigerate. It will last for a few days.

Bergamot Charmoula

Makes about 1½ cups (375 ml)

Charmoula (sometimes spelled *chermoula*) is a mildly spicy, oil-based condiment, usually spiked with oregano. Here I use dried bergamot instead, but you could use either, or even another dried herb that keeps its flavor, such as dill. It's great tossed with hot potatoes right out of the oven, drizzled over grilled meat or vegetables or steamed fish, added to dips like hummus, or drizzled on soups or stews. Watching the hot oil sizzle as it hits the paprika, garlic, and chili is always exciting.

½ cup (135 ml) mild oil, such as grapeseed
  or sunflower
2 tablespoons smoked paprika
½ teaspoon red pepper flakes or cayenne,
  plus more to taste
½ tablespoon finely grated garlic
  (about 3 small cloves)
½ cup (135 ml) flavorful oil, such as
  extra-virgin olive oil
1 teaspoon cumin seeds, toasted and
  coarsely ground
1 tablespoon dried bergamot, crumbled
2 tablespoons chopped fresh bergamot
  (optional)
1 bunch cilantro (a good handful), minced
  (with flowers and green seeds if available)
½ teaspoon kosher salt
Zest of ½ large lemon

Heat the mild oil until hot, but not smoking. Combine the paprika, red pepper flakes, and garlic in a heatproof bowl, then pour the hot oil over it—it should sizzle. Allow to cool for a minute, then add the flavorful oil and the remaining ingredients and stir. Store in the fridge. It will improve in flavor after sitting overnight.

Tomato Sauce with Wild Herbs

Makes about 1 quart (945 ml)

This simple tomato sauce scented with dried ramp leaves and bergamot is based on a spicy version I used to make under my old Chef Angelo Volpicelli from Rome. If you like the flavor of this sauce, take a look at Eggplant Baked with Wild Herbs and Tomato, too (page 94).

1 can (32 ounces / 900 g) whole
  peeled tomatoes
3 large cloves garlic, sliced as thin
  as possible
¼ cup (60 ml) blended olive oil or
  mild olive oil
½ teaspoon red pepper flakes
½ tablespoon crumbled dried ramp leaves
½ tablespoon crumbled dried bergamot
  leaves, any large stems removed
¾ teaspoon kosher salt, or to taste
¼ cup (60 ml) dry white wine

Purée the tomatoes in a blender or food processor, then strain out the seeds through a food mill (optional, but recommended).

Sweat the garlic in the oil very slowly, until lightly browned and aromatic. Remove the pan from the heat and add the red pepper flakes, ramp leaves, bergamot, and salt; stir for a minute. Returning the pan to the heat, add the wine and cook for 2 minutes.

Add the tomatoes and their juice, cover, and simmer the sauce over medium-low heat for 20 to 30 minutes. Finally, purée the mixture until very smooth using a using an immersion or handheld blender.

Cool the sauce, then transfer to a labeled, dated container and refrigerate until needed.

Prickly Ash

Imagine this: You bite into a piece of seared meat covered in crunchy peppercorns and hot chilies. Immediately you feel the heat and punishment you know and love from the capsaicin in the chilies, but there's a different flavor, too—one you can't quite place. Cascading among the fruity notes from the chili are blasts of citrus, followed by a numbing sensation that combines into a sort of tongue-twisting alchemy as you chew.

The heat reaches its crescendo and you start to salivate profusely, followed by a pleasant but numbing sensation. You've just taken a ride on the mala train. *Mala* is the Szechuan term for the taste combination of Szechuan peppercorns with hot chilies, and if you're like me, you might begin to crave it.

In Minnesota and Wisconsin, where I roam, we don't have lemons and limes, but we do have *Zanthoxylum americanum*, which is also from the rue/citrus family. Most people know it as prickly ash, and it's a close cousin

Mature fruit. The aroma is strongest when red, but I wait to harvest until the seeds, which are gritty tasting, have dropped.

to the plant that bears Szechuan peppercorns sold in stores and used throughout Szechuan cuisine. I'd lived next to the plant my whole life, but it wasn't until my girlfriend's mother, who'd used prickly ash for years, introduced it to me that I really took notice.

Since then, I've spoken with local hunters in my area about the plants, and they often reply with comments such as, "So that's why it smells like limes when I get caught in the prickly bushes!" And yes, the shrub is full of thorns, but the peppercorns/berries are delicious when used with care. When you eat them raw, the flavor is stronger and more numbing than when you chew them with other ingredients. When I first experimented with prickly ash berries, I would trick servers into eating a handful of them just to watch what they would do. (If you like having friends, maybe don't do that.)

The prickly ash plant offers more than just numbing peppercorns, though. If you visit an Asian market, you'll notice that the fruits are harvested and sold at different stages of growth, my favorite being when the fruit is still green, unripe, and tender. Since the seeds are undeveloped at that stage, you can eat them whole. Each one is like a small citrus bomb; they're one of the greatest complements for raw fish I've tasted, and a great candidate for fermenting in brine, too. The leaves, when very young, can also be good, but aren't exactly the same as the young leaves used in the Far East, and quickly develop a soapy taste as they age.

As for harvesting the seeds, I'm lazy. The peppercorns have the most intense flavor when they're bright red, but they also have a giant, gritty seed inside, and I don't like giant gritty seeds. To save myself the trouble of winnowing them, I wait until the seed has dropped and the outer husk has turned brown, then I gather as many of the husks as I need, dehydrate them, and store in a jar in the fridge or freezer. They'll lose their potency stored at room temperature.

Prickly Ash Peppercorn Jerky

Serves 4 as a snack

Here's another great way to use dried Szechuan peppercorns and the mouthwatering mala flavor that comes from spicy chilies and the numbing of the prickly ash berries. Maple sugar is a delicious and versatile dried, granular version of maple syrup; you'll find it in larger grocery stores or specialty spice stores.

2 tablespoons whole black peppercorns

1 tablespoon coriander seeds

2 tablespoons dried prickly ash berries, picked over, any black seeds discarded

1 teaspoon red pepper flakes, or other dried chili you like (to taste)

¼ teaspoon pink salt / sodium nitrite (optional)

1½ tablespoons kosher salt

1 tablespoon maple sugar or brown sugar

2 pounds (910 g) lean red meat (beef, venison, buffalo, or whatever you like, as long as it's completely lean)

Toast the black peppercorns, then crush them as coarse as you like. I like to use a molcajete (traditional Mexican mortar and pestle) for this. Reserve the peppercorns and repeat the process with the coriander. Grind the prickly ash berries in a spice grinder as finely as possible, then mix all the spices together.

Slice the meat against the grain into ¼-inch (6 mm) slices. Cut the slices roughly 2 inches by 3 inches (5 × 7.5 cm), then toss with spice mixture, massaging it a bit to help the seasonings penetrate, and refrigerate overnight.

The next day, remove the meat from the fridge and put the pieces into a dehydrator set at 150 to 160°F (65–70°C), or into an oven on the "warm" setting, or into a warm oven with the door ajar if you don't have a dehydrator. Allow the meat to dry for 2 to 3 hours (depending on the its thickness) or until firm but still a little pliable. Taste some of the jerky to check the texture and see if you like it, or if you'd prefer it a bit drier. If you dry it a little too much, try vacuum-sealing it for 24 hours and refrigerating it, which can help it soften a bit. This is a subjective process. If you dry your jerky in an oven it may dry much faster, since the temperature can run hotter than a dehydrator. The jerky will last for weeks if not longer under refrigeration.

Raw Fish with Green Szechuan Peppercorns, Rue, and Lemon Jam Aioli

This was one of the most successful prickly ash berry dishes I ever served. Think of it more as an example than a specific recipe. Cut high-quality tuna or sashimi-grade fish into fine cubes, put in a bowl, and season with salt, pepper, and a few unripe Szechuan peppercorns. Put a dollop of Lemon Jam Aioli (recipe follows) on a plate, then mound the tuna on top attractively and garnish with kinome (very young prickly ash leaves) or rue, or whatever tender, aromatic herbs you have. Rue (*Ruta graveolens*) is a perennial herb I learned about from reading *Apicius*, one of the world's oldest cookbooks. Like lovage, rue was enjoyed by the Romans, and they used it in all kinds of dishes. The smell is sharp and potent; a little goes a long way. If you like growing and cooking with herbs, I highly recommend planting some.

Serve with crackers or flatbread. Top the fish with a drizzle of toasted sesame oil, if you like. Good sushi-grade tuna is my favorite fish for this dish.

Rue (*Ruta graveolens*)

Lemon Jam Aioli

Makes about 2 cups (225 g)

Lemon jam is one of those secret condiments chefs keep in their back pocket. A purée of cooked, juiced lemons—skin, pith, and all—might sound odd, and the flavor is a bit bitter and intense by itself. But mixing the purée with mayonnaise or sour cream tames the flavor, turning it into a zippy condiment. It's good as a dip for raw vegetables or a sandwich spread, with fish or chicken, and all kinds of other things.

12 ounces (340 g) lemons (roughly 3 medium lemons)
¼ cup (60 ml) warm water
Pinch of salt
¼ cup (60 ml) flavorless oil

Quarter the lemons and juice them, reserving the juice for another purpose. Cut the lemon quarters in half lengthwise (making eight narrower wedges from each lemon), put them in a small pot, cover with water by an inch (2.5 cm), bring to a rapid boil, drain, and cover with fresh water. Bring the pot back to a simmer, turn the heat to low, cover, and cook until the lemons are tender when pierced, about 30 to 45 minutes. Remove the lemons to a blender, add the ¼ cup of warm water and a pinch of salt, pulse, then purée as well as you can, scraping down the sides as needed. Finally, drizzle the oil in slowly until you get a smooth purée. If the jam doesn't want to move in the blender, drizzle in more oil, 1 tablespoon at a time, to help the blades move and make the mixture smooth. Remove the purée to a bowl, press cling film on the surface, and cool until lukewarm, then refrigerate. One the jam is cold, mix it in equal proportions with mayonnaise and season with salt and fresh lemon juice to refresh the flavors.

Kinome-Ae

Makes about ½ cup (135 ml)

Besides using herbs I like as raw garnishes, I experiment with making sauces out of them, too. Kinome-Ae is a traditional Japanese sauce used to dress vegetables. It specifically calls for the leaves of Szechuan peppercorn plant. Given that it might be difficult for you to find Szechuan peppercorn leaves that taste exactly like the ones I use (most are soapy tasting if you don't harvest them very young), this recipe calls for easier-to-source green prickly ash seeds (or cilantro). One of my readers from Japan suggests crushing very young prickly ash leaves to a paste, then adding white miso, rice wine vinegar, and a touch of sugar and using as a sauce for fish or grilled meats, which sounds great, too.

½ cup (30 g) kinome leaves (or cilantro)
3 tablespoons prickly ash / green Szechuan
   peppercorns
1 pinch chili flakes, or equivalent
1 tablespoon toasted sesame seeds
2 tablespoons toasted sesame oil
3 tablespoons soy sauce

Using a food processor or mortar and pestle, grind or pound the leaves, green peppercorns, chili, and sesame seeds, then drizzle in the oil and soy sauce. If you use kinome, the sauce is best the day it's made; when made with cilantro, it will retain a good flavor for a few days in the fridge.

Prickly Ash Chili Sauce

Makes 1 cup (240 ml)

Hot, gently numbing, and packed with umami, Szechuan chili crisp is a new-old condiment that's delicious on everything. I love the stuff, and I have my favorite brands, but after I noticed how much I was spending on it, I had to reverse-engineer my own version. It isn't exactly the same as the product you might see in a store, but I can guarantee you it's just as addictive. Instead of red pepper flakes, whose heat can vary from mild to nuclear (often due to age), mine relies mostly on guajillos or another mild chili (anchos or puyas could work), with mushroom powder and its added umami providing the backbone of the sauce, which lets you spoon more of the "goodies" on each bite. The real secret, though, are fermented black beans, or douchi, that, while difficult to find in stores, are widely available online—my favorite brand is Pearl River Bridge. The sauce will still be good without the fermented beans, but you should try it with them at least once.

5 whole (15 g) dried guajillo chilies,
   or more to taste
2 teaspoons red pepper flakes (recently
   purchased—make sure they're hot!)
1 cup (240 ml) flavorless cooking oil
   such as grapeseed or soybean
1 tablespoon dried prickly ash / Szechuan
   peppercorns
3 tablespoons ground mushroom powder
   such as shiitake or porcini
2 large cloves garlic (8 g), trimmed
½-inch (1.25 cm) piece fresh ginger (3 g),
   coarsely chopped
1 small shallot (18 g), coarsely chopped
2 teaspoons soy sauce
2½ tablespoons fermented black beans
   (douchi)

Toast the guajillos in a 300°F (150°C) oven for 10 minutes, then cool. Break the stem off each chili and shake out the seeds. Discard the stems and seeds. Crumble the chilies well, mix with the red pepper flakes, and reserve. Combine all ingredients except the chili mixture and black beans in a blender and purée until smooth, about 30 seconds. Pour the mixture into a small 2- to 3-cup (480–720 ml) capacity saucepan, add the chili mixture, bring to a simmer, and cook on low until starting to foam, about 25 to 30 minutes. Watch the mixture carefully, as you don't want to burn it. When in doubt, undercook it a bit; you can always gently simmer it for a bit longer. When the mixture is barely starting to color, stir in the beans, then set aside the pan to cool, and marvel at how great the kitchen smells. The sauce will last for a month in the fridge—longer if you make sure the solids are always covered by a layer of oil in the jar. Stir it before using.

Wild Peppercorn Crust

Makes a scant ⅓ cup (30 g), enough to generously crust 2–4 steaks, depending on size

One of my favorite ways to use and serve the peppercorns I harvest and dry is this spicy, fiery crust for meat or fatty fish, such as tuna or swordfish. If I'm feeding people who like spicy food, I might serve a whole piece of meat crusted with it. If I want to share the flavor with a crowd, I'll crust small pieces of meat and serve them as a small, single-bite appetizer. Adding a few different seeds or spices is a great variation here, too—especially cumin, dried green peppercorns, caraway, and sesame seeds. Feel free to adjust the proportions to your taste. You can substitute commercial Szechuan peppercorns, but it's not as fun as harvesting your own.

2 tablespoons prickly ash / Szechuan peppercorns
2 tablespoons black peppercorns
1 tablespoon dried coriander
¼ teaspoon red pepper flakes (optional)

In a mortar and pestle, preferably a molcajete, crush each spice individually. First, crush the prickly ash, grinding them as fine as possible to break up the covering that protects the seed. Some people sift out the shells, but I don't find them offensive. If you don't have a molcajete, use a spice grinder to get them finely broken up, or crush them with the back of a sauté pan. Next, crack the black peppercorns. Here you're looking for a rough crack, or what's known as butcher's crack (or grind, or cut)—not whole corns, but definitely not powder, since part of the fun of a peppercorn crust is crunching on pieces of peppercorns. Finally, crush the coriander, and then the red pepper flakes, which should be fine, like the Szechuan peppercorns. Combine all the crushed spices, and store in a small glass jar in the refrigerator, where the blend will keep a good aroma for a week or two.

To use the blend, take a piece of meat without too much surface area—a tenderloin, medallions of pork tenderloin, or hunks of tuna are all good choices. Season the meat all over with salt, then press one side into the peppercorn mixture. Sear the meat crust-side down in a pan, in hot oil, then flip and bake in a hot oven until done to your liking, allow it to rest off the heat for a few minutes before cutting, and serve.

Ramps

Onions are a cook's best friend, and they make just about everything taste better. Mostly, this section features some of my favorite ramp and wild onion recipes and techniques, but some of the techniques, like working with scapes, can be applied to garden-variety alliums such as chives, too.

I harvest more ramps (*Allium triccocum* and its white variant *A. t.* var. *burdickii*) than any other type of allium. These wild spring leeks are now so popular with chefs and foodies that some people think they're cliché, but I doubt I'll ever fall out of love with them. They offer many gifts: first the leaves and bulbs, then later in the season scapes (unopened flowers), flowers, and finally young, potent green seeds. Every part of the plant is a powerhouse of wild onion flavor. Ramps are only one onion though, and around the world, similar plants are harvested, including *A. ursinum*

(wild garlic), *A. victorialis* (victory onion), and many others. You can substitute a lot of different leafy-green-oniony plants for ramps in any recipe in this chapter.

There's a growing trend of calling out among foragers for harvesting ramps, and I can understand why, especially if you're digging up bulbs from ramp patches on public land, which is illegal where I live. Personally, I still dig some bulbs every year from private land, but mostly I harvest leaves. Harvesting ramp scapes and green seeds are other options to consider to get your rampy fix if you don't have access to private land. Clipping a few ramp leaves here and there is the most bountiful harvest, though, and can be done quickly—there's no shovel, no mud, and because the bulbs weren't uprooted, the plants survive to see the next year, allowing them to reproduce and spread, ensuring their survival for years and generations to come.

Ramp Vichyssoise

Makes about 7 cups (1.75 L)

Smooth as velvet and green as a spring ramp patch, a good vichyssoise—the classic soup made from potatoes and leeks—is worthy of a cult following when made with ramps. Back in the day, thinking I was being creative, I served this soup warm, which was a mistake. The success of the soup relies on how the potato tightens when the soup is cool, giving it a silky, luxurious feel.

10 ounces (285 g) ramps, with leaves,
  or just leaves
1 pound (455 g) russet potatoes,
  peeled and diced
4 tablespoons unsalted butter
¼ cup (60 ml) dry white wine
4 cups (945 ml) good chicken stock
1 cup (240 ml) heavy cream, chilled
A few scrapes of fresh nutmeg, to taste
1 teaspoon kosher salt, plus more to taste
Ground white pepper, to taste (optional)
Croutons lightly browned in oil, for serving
  (optional)

Remove the tops from the ramps, leaving the red stems and bulbs. Chop the stems and bulbs roughly. Sweat the peeled, diced potatoes in the butter for 5 minutes, then add the chopped ramp bulbs and stems, and sweat for a few minutes more.

Add the wine and cook down by half. Add the stock, bring the mixture to a brisk simmer, and cook for 20 minutes, uncovered, then turn off the heat and allow to cool for 20 minutes. While the soup is cooling, bring a quart or two of lightly salted water to a boil and blanch the ramp leaves for 1 minute, then drain and refresh immediately in cold water until cool. Squeeze the ramp leaves dry, chop them medium-fine, and reserve.

Fill a sink with 5 or 6 inches (12.5–15 cm) of cold water. While the soup is still quite warm, purée it until very smooth using an immersion or other blender, adding the cream as you go. Work carefully, in batches if needed. Pour the soup into a metal bowl or pot in the sink with cold water, then stir for a minute or two to help distribute the heat and cool it down quickly to preserve the green color.

When the soup is cool, double check the seasoning and adjust as needed for a touch of nutmeg, salt, and pepper. Soups that are served cold or room temperature should be more heavily seasoned than hot ones. Serve the soup at room temperature, with the croutons. Vichyssoise can be served hot, but part of what makes the soup special is its texture, which is creamiest at room temperature.

Ramp Leaf Dumplings

**Makes about 20 dumplings,
or 4 modest servings**

The Italian name for these is *gnudi*, literally "nude ravioli filling." They're tender, fluffy little pasta-type dumplings. You can use wild greens other than ramps here, but make sure they're cooked until soft and tender before chopping and adding them to the dough. The most basic way to serve these dumplings is with a butter and sage sauce, but for a real treat drizzle some melted sage butter over the dumplings nestled in a pool of simple tomato sauce. You can easily double the recipe to serve more people.

8 ounces (225 g) high-quality ricotta,
    preferably Calabro brand
6 ounces (170 g) fresh ramp leaves
1 large egg
½ teaspoon kosher salt
¼ teaspoon fresh-ground black pepper
¼ cup (25 g) grated Parmesan cheese
A few gratings of fresh nutmeg
¼ cup (30 g) flour, plus more for rolling
    the dumplings

Sage sauce, for serving
4 tablespoons unsalted butter
2 teaspoons sliced fresh sage
¼ cup (60 ml) dry white wine
Pinch of kosher salt and fresh-ground
    black pepper
2 tablespoons grated Parmesan cheese

If possible, drain the ricotta for a few hours or overnight. Blanch the ramp leaves in boiling salted water, then chill in cold water, drain, and drain again, pressing down on the leaves with a towel to remove as much moisture as possible. Chop the greens fine, then purée in a food processor with the egg, salt, pepper,

Parmesan, nutmeg, and ricotta; transfer to a bowl and stir in the flour. Allow the mixture to rest for a few minutes while you bring a wide pot of salted water to a simmer, as for pasta. Taste a tiny bit of the mixture, adjust the seasoning as needed, then taste again to make sure it tastes really good. Form tablespoons of the mixture into balls, then roll each ball in flour, tap off the excess, and place on a floured cookie sheet. Drop the dumplings into the simmering water, making sure not to overcrowd the bottom of the pan. Cook the dumplings for a few minutes until they float, then a few minutes more to help them hold their form.

Meanwhile, melt the butter and sage together in a sauté pan until the butter browns. Deglaze the pan with the wine, season to taste with salt and pepper, then add the dumplings to the pan and toss to coat. Serve drizzled with the sauce and Parmesan cheese.

Ramp Leaf Pierogi

Makes about 40 pierogi (serves 4–6)

These pierogi are reminiscent of fried ravioli, and the potato and cheese in the filling are a great way to smooth out the powerful flavor of Tjeremsha (fermented ramp greens). If you flour the raw dumplings, freeze them in a single layer on a cookie sheet, then put them into a freezer bag, you can cook them straight from frozen—just account for a little longer cooking time, and make sure your water is at a full, rolling boil before adding the dumplings.

Filling

8 ounces (225 g) cream cheese or chèvre
12 ounces (340 g) cooked russet potato, riced or mashed
1 tablespoon chopped fresh dill
2–4 ounces (55–115 g) Tjeremsha (page 169), minced (use the larger amount if you really like fermented ramps), divided

Dough

1 cup (220 g) sour cream
1 large egg
1 tablespoon unsalted butter, softened
2½ generous cups (300 g) flour, plus more for dusting the work surface
1 teaspoon kosher salt

For the filling, mix the cheese, potato, dill, and half of the Tjeremsha. Taste the filling, and add the rest of the ramps, if you like.

For the dough, whisk the sour cream and egg together, add the butter, flour, and salt, and knead into a soft dough. Allow the dough to rest for 30 minutes.

Divide the dough into four equal parts. Working with a quarter of the dough at a time, use a pasta roller or a rolling pin to roll the dough out a little thicker than you would fresh pasta, about ⅛ inch (3 mm)—it doesn't have to be perfect. Flour the work surface as needed to keep the dough from sticking. Use a drinking glass or ring mold to cut out roughly 3½-inch (8.5 cm) rounds, saving the scraps to re-roll. Place about 2 generous teaspoons of filling in the center of each circle of dough, fold them closed, and crimp the edges with a fork.

Cook the pierogi in boiling water until they float, then remove to an oiled pan, and refrigerate until needed (2 to 3 days), or cook right away. To serve, brown freshly cooked pierogi in a little oil until browned on both sides. Because pierogi are rich, I like to serve them with lighter sides, such as freshly cooked vegetables—especially wilted greens, cherry tomatoes, and sautéed mushrooms.

Across, fermented Ramp Leaf Pierogi with venison bratwurst, tomato jus, cabbage, chickweed, and chicken of the woods mushrooms. From my first restaurant, The Salt Cellar (2016).

Ramp Leaf Sausage

Makes 5 pounds (2.25 kg)

Besides burgers, this was one of the first things I ever made with ramps. It may look like a sausage Dr. Seuss would make, but once your friends taste it you'll be able to barter links for goods and services. If I have a small tasting outdoors, I might serve it like a cold cut; if I'm grilling out, I'll char and eat them like any other sausage. They're rich, made for eating with a knife and fork, but if you really love ramps, you could put them on a bun. Just be prepared to take a nap afterward. If you don't have sausage casings, you can make patties, but they're not quite the same. Ask your butcher for sausage casings—or better yet, order them from butcherpacker.com.

5 pounds (2.25 kg) pork shoulder
1 ounce (28 g) chopped ramp bulbs or
  2 ounces (55 g) chopped fresh ramp leaves
1½ tablespoons kosher salt
1 tablespoon fresh-ground black pepper
8 ounces (225 g) ramp leaves
1 large egg
Hog sausage casings, as needed, soaked in
  water to remove salt

Dice the meat into 1-inch (2.5 cm) cubes. Combine the chopped ramp with the meat, salt, and pepper. Chill the meat in the freezer for an hour or two if possible, or refrigerate to keep cold. Blanch the ramp leaves in salted water, then shock in an ice bath, remove, squeeze out as much water as possible, and purée with the egg in a blender. A food processor can work, too, but the purée might not be as fine. Grind the meat and ramp bulbs through the coarse die of a meat grinder, then mix with the ramp purée. Allow the mixture to sit overnight, then pack into casings the next day. I like to tie them off at 4-ounce (115 g) links.

Ramp Leaf Salsa Verde

Makes 1 pint (480 ml)

A punchy, aggressive condiment that will make just about anything taste better. Use it as a finishing touch for vegetables of all kinds, steaks, soups and stews, fish—this stuff could make a boot taste good. The salsa will be slightly spicy from the raw ramps at first, but will mellow as it ages over time.

2½ ounces (70 g) ramp leaves, divided,
  half whole and half coarsely chopped
½ teaspoon kosher salt
2 teaspoons anchovy paste or finely
  chopped anchovies
¼ cup (60 ml) fresh lemon juice, plus the
  zest of 1 lemon (red wine vinegar is a
  good substitute)
1 tablespoon capers
¼ teaspoon red pepper flakes
¾ cup (180 ml) blended olive oil or
  cooking oil
¼ cup (60 ml) water

Bring roughly a quart of salted water to a boil. Blanch the whole ramp leaves in the water for 10 seconds, then remove and refresh in cold water, squeeze dry, and chop. Combine all the ramp leaves and remaining ingredients except the oil and water in the bowl of a blender, then purée, drizzling in the oil, until very smooth. At the end, add the water and purée for a second or two more. Transfer to a pint jar and store in the fridge. The salsa will lose its bright green color after a few days but will be good for weeks. As it sits under refrigeration, some oils will get firm; simply bring it to room temperature and give it a stir to restore the consistency.

Basic Pickled Ramps

**Makes about 3 pints (1.5 L),
depending on the ramps' size and age**

Everyone has a recipe for pickled ramps, and mine has served me well over the years. You can jazz it up to your liking by adding different things, if you must, but I like the dependable taste of pickling spices. The hidden bonus with pickled ramps is that you get their juice—a sharp, rampy nectar essential for making a great Pickled Ramp Aioli (recipe follows).

1½ tablespoons pickling spices
3 cups (720 ml) water
1 tablespoon kosher or sea salt
½ cup (100 g) sugar
1 tablespoon chopped fresh ginger
1 small handful fresh dill sprigs (optional)
1 pound (455 g) ramp bulbs, trimmed of their taproot, red portion of the stem still attached
1½ cups (375 ml) apple cider vinegar

Toast the spices over medium heat in a sauté pan until aromatic, then cool.

Heat the water, salt, sugar, ginger, dill, and spices over low heat in a lidded pot wide enough to accommodate the ramps. When the mixture begins to steam (about 5 minutes), place the ramps in and cover tightly. Steam the ramp bulbs for 5 minutes, until they wilt a bit but are still crunchy and raw in the middle.

Add the vinegar, then bring the mixture to a boil and turn off the heat. Pack the hot ramps into sterilized jars, fill with liquid nearly to the brim, screw on the lids tightly, then turn the jars upside down and allow to seal. Like this, rather than in a hot-water bath, the ramps will stay crisp and the jars will seal from the heat.

Alternatively, store the ramps covered in their liquid in your fridge. As long as they're covered by liquid, they'll last a long time—at least until next ramp season.

Pickled Ramp Aioli or Sour Cream

Makes about 3 cups (720 g)

This is how you use that ramp pickling liquid you just made. This is one of the best-ever garnishes for fried fish—especially panfish such as sunnies (sunfish) and perch. It's also great with warm, lightly buttered, roasted beets or fried potatoes, root vegetables, and other vegetables.

1 cup (240 ml) ramp-pickling liquid
  (reserved from the previous recipe)
2 cups (440 g) thick mayonnaise
  (or sour cream), preferably homemade
½ tablespoon each chopped tarragon,
  cilantro, and chives, or ½ tablespoon
  chopped fresh dill, or your favorite herbs
½ cup (70 g) chopped Basic Pickled Ramps
  (page 165)

Gently cook the pickling liquid down until only ¼ cup (60 ml) remains, being careful not to scorch or brown the liquid. Cool the liquid until just warm, then add it to the mayonnaise or sour cream, stirring to combine. Fold in the herbs and chopped pickled ramps. Transfer to a container (a Mason jar works well) and refrigerate until needed.

Ramp Leaf Sriracha-Style Sauce

Makes about 3 cups (720 ml)

Another great thing to make with ramp leaves is a simple sriracha-style hot sauce. The fermentation only takes a few days, and the sauce picks up plenty of rampy funk in the process.

12 ounces (340 g) ramp leaves,
  washed and dried
3 pounds (1.3 kg) jalapeños
Scant 2 ounces (55 g) salt
4 ounces (100 g) sugar
1 ounce (28 g) ramp bulbs, chopped
  (optional)
¼ cup (60 ml) flavorless oil

Slice the ramp leaves into 1 inch pieces. Wearing gloves, coarsely chop the jalapeños. Toss the peppers with the salt, sugar, ramp leaves, and bulbs.

Place the mixture in an airtight container, preferably a vacuum-sealed bag, or in a container such as a Mason jar with plastic wrap pressed onto the surface to remove excess air. Allow the mixture to ferment for at least 5 days and up to 14 in a cool, dry, place away from light and heat.

Transfer the jalapeño mixture and all the accumulated juices to a saucepan and cook on medium, covered, stirring occasionally until very soft and most of the juice has evaporated, about 30 minutes.

Carefully purée the pepper mixture in a blender until very smooth, starting on low and working up to high, drizzling in the oil to make a smooth purée. Pass the purée through a strainer (optional) and chill. The sauce will last for a month in the fridge.

Dried Ramp Leaves

One of my favorite ways to preserve ramp leaves is to dehydrate them, then crumble them before adding to recipes. Dried ramp leaves lend a telltale aroma to foods but are milder in flavor than either onion or garlic powder, so you can use more of them in your cooking. They also make a good base ingredient for rubs and seasonings. To dry them, put clean leaves in a dehydrator, making sure to use high heat (145°F/60°C or higher) until the leaves are cracker-dry. Drying at lower temperatures can yield chewy, soft leaves—still delicious, just chewy and difficult to grind to a fine powder. Once dehydrated, store the leaves in an airtight bag or jar, and crumble as needed. For a fine powder for making rubs, grind the dried leaves in a coffee grinder or high-speed blender. See Dried Ramp Leaf Rub (page 168) for my favorite blend.

Dried Ramp Leaf Rub

Makes about 1 cup (115 g)

An all-purpose seasoning made from dried ramp leaves. This rub is great dusted on meat and fish as well as vegetables, and is an all-purpose seasoning for soups and sauces.

½ cup (55 g) ground dried ramp leaves
  (see the sidebar on page 167)
1 tablespoon black peppercorns
2 tablespoons whole cumin seeds
2 tablespoons whole coriander seeds
2 tablespoons sweet paprika
1 tablespoon whole fennel seeds

Combine all ingredients and grind to a fine powder in a spice grinder (working in batches) or in high-speed blender. Store in an airtight container in a cool, dry place. The seasoning keeps a good flavor for a month or two at room temperature, and can be frozen or refrigerated for longer storage.

Dried Ramp Ranch Dressing

Makes about 1½ cups (375 ml)

One of the best condiments made from dried ramp leaves (see the sidebar on page 167). Dairy, as a general rule, is a sponge for aromas, and having it absorb the essence of dried ramp leaves makes for an addictive ranch dressing you can dip anything into. Try it with Cornmeal-Fried Milkweed Pods (page 119).

¾ cup (165 g) mayonnaise
½ cup (135 ml) buttermilk
¼ cup (55 g) sour cream
½ teaspoon kosher salt
1 tablespoon sliced chives
2 teaspoons dried powdered ramp bulbs,
  finely ground (optional)
1 tablespoon chopped fresh tarragon
1 tablespoon fresh lemon juice
1–2 tablespoons dried, crushed ramp leaves,
  to taste

Combine all ingredients and mix well. Store in an airtight container in the fridge. The dressing will last for a few weeks.

Tjeremsha: The Siberian Wild Onion Delicacy

Makes roughly 1 cup (240 ml)

One of the ultimate incarnations of ramps and their cousins. The first time I cut open a bag of fermented ramp leaves, the smell was so powerful, so unexpectedly strong, all I could do was howl laughing. If there were weapons-grade aromas, this would be one. I started experimenting with fermenting ramp leaves to make sauces and condiments, but while reading Stephen Barstow's great book *Around the World in 80 Plants*, I found they have a name. In Siberia the soured onion leaves are known as Tjeremsha or Cheremsha, the name referring specifically to *Allium victorialis* (a larger cousin of ramps) as well as the final lacto-fermented product itself. Mixed with equal parts crème fraîche or sour cream and eaten on a cracker, it's a delicacy, and calling it "wild onion caviar" isn't out of place. Part of what I love is the texture of the leaves after fermentation: Not quite soft, but not tough, they have a special, meaty texture to them that will be lost with the traditional pounding and mashing à la sauerkraut.

Traditionally, these fermented leaves are used to garnish dishes like pierogi, or made into a sort of egg salad (also known as Cheremsha), but once you taste them you'll understand the possibilities are endless. Most people who taste the dish will proclaim it delicious, as long as they're not allowed to smell it first. Unless you live alone, or would like to, I highly recommend vacuum-sealed fermentation here to control the aroma. Ramp bulbs and pieces of firm stem can be fermented similarly.

8 ounces (225 g) fresh ramp leaves
2 scant teaspoons (11 g) salt

Cut the ramp leaves into 1-inch (2.5 cm) pieces and massage gently with the salt, then seal in a vacuum bag for the strongest flavor and best texture, or place in a jar, weighted down as for Grape Leaves Fermented in Brine (page 26). Ferment for at least 2 weeks in a cool, dry place, then refrigerate for the most potent aroma. Kept wet with their juice in a jar or another container, they will keep for a very long time.

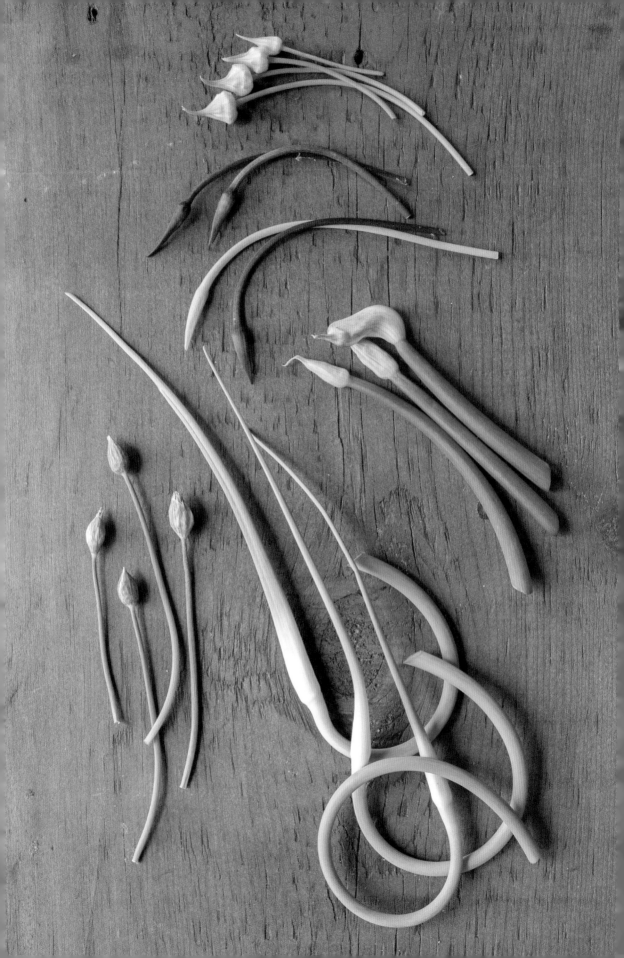

Fermented Scapes, Green Ramp Seeds, and Onion Bulbils

My first choice for preserving these oniony things is to sour them in brine. The brine that comes off ramp seeds and scapes, in particular, is really powerful stuff, perfect for adding to marinades, seasoning dips—all kinds of things, a great example being the Forager's Pub Cheese. The easiest way to make this dish is to follow the method in Grape Leaves Fermented in Brine (page 26). If I have grape leaves available, I'll add one or two to help ward off kahm yeast, too. If you like really strong oniony flavors, dry ferment the onion as for Dry-Fermented Grape Leaves (page 26). Without the added liquid absorbing some of the flavor, all of the aroma stays inside the bag to make an onion concentrate.

Forager's Pub Cheese (with or without sour ramp seeds)

Makes about 2 cups (425 g)

Spreadable cheese is one of the most addictive things in the world, and I've served countless versions of this recipe—flavored with horseradish, bourbon-aged Worcestershire, or other umami-packed things. It's the perfect canvas for taming the flavor of fermented ramp leaves or green seeds, but is perfectly snack-worthy without them, too. I was inspired to create this recipe by Wisconsin's famous brick cheese—and the very stinky cheese spread made from it you can still find at bars and restaurants around the state.

8 ounces (225 g) good white cheddar,
   or a softer cheese such as Wisconsin brick,
   at room temperature
4 ounces (115 g) cream cheese,
   at room temperature
½ cup (110 g) sour cream
¼–⅓ cup (35–45 g) chopped, fermented
   onion seeds, or 1 teaspoon grated garlic
¼ teaspoon cayenne or hot chili sauce
2 tablespoons fermented brine from ramps
   or another preserve (optional)

Grate the cheddar, then combine with the cream cheese in a food processor and process until smooth, scraping down the sides occasionally. Add the remaining ingredients and process until very smooth, then double-check the seasoning, adjust as needed, and refrigerate. The cheese will keep for a week.

Across, Various edible parts of alliaceous plants: unopened chive blossoms, garlic scapes, ramp scapes, and wild allium bulbils. When I see garlic scapes forming, I know it's time to check the wild patches.

Ramp or Wild Onion Leaf Butter

Makes about 1 cup (225 g)

One of the most versatile and popular ways to preserve ramp and wild onion greens, this is a basic compound butter that's good on everything. Melt it on steak or fish, toss it with pasta or vegetables, spread it on toast or the inside of a grilled cheese, or simply melt it and use as a dip for steamed artichokes. This is about the smallest amount you can make, so feel free to double the recipe or scale to your needs. The smell of it hitting a hot pan (or even getting microwaved) will fill the air with a beguiling cheesy, garlicky aroma.

8 ounces (225 g) salted butter
2 ounces (55 g) sliced ramps or other onion leaves
½ tablespoon cold water
A few cracks of black pepper
½ tablespoon chilled lemon juice (or water)

A few scrapes of fresh lemon zest

Cut the butter into tablespoon-sized pieces and bring to room temperature. Bring a pot of water to a boil and blanch half the ramp leaves for 5 seconds, just until wilted, then refresh in cold water. Squeeze the leaves dry, then mince fine on a cutting board with the fresh ramp leaves. In the bowl of a food processor, pulse the ramp leaf mash to smooth it out, then gradually add half of the butter, processing to make a smooth paste (it may take some time if your butter is cold), gradually adding the water and the rest of the butter and continuing to process until the butter is light green and fluffy. Finally, add the pepper, and drizzle in the lemon juice and zest, processing for a few more seconds to lighten it. Spread the butter in a thick line onto the middle of a piece of parchment, roll into a log shape, and refrigerate, then cut into portions and freeze. The butter will keep for a few weeks in the fridge, and months in the freezer.

Tabasco-Style Ramp Hot Sauce

Makes about 3 quarts (3 L)

The holy grail of ramp sauces in my world: a long-fermented hot sauce modeled after Tabasco. This makes 3 quarts (3 L), so consider making a half recipe if you don't want a lot of hot sauce, or if it's your first time making it. That being said, once you taste this sauce on a plate of eggs, you might want to start doubling the recipe. It's a great DIY project to start in the spring and enjoy in the cold months.

1 ounce (28 g) kosher salt
2 cups (480 ml) water
14 ounces (400 g) ramp leaves
2 pounds (910 g) jalapeño peppers, stemmed and chopped, seeds included, to yield about 1¾ pounds (795 g)
3½ cups (850 ml) cider vinegar
1½ teaspoons xanthan gum

Add the salt to the water, and whisk to dissolve. Chop the ramp leaves, combine with the jalapeños, and pack into a 3-quart (3 L) (or larger) container. Pour the salt water over the ramp mix, cover tightly, and store in a cool, dark place for 2 weeks, stirring every few days. After the fermentation stops, the mixture will be stable, and you won't need to stir it (or "burp" it, as chefs say) regularly. Continue aging the mixture for at least 2 months, and up to 6.

To finish the sauce, add the cider vinegar and purée 4 cups (945 ml) at a time (or less, if you have a small blender), adding ½ teaspoon of xanthan gum to each 4-cup batch to thicken it slightly. Strain the sauce for the smoothest finished product, discarding the leftover solids. From here, the sauce can be canned and processed in a water bath, which I recommend if you're giving it as a gift. It's fine stored at room temperature, but will keep the brightest flavor if refrigerated after opening. It will keep indefinitely.

Sauces made from ramp leaves: ramp mole, steak sauce, and Tabasco.

Ramp Steak Sauce

Makes 2½ cups (625 ml)

I like this sauce made from fermented ramp leaves so much, I've considered selling it. It's basically a condiment I engineered after seeing "ramp sauce" being sold at a store while I was on vacation. I bought a bottle, brought it home, and was pretty disappointed—it tasted of vinegar and was weak on ramps, aside for a few stringy pieces in the bottom. It was basically forgettable.

The version I developed goes like this: Mix ramps with 3 percent of their weight in salt (a kitchen scale that weighs items in grams helps here, and is well worth the minor investment), and let them ferment for 2 weeks or more, then purée and bottle them. It ends up tasting a bit like Worcestershire, but with a very strong umami quality that's almost oceanic from the fermentation. If you don't want to use a vacuum sealer, you can weigh down the ramps in a jar or fermenting vessel, but it's more difficult to keep the ferment clean and pure, as mold forms more easily without brine. The finished sauce is excellent drizzled over mild things like fish, poultry, and eggs, or warmed, whisked with a knob of butter to mellow and round out the flavor.

250 grams (roughly 9 ounces) fermented
    ramp leaves
7.5 grams (1½ teaspoons) salt

Final sauce
10 cloves or allspice berries, or a
    combination of the two
30 black peppercorns
300 grams (1¼ cups) apple cider vinegar
20 grams (4 teaspoons) kosher salt
½ teaspoon xanthan gum
60 grams (¼ cup) reserved brine from
    fermented ramp leaves, or water

Mix the ramp leaves and salt, vacuum-seal, and allow to ferment for 2 weeks, following the directions for Dry-Fermented Grape Leaves (page 26).

Once the ramps are fermented, make the sauce. Toast the cloves and the peppercorns, grind to a fine powder, then cool. Put all ingredients in a blender and purée until very smooth, then transfer to a Mason jar or other container and refrigerate until needed.

Cow Parsnip

Cow parsnip (*Heracleum maximum*) looks like a plant from another world, towering over other flora with its giant palm-shaped leaves. Just as with a parsnip grown in your garden, the juices of the cow parsnip, exposed to skin and sun, can cause a phototoxic burn on the skin that can last for a while. Even so, that hasn't stopped cow parsnip and its similar-tasting cousins from being used as a food plant around the world, and if you look at what the plant gives, it's easy to see why.

The dried seeds are probably the most widely used part of the plant around the world. After the plant makes flowers, its final and most important gift is a spice. *Golpar* is the Persian name for the dried seed of a cousin (*H. persicum*), confusingly sold under the name *angelica seed*. In India it's known as chimping. Drying the seeds and grinding them in a spice grinder gives off a potent aroma that's hard to describe, and, at first for me, even harder to cook with.

How's a spice hard to cook with? Well, for one, golpar doesn't like to be toasted. Chefs are told to always toast their spices. Secondly, and most important, too much of it is soapy tasting—not a label I want attached to my food. The first dishes I created with it were okay, but I knew there was something I didn't understand, and I gave up on it for a while. Then I read about Persian recipes using ground angelica seed and, because that seed is arguably even more difficult to use, I ordered some online to see what it tasted like. *Who knows?* I thought. *Maybe they're using a different species that tastes better than the angelica seed I harvest in Wisconsin.*

A few weeks later, a plastic jar of light brown powder showed up, and cracking open the seal sent a familiar aroma wafting into the room. It was nearly identical to the cow parsnip seeds I harvest—it was definitely not angelica. After that, I made a few recipes I found online that used golpar, and then I started creating my own. It's one of the best seasonings for beans I've come across, but this spice really shines when blended in equal parts with other aromatic seeds from the Apiaceae family: Cumin seems the most traditional, but caraway, coriander, fennel, or a combination of a few would be equally good. There's also a seasoning mix called Advieh, similar to garam masala, that uses golpar in combination with other things. Mixing with another spice helps calm the flavor of the cow parsnip seeds, making them less intense than they are by themselves. I've included a few of my favorite combinations here, but it's also great added to vegetable pickles and relishes such as CSA Fermented Giardiniera (page 71).

As a safety note, I've read some anecdotal information saying that consuming golpar in larger amounts, just like carrot seeds, could possibly interfere with beginning a pregnancy, or with the early stages of pregnancy. I can't speak to the science or medicinal properties of plants, but I'd wager it's better to avoid it if you're trying to get pregnant, or serving to someone who is—just as you might with alcohol.

Here are a couple of my favorite recipes.

Dried cow parsnip seeds.

The Botany of Spices

Golpar is a perfect example of how you can construct flavors in food using a botanical lens. As I mentioned before, mixing golpar and cumin together in equal parts is really good. Exactly *why* they complement each other is hard to explain, but they both share the same sort of high volume on the palate—they're strong flavors. Cumin, coriander, fennel, aniseed, dill seeds, cow parsnip seeds, caraway . . . these are all from Apiaceae plants, and most can be substituted for one another, or could taste good mixed.

For example, marinated feta cheese, goat cheese, potatoes, or warm olives would all taste fine seasoned with cumin or fennel seeds, but they'd also be good with coriander mixed in equal parts with dill seeds. Thinking about the familiar relationships between plants unlocks lots of doors, and is a way of pairing flavors no chef has ever described to me. So as a fun experiment, the next time you're cooking and you reach for one of the spices mentioned here, consider its cousin spices: They might taste good either in addition to, or as a substitute for, the seasonings called for in whatever you're making.

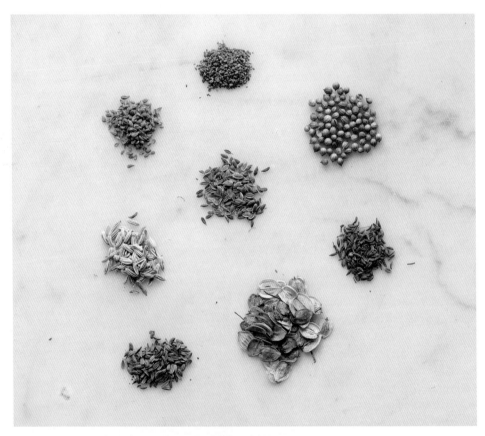

Clockwise from top: Celery seed, coriander, wild caraway, cow parsnip, wild fennel, fennel, aniseed, and dill.

Lentil Salad with Golpar

Serves 5–10, depending on the size of the portion

This was one of the first recipes I made in which, instead of trying to cover up the flavor of the cow parsnip seeds, I used it—combining the seeds with a little cumin—and watched a group of hungry people gobble it up. After I tested the recipe on family, I liked it enough that I served it to around 200 people for the Wild Harvest Festival in 2019. You want lentils that hold their shape really well; black lentils are my favorites, or the tortoiseshell-green lentils du puy. Cheap brown or red lentils won't work here.

1 cup (200 g) black or French green lentils
2 cups (480 ml) stock or water
Kosher salt, to taste
1 ounce (28 g) shallot, in ¼-inch (6 mm) dice (or ½ small onion or leek)
1 tablespoon flavorless oil, such as grapeseed
3 tablespoons roasted walnut or another nut oil, or good-tasting olive oil
¼ rounded teaspoon ground cumin
¼ rounded teaspoon ground cow parsnip seeds (golpar)
1½ tablespoons fresh lemon juice, or to taste
1½ tablespoons Fermented Lemon Confit (page 45), in ¼-inch (6 mm) dice (or preserved lemons soaked in water, or grated lemon zest, to taste), for serving (optional)
Chopped fresh cilantro (or dill or mint), to taste, for serving (optional)

Bring the lentils to a simmer with the stock and a pinch of salt, then cook, covered, at a slow simmer, until the lentils are just cooked, about 20 minutes. Meanwhile, sweat the shallot in the flavorless oil for a minute or two to tame it, then transfer to a bowl large enough to accommodate the lentils. Drain the lentils and combine with the shallot and remaining ingredients. Double-check the seasoning and adjust as needed. Serve sprinkled with a few extra pieces of Fermented Lemon Confit or chopped herbs. This dish is delicious served warm or at room temperature, and it travels well.

Marinated Feta with Golpar

Get the best feta you can find—I like Israeli or Bulgarian, but any kind of feta sold in a block or cut for you to order can do in a pinch, and if it is packed with whey, even better.

Cut the cheese into bite-sized pieces, then season with freshly toasted, coarsely ground cumin seeds, a tiny bit of grated garlic, a few good glugs of olive oil, chopped cilantro or parsley or other herbs to taste, crumbled dried hot pepper, grated finely diced lemon zest, and equal parts ground cumin and cow parsnip seeds (golpar), to taste. Gently spoon the marinade over the cheese, which will gradually absorb some of the spices as it sits. Cover the cheese and allow it to marinate in the refrigerator for at least 30 minutes, or up to overnight, tossing before serving to coat the cheese with the juices. Serve with toothpicks, either by itself or as part of a large appetizer platter with hummus, olives, grape leaves, and soon. For a more refined version of this dish, you can cut a 4-ounce (115 g) block of feta into ½-inch (1.25 cm) slices, keeping it whole, then cut each slice into thirds, and sprinkle the seasonings and marinade on top, as pictured.

Angelica

Just the word *angelica*, at least for me, has long conjured up images of arcane herbs and plants lost to time, and my love for the plant has only grown as I've learned more about it. I'd read about angelica in older French cookbooks, and I knew the Vikings cultivated the plant (a supposedly candy-sweet variety called vossakvann, which they tamed to have a semi-solid stem). Since Minnesota shares a similar climate with parts of Scandinavia, I knew angelica was a possibility in my region, but I'd already searched for the plant for years in Minnesota during the spring morel season, without success.

Then, as luck would have it, one summer I noticed a colony of strange, tall plants that looked like something from a Dr. Seuss book growing along a back road on my girlfriend's farm. I watched the plants closely, waiting for them to show their flowers (a helpful tool in identification, as the flower umbels are distinctly round), making sure I could distinguish it from the common and poisonous hemlock (*Conium maculatum*), which has clusters of white flowers (instead of angelica's green flowers) and leaves that are finely divided, like carrot leaves. Be absolutely sure before harvesting and consuming so that you know the difference; it is also helpful to seek a second opinion from an experienced forager.

I'll never forget the first time I held a cut stem up to my nose. The smell was incredible, a powerful aroma evoking the soul of gin, with a perceptible carrot-y undertone. It's unforgettable. A few years later I can look at a plant during any stage of growth and tell you if it's angelica or not—like seeing an old friend. There's no reason to be scared of this plant, but as with other members of the carrot family, juice from its green parts can and will cause photodermatitis, or sun rash, so be mindful when you harvest it, and wash your hands as soon as you get inside.

Now, you may find yourself saying, "Sure, Alan, but what about the rest of us who aren't wandering around the woods all day? How can we taste this plant? And more important, how can we avoid accidentally tasting hemlock?" Easy: Angelica is a great plant to grow in a garden, and it can take up space just like a small apple tree, becoming a beautiful perennial fixture in a yard. One of the most beautiful edible ornamentals I've ever seen is an angelica that grows in my friend's garden in full sun. More than 7 feet (2.1 m) tall, its giant purple flower stalk seems to reach up to the sky and is nearly as thick as my forearm; I call it the Methuselah.

To plant your own angelica, you could order seeds online, or harvest some wild. The species of seeds you get may not be exactly what grows wild near you. (There are a number of wild species, and flavors can vary among them. For the record, I've only eaten *A. atropurpurea*, and I recommend searching it out.) The easiest seeds to get are probably from domestic *Angelica archangelica*, which I've heard tastes similar, if milder.

The plant smells incredible, but cooking with it takes some experimenting. Generally, the stems are harvested, but the leaves can also be tasty when blanched and added in tiny quantities to dishes such as fruit salads. The seeds are edible, too, but are an acquired taste. The root is commercially harvested, and is probably one of the key ingredients in any gin you purchase. (Bombay Sapphire, especially, tastes of angelica root to me.) Raw, the flavor of the stem is so strong that it's reminiscent of medicine, but cooking with it is kind of a misnomer—the aroma, at least from leaves and stems, weakens greatly after heating, with the exception of candying in syrup (arguably the most famous preparation), which holds the aroma trapped in the sweet, dense liquid. You can harness the flavor with cold infusions, too, especially by fermenting the stems into crème fraîche. I like to compare cooking with angelica to cooking with truffles: instead of finding a way to use the plant per se, you're trying to find a way to harness the flavor, potentially into another medium, such as dairy or alcohol. Here are some of my favorite things to do with this incredible, ancient herb.

Fennel Salad with Apples and Pickled Angelica

Angelica isn't something you're just going to toss into any salad, but it pairs perfectly with sweet apples, and crisp, crunchy fennel. To make this salad, take a bulb or two of fennel, cut them in half vertically, then shave the short way ⅛ to ¼ inch thick (3–6 mm) on a mandoline, or cut with a knife. Don't shave the fennel paper-thin; it should be thick enough to be a bit crunchy. Cut a good eating apple, like a Honey Crisp, peel it (optional), core it, and cut it into slices about the same size as the fennel. Pare an orange and cut it into slices or skinless wedges. Chop a few fennel fronds for color. Add a few slices of Pickled Angelica (recipe follows) to taste, put the ingredients in a bowl, season gently with oil and a dash of lemon juice or vinegar and salt to taste, and serve. It's excellent with fish or poultry, or all by itself.

Pickled Angelica

Makes 1 quart (945 ml)

This is a delicious way to preserve angelica stems, especially if you don't want to take the time to candy them. Toss Pickled Angelica with fennel salad or slaw for a refreshing salad. In the right place, this pickle could even be sneaked into a dessert with fruit, preferably alongside citrus, but it pairs well with fresh red berries and fruit, especially when served with yogurt. Scandinavian cuisine and flavors—especially fish, dill, onions, and sour cream—pair well with Pickled Angelica.

1 tablespoon pickling spices
1¼ cups (300 ml) water
1 cup (240 ml) apple cider vinegar
2 teaspoons kosher or sea salt
1 cup (200 g) sugar
12 ounces (340 g) tender angelica stems

Toast the pickling spices and mix with the water, vinegar, salt, and sugar. Bring the mixture to a boil. Meanwhile, cut the angelica into ¼-inch (6 mm) slices, add to the pickle liquid, and cook until tender, about 5 to 10 minutes. Strain out the stems and pack them into a quart jar, then cover completely with liquid. Seal the jar, then can it in a water bath—or simply cool, pour into a jar, and refrigerate. The angelica will last for months and will mellow a bit as it sits. Refrigerate after opening.

Zavirne

Zavirne, besides being one of the coolest names for an edible plant part, is what the people of Salento, Italy (on the Adriatic coast), call unopened angelica flower blossoms. I knew cow parsnip blossoms were edible (and delicious), but since raw angelica stems are very strong tasting, I thought angelica blossoms would be worthless as a culinary product. How wrong I was! For whatever reason, angelica blossoms don't taste as strong once they're cooked. They're delicious grilled, served with nothing more than lemon or a dash of vinegar and oil, but for a real treat, cook them or cow parsnip blossoms in tempura, or your favorite batter. Angelica blossoms, with their subtle perfume, make a very special dessert cooked this way.

Zavirne. Also known as cocoon broccoli. One of the first guests I ever served them to said it was like eating a vegetable from Harry Potter.

Fried Zavirne

**Makes enough batter to fry
10 or more blossoms**

This is just a simple batter for a handful of blossoms; feel free to double it to feed a crowd. Serve it with lemon wedges, lemony aioli, or mayonnaise. Angelica blossoms should be blanched and cooled in their liquid to calm their flavor, but if you're making this from cow parsnip, you can cook them directly from their raw state.

1 scant cup (120 g) flour or equivalent
½ teaspoon paprika
¼ teaspoon fresh-ground black pepper
¼ teaspoon kosher salt
¼ teaspoon onion powder
¾ cup (180 ml) soda water
1 large egg
Fresh angelica blossoms
Cooking oil, as needed for frying the zavirne
Crunchy salt and lemon wedges, for serving

Combine the dry ingredients. In a separate bowl, combine the wet ingredients, then fold them into the dry ingredients. Keep the batter cold until ready to use. Dip the zavirne into the batter just to coat, then fry in a few inches of oil, turning occasionally, until golden. Serve hot with salt and lemon on the side.

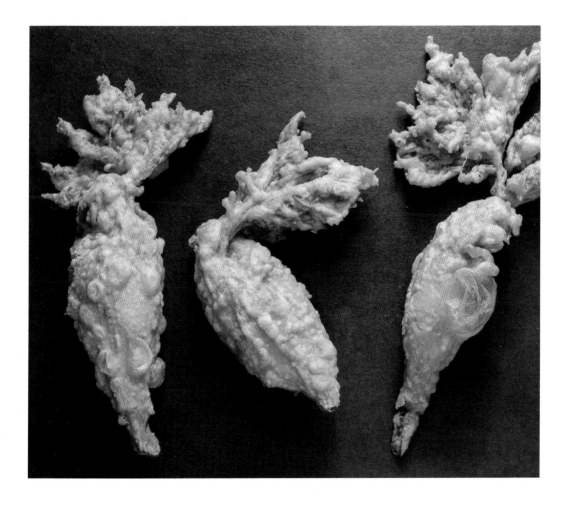

Sweet Fried Angelica Blossoms (Zavirne Dolce)

Angelica blossoms differ from cow parsnip blossoms in that they can double as a dessert. To make them, blanch the angelica blossoms in a pot of boiling water for 5 minutes, then turn off the heat and let the blossoms cool in the liquid until you can handle them. Dry the blossoms thoroughly, pressing them gently between towels. Heat some oil (a shallow frying pan or skillet will work, but for big batches I recommend using a deep-fryer or a deep skillet) until hot but not smoking (about 350°F/180°C). Dip the blossoms into all-purpose flour seasoned with a pinch of cinnamon, then into beaten egg whisked with a dash of sweet liqueur such as sambuca or limoncello. Dip the blossoms a final time into the flour, then fry until golden and crisp. You can serve them whole or cut into pieces. Drizzled with honey and a dusting of powdered sugar, they make a very special dessert.

Classic Candied Angelica

Makes 1 quart (945 ml), enough to last through the winter when used in small amounts

The classic way to prepare angelica stems is time consuming but makes a great after-dinner conversation piece or addition to special desserts. If your stems are thick or slightly mature, blanch them in the water first, then peel them carefully with a paring knife. After the stems are peeled, add the sugar to the cooking water and proceed as follows.

1 pound (455 g) thick, tender angelica stems, trimmed of leaves (a finger's width is good)
4 cups (945 ml) water
6 cups (1.2 kg) white sugar, plus extra for coating the stems

Cut the stems into pieces about 3 to 4 inches (7.5–10 cm) long, or whatever size you'd like, depending on the container you will store them in.

In a large pot, bring the sugar-water mixture to a rolling boil, then add the angelica stems (you may have to add them a few at a time to make room) and cook for 3 to 4 minutes until wilted. Turn off the heat and remove the angelica to a bowl or other container.

Bring the syrup back to a rolling boil for a minute or two, pour it over the stems and allow to cool to room temperature, then chill, covered, for at least 12 hours. The next day, drain off the syrup, bring to a boil again, pour over the stalks, cool, and refrigerate. Repeat the process one more time. After the last time, remove the stems and blot them dry.

Toss the stems with sugar, then dry the sugared stems in a dehydrator on the lowest temperature setting, or leave them on a cooling rack at room temp until dried, but still slightly pliable. When the stems are dried, refrigerate until needed in a tightly sealed container. Refrigerated, vacuum-sealed stems will keep the best texture and flavor.

Strawberry Rhubarb Crisp with Angelica

Serves 8–10

One of my trademark desserts. Angelica has a natural affinity for rhubarb, and both of them shine in this slight update of the American classic. Instead of using candied angelica, which won't work in this recipe, you'll mix together the rhubarb and fresh angelica, allowing the angelica to perfume the rhubarb with its aroma, a technique I came up with after cooking with truffles.

Filling

1⅓ cups (270 g) sugar (preferably organic), divided
2 pounds (910 g) rhubarb
1 pound (455 g) strawberries
1 tablespoon lemon juice
3 tablespoons cornstarch
5 tablespoons fresh angelica stem, in ¼-inch (6 mm) dice

Crumb topping

1¼ cups (125 g) rolled oats, preferably the thick, old-fashioned kind
1½ cups (180 g) flour (or equivalent)
6 tablespoons unsalted butter
½ teaspoon salt
½ teaspoon ground cinnamon
¾ cup (160 g) brown sugar

If you're using organic sugar with large granules, grind it in a blender or food processor to break it up, which will speed the maceration process. Wash the rhubarb, then trim any tough stems and leaf particles. Cut the stems into ½-inch (1.25 cm) pieces and toss with 1 cup (200 g) of the sugar and allow to macerate for 30 minutes, tossing occasionally, preferably in a place with ambient warmth. (I used to put hotel pans on top of a cool oven in kitchens, but you could turn your oven on warm and set the rhubarb near the vent.) Meanwhile, trim and quarter the strawberries and toss them with the remaining ⅓ cup (70 g) sugar. Drain the rhubarb, discarding the juice, then combine with the strawberries, lemon juice, cornstarch, and angelica. Combine well, then rest the mixture in the fridge for at least a few hours or overnight, to allow the angelica's perfume to penetrate the rest of the ingredients.

While the filling rests, make the crumb topping: Toast the oats in a 350°F (180°C) oven for 15 minutes, then allow to cool. Combine the cooled, toasted oats with the remaining topping ingredients, mixing them together gently by hand—clumps are all part of the rustic charm here.

To bake the crumble, increase the oven temperature to 375°F (190°C). Pour the filling into a 8 × 12-inch (20 × 30 cm) baking pan, covering it with a layer of the crumb topping. Bake for 30 minutes, then reduce the heat to 325°F (160°C) F and bake 20 to 30 minutes more, or until golden and bubbly. Allow the crisp to rest a bit before serving. Serve with vanilla ice cream or whipped cream. It's also great the next day for breakfast with thick Greek yogurt.

Sweet Galium

Sweet galium (*Galium triflorum*) is one of the greatest wild herbs I've encountered. Sweet woodruff (*G. odoratum*, a cousin) is an herb that's been used in Europe for a very long time. It is loved for its incredible aroma, which is a combination of vanilla and fresh-cut grass. I knew the plant didn't grow in the Midwest, so imagine my surprise when another chef in town put sweet woodruff on his menu. I needed to have this herb. The only problem was finding it.

I knew from images that woodruff was a type of cleaver or bedstraw, an ubiquitous weed easily identified through its creeping, vine-like structure and the whorls of leaves that circle the stem. Every type of bedstraw I smelled, though, just smelled like grass. I thought it must be some incredibly rare cousin I'd need to find, a botanical needle in a haystack. On a whim, I brought a handful of some of the most common galium home, tossed it unceremoniously into the dehydrator, and went into the other room to work.

Not 20 minutes later, a strong vanilla scent crept out of the other room, calling to me, pulling me like the white fingers of aroma in a cartoon. I jumped up and down—I'd found it! It was just a common weed, and it was *everywhere*! I couldn't believe it. The entire top floor of my apartment building reeked of vanilla for hours. It's one of the most powerfully aromatic plants I've ever come across, and it was hiding in plain sight.

Since then, my love for this common weed has only grown, and I use it in all kinds of things. Harvesting, storage, and cooking with it couldn't be easier, and it can be used anywhere you'd like the taste of vanilla. The aroma is so strong, in fact, that you can make your own homemade vanilla extract from it! I've included a few simple recipes here to get you started, but the only limit to how this herb can be used is your imagination. Besides the simple panna cotta and extract below, add a handful to Black Walnut Preserves (page 252) or any sort of homemade alcohol infusion, for the delicious vanilla note it imparts.

Sweet Galium Panna Cotta

Serves 8

A tribute to the panna cotta that Chef Jim Christiansen, formerly the chef of Heyday in Minneapolis, used to run on his menu. Sweet galium would love to be infused into just about any dairy-based dessert, but it's hard to beat a good panna cotta, the classic Italian, scented-cream dish that just might be the most perfect summer dessert out there when paired with fresh berries or a fresh fruit sauce. You can halve this recipe using two sheets of gelatin or 2 teaspoons of powder.

¼ cup (3 g) packed (a good handful)
  dried galium leaves and stems
3 cups (720 ml) heavy cream
½ cup (135 ml) maple syrup or sugar
3½ sheets gelatin or 3½ teaspoons
  of powdered gelatin
1 cup (220 g) thick Greek yogurt

Wrap the galium in cheesecloth for easy removal later. Heat the cream, maple (syrup or sugar), and galium until steaming, then remove from the heat and cool to room temperature, allowing the galium to infuse for at least an hour or so, or up to 8 hours. Afterward, remove the galium and discard. Soak the gelatin in ice water until soft, about 4 or 5 minutes, then add it to the cream mixture and reheat it gently, whisking to dissolve the gelatin. If you use powdered gelatin, purée this with a hand blender to break up any lumps. Finally, whisk in the yogurt. Pour the mixture into ramekins or other small vessels (jam jars, custard cups, teacups) to set, and refrigerate overnight. To serve, unmold the panna cotta by sliding a paring knife around the edge and gently releasing them, or serve them in their individual vessels, topped with a dollop of jam or fruit sauce and fresh berries.

Sweet Galium Panna Cotta with black cap raspberries and milkweed flowers.

Galium Vanilla Extract

Makes 2 cups (480 ml)

I knew from the German tradition of Mae-bowle, or May or spring wine infused with sweet woodruff, that the scent of galium should be alcohol-soluble. I used to have my pastry chef save empty vanilla pods and put them in a bottle of brandy, which worked like a charm and was a good way to stretch the beans she seemed to fly through with no thought to our bottom line. With the price of vanilla currently sky-high, I thought I'd try to make a vanilla extract with galium in place of vanilla beans. Wouldn't you know it? The galium worked, much better than I expected. To ensure a super-strong extract, I do a double infusion. It's almost shocking how good a substitute galium is for vanilla, and instead of hundreds of dollars a pound, you can get it for free outside. It's strong, but I do use slightly more of it than I would vanilla extract. Simmering the finished extract in a water bath is optional, but makes it more versatile since it may curdle cream in its raw state. I've made a similar extract with fresh leaves, but it wasn't quite as potent. A one-time maceration of leaves and alcohol can work, too, but isn't quite as strong.

4 packed cups (945 ml) dried galium*
2 cups (480 ml) brandy

Pack half of the galium leaves in a quart Mason jar or similar glass container, then cover them with the brandy and screw on the lid. Leave the jar out at room temperature for a week, shaking it occasionally. After a week, remove the leaves, squeezing them to extract as much infused brandy as possible, and discard. Repeat the maceration process with the other half of the galium leaves and the infused brandy, allowing them to infuse for a week, then pour the brandy and leaves into a double boiler (or a small bowl set into a saucepan over—but not touching—simmering water) for 30 minutes to gently cook off a bit of the alcohol. Cool the extract, strain out the galium and discard, then bottle the infusion and store it in the fridge. Use wherever you'd use vanilla, especially in dishes such as whipped cream, baked goods, and sweet sauces.

---

* Because dried galium is extremely light, measurement here is provided in volume.

Wild Seed Cake

Makes 1 loaf-shaped cake

I spent weeks working on this pound cake to showcase the entire angelica plant for a few hundred people at a Slow Food dinner. Later, a friend from Wales turned me on to "seed cake," typically made with caraway seeds, which is common in the United Kingdom. I often serve this cake with a compote of angelica and rhubarb, but any stewed fruit would be delicious. You can also replace the almond meal with an equal amount of additional cake flour or all-purpose flour, just as with a regular pound cake.

1 cup (120 g) cake flour or all-purpose flour
½ teaspoon baking powder
1 cup (200 g) sugar
2 teaspoons Galium Vanilla Extract
    (page 190) or 1 teaspoon vanilla extract
5 scrapes *each* orange and lemon zest
8 ounces (225 g) unsalted butter
1 cup (85 g) almond meal
1 tablespoon ground angelica seeds, or 4 teaspoons dried whole seeds, such as caraway
Pinch of kosher salt
4 whole eggs plus 1 egg yolk
½ cup (135 ml) milk

Sift together the flour and baking powder and reserve. Cream the sugar, vanilla, zests, and butter in a stand mixer with the paddle attachment, scraping down the sides as needed to clean the bowl, until the mixture is lightened in color and fluffy, about 5 minutes, then add the almond meal, angelica seeds, and salt, and mix for another minute. Add the eggs and egg yolk, one at a time, waiting until each is fully incorporated before adding the next. Add the milk and mix a moment more, to combine. Use a spatula to fold in the flour mixture by hand until just combined. Spread the batter into a loaf pan and bake at 300°F (150°C) for 60 minutes, or until a cake tester comes out clean. Cool the cake on a rack before slicing.

Seed cake, made with wild caraway and black walnuts.

Sweetfern and Sweetgale

If I close my eyes, I can picture blueberry picking in the summer. As I walk, hunting the next patch of ripe fruit that tastes like sunshine, a perfume wafts up from the sweetfern crushed underfoot. It's a special aroma, hard to describe, but one it shares with its cousin sweetgale. There are other plants in the same family (Myricaceae), but the only ones I've worked with are sweetgale (*Myrica gale*) and sweetfern (*Comptonia peregrina*). I use the fruits of the two interchangeably as a spice.

The aroma of the plants, to me, is a combination of smells reflecting the terrain it grows in, which is acidic, rocky, and surrounded by coniferous trees. Saying it's "piney" isn't quite right. *Resinous* is a more specific term, but one that doesn't exactly stir up appetites. Either way, it's a great aromatic.

I know a few people who harvest the leaves of sweetfern to use as a seasoning, but besides tea, I don't do much with them. For me, the real prize of this plant is found in its nutlets: small, bright green orbs covered in tiny green hairs, almost like miniature chestnuts in their spiny green burrs. Fresh, their aroma is potent, lingering.

Most people will dry the leaves for future use, but I find they lose flavor quickly after drying. Nutlets keep their aroma well and, after drying, can be crushed and used whenever, although the burrs surrounding the nutlets tend to crumble a bit when dried. Sweetgale fruits will keep their shape. I find sweetfern to be in the same taste realm as sweetgale, but subtler. I dry my nutlets and store them in a plastic bag inside a hard-sided container in the freezer, or vacuum-sealed, but room temperature is fine for a month or two.

Simple cookies are a great way to enjoy the subtle flavor of sweetfern and sweetgale, but the nutlets can also be infused into cream many different ways, as in the dairy-based fermentation I use with Wildflower Crème Fraîche (page 200). Historically, the plants are used in Scandinavia in the form of gotlandsdricka and gruit—brews rumored to date back to the Vikings, scented with sweetgale and other herbs.

Dried sweetfern and sweetgale nutlets have a distinct, similar flavor, although I find sweetgale stronger.

Sweetfern Cookies

Makes about 15 small cookies

A simple shortbread cookie that tastes like sweetfern smells. They're great with coffee or tea, or crumbled into ice cream.

2 teaspoons dried, ground sweetgale or sweetfern nutlets
4 tablespoons unsalted butter, diced small
¼ cup (30 g) all-purpose flour
¼ cup (30 g) whole wheat or other interesting flour
Pinch of salt
2 tablespoons maple sugar or brown sugar

Grind the nutlets, crumbly husks and all, to a fine powder in a coffee grinder, then combine with the remaining ingredients and work gently into a smooth dough. Form the dough into a log, wrap in cling film, and refrigerate overnight (or at least a few hours) to hydrate the flour and ensure even cooking. Preheat the oven to 350°F (180°C), cut the log into ¼-inch (6 mm) slices, and bake for 8 to 10 minutes or until lightly browned. Cool the cookies on a rack, then store at room temperature in a covered container.

Sweetgale Schnapps

Makes about a pint (480 ml)

An ode to the Scandinavian tradition of infusing liquor at home—and for me, a taste of the Boundary Waters where I usually harvest the plant with my father. Liquors infused with sweetgale are still sold commercially in Europe, although they will probably come flavored with herbs as well, so think of this as a simple method to build on. Typically the leaves are used in the maceration/infusion process, but I like the berries since they're so potent—just a few will infuse a good amount of liquor. My Scandinavian ancestors would probably have taken it straight as a shot after yelling, "Skol!," but I've enjoyed it with soda or on the rocks, too, as a digestif. Another combination, similar to a historical beer made with the plants called gruit, would be to use a few leaves of yarrow and creeping Charlie (historically used before hops) in addition to sweetgale or sweetfern fruit or leaves. I've read that sweet galium is also used, and an inch or two (2.5–5 cm) of dried leaves added to the version below can be very nice. This liquor is also good used in place of brandy for desserts—say, if you're adding a bit to fruit sauces. If you want to drink it and find the flavor too strong, try tinkering by mixing it with other macerated spirits to make a blend, or using it as a flavoring agent in place of gin. Sweetfern will make a milder version than sweetgale.

1 generous tablespoon crushed fresh sweetgale fruit or sweetfern nutlets

2 cups (480 ml) vodka or another neutral spirit

2 tablespoons maple syrup or honey, or to taste

Gently pound the nutlets with a mortar and pestle to release their aroma, then combine with the vodka and maple syrup; allow to macerate at room temperature for a week. Strain the liquid, then bottle it and store in the pantry or fridge.

Flowers

Inspired by Chef Michel Bras and his signature dish, The Gargouillou; he was compelled to create the dish after running through a field of wildflowers in bloom. I can remember a time when I wished I knew of just *one* kind of flower I could eat outside. Look at foraging books and field guides, and you're going to see mostly plants, roots, nuts, and tubers—things that can, and will, sustain you. Flowers aren't going to make up a large portion of your diet. They're never going to be championed by hard-core foragers hunting for calories, and some people think harvesting flowers is a waste of precious time. Most flowers are just pretty, and a few of them taste good—some of them, really good. In my mind, though, knowing a few flowers, especially edible ones, is a part of the native landscape knowledge we're quickly forgetting and, honestly, eating flowers is just fun, almost like playing with your food—ask anyone who's ever tasted the spicy, sweet flavor of a nasturtium flower.

As a chef, I'm concerned with beauty, and I know if I put a plate of food in front of someone they will eat with their eyes first. No one will say a rose is ugly, but they might shy away from eating a bowl of nettles or anything else that gets labeled as a weed. Flowers make food look delicious. They're colorful and attractive, and when something looks delicious to you, barring some horrible seasoning job, you're much more likely to enjoy it.

I want more people to appreciate and know about wild foods, to get excited by nature, to want to go outside and explore. I like to think putting a handful of flowers on a salad, and listening to the oohs and ahhs when the plate is brought to the table, is a small way of inviting people to do that. Here are a few of my favorites.

Virginia waterleaf (*Hydrophyllum virginianum*)

Comfrey (*Symphytum officinale*)

Mustards (*Sisymbrium* and *Brassicas* spp.)

Deadnettle (*Lamium purpureum*)

Chive and onion (*Allium* spp.)

Lilac (*Syringa vulgaris*)

Campion (*Silene* spp.)

Daylily (*Hemerocallis fulva*)

Roses (*Rosa* spp.)

Vetch (*Vicia americana*)

Hosta (*Hosta* spp.)

Columbine (*Aquilegia canadensis*)

Nasturtium (*Tropaeolum* spp.)

Bergamot (*Monarda fistulosa*)

Elder (*Sambucus nigra*)

Bellflower (*Campanula* spp.)

Borage (*Borago officinalis*)

Violets (*Viola* spp.)

Black locust (*Robinia pseudoacacia*)

Scarlet bee balm (*Monarda didyma*)

Signet Marigolds

There is one species of marigolds that features a pungent citrus flavor, called gem, or signet marigolds (*Tagetes tenuifolia*). I've tasted tangerine and lemon gem species, both have an equally intense taste and aroma. Their power is a secret I've been keeping, bringing it out here and there when I really want to knock people's socks off. To sweeten the deal, they can be as good with dessert as they are with savory courses.

Like other powerful aromatics, such as rosemary or sage, you can overdo it with marigolds, and a little goes a long way. When you use just enough, in the right place, these citrusy little flowers are fantastic, and those little green leaves are worth their weight in gold.

Marigolds will taste great anywhere there's fruit, or where a concentrated orange flavor would be welcome. Tuck a few leaves or flowers into a salad, maybe with a few slices of pared oranges or tangerines; infuse them into schnapps or orangecello; use them as a garnish for a bowl of fruit salad, or in Roasted Carrot Salad with Marigolds.

To sneak the flavor into something for first-timers, use it for Marigold Dressing. It's an all-purpose salad dressing, and the best way I've found to use marigolds if I want to mute their flavor a bit. To make this dressing, follow the recipe for Goddess Herb Dressing (page 43), substituting 1 tablespoon (4–5 g) roughly chopped signet marigold leaves, or to taste, for an equal amount of the tarragon or other herbs.

Roasted Carrot Salad with Marigolds

My favorite way to cook carrots is probably the easiest, and lends itself beautifully to this simple salad. Cooked whole, the carrots steam inside their skins, concentrating their aroma and color. Because carrot sizes vary, I usually just tell people to cook these "until they're done"—when a knife can just barely pierce them. After cooling, the carrots shouldn't be mushy, but just al dente. Try it with parsnips, too.

Whole carrots, preferably fresh from the garden, on the large side, greens removed down to ½ inch (1.25 cm), skins gently scrubbed
Flavorless oil, just enough to lightly coat the carrots
Kosher salt, fresh-ground black pepper, cumin, maple syrup (or sugar), finely grated orange zest, and apple cider vinegar, to taste
Marigold leaves, chopped, to taste
Marigold flowers, whole, to taste

Preheat the oven to 400°F (200°C). Toss the carrots with enough oil just to barely coat them, then season lightly with salt. Lay the carrots in a cast-iron skillet or on a baking sheet, then roast just until they can be pierced with a knife, 20 to 30 minutes, depending on the size of your carrots. Remove the pan from the oven and cool the carrots to room temperature. They should feel slightly underdone, and will continue to cook from the pan's residual heat as they cool. When in doubt, undercook them.

Cut the roasted carrots on the bias into ½-inch (1.25 cm) thick slices, season well with salt and pepper, a little cumin, a dash of maple syrup, and some finely grated orange zest to taste, then sprinkle on a little apple cider vinegar. Double-check the seasoning and adjust as needed, making sure it's well seasoned, since you'll serve it at room temperature. Garnish with chopped marigold leaves and whole flowers to taste.

Wildflower
Crème Fraîche

Makes enough for a quart (945 ml) jar

This is another example of how you can harness delicate flavors—ones that might not want to be heated—by using a quick ferment in dairy. The cream acts as an aroma sponge, soaking up the scent of whatever it contacts. It's magic, really. Once the dairy base is infused, you can use it anywhere you'd like the flavor of your ingredient. If the aroma can stand some heat, like galium, vanilla, elderflower, or meadowsweet flowers, you can heat the whole thing and make a dish like Spruce Tip Panna Cotta (page 208).

If the aroma of whatever you're using would diminish more than you'd like when heated, as with, say, wintergreen or angelica, you can sweeten the cream and whip it, then use it wherever you'd like some floral-tasting whip. As you'll notice, it's also in the ice-cream-esque semifreddo that follows. Wildflower Crème Fraîche is an incredibly versatile, practical way to capture aromas and a great way to share them with others, especially flower-cooking skeptics. Don't stop with flowers, though; the scent of many things can be captured this way. Use your imagination.

3 cups (720 ml) heavy cream
3 tablespoons full-fat Greek yogurt
  (I like Fage) or buttermilk
½–1 ounce (14–28 g) dried or fresh flowers

Combine the cream and yogurt, then pour the mixture into a widemouthed Mason jar or similar container. Wrap the dried or fresh flowers in cheesecloth before adding them to the cream. Tie some cheesecloth or a towel around the top, and allow the mixture to ferment overnight at room temperature. The cream should visibly thicken; if it doesn't, stir it a bit and leave out for another 24 hours, then store it in the fridge. Once the cream chills it will be like very thick yogurt or sour cream. You can leave your crème fraîche out for longer, but eventually it will develop bitter notes. Sometimes I sweeten it with maple syrup or sugar, sometimes not, but typically I serve it with something sweet. It can be used to flavor all kinds of dairy-based desserts where cream or sour cream might be used, and the simplest way to enjoy it is just to whip it, like regular cream.

Meadowsweet:
Move Over, Elderflower

Meadowsweet, also known as queen of the meadow (*Filipendula ulmaria*), is an unassuming flower I learned about from reading Chef Magnus Nilsson's *Fäviken*. Although the book didn't include any recipes or techniques for cooking with the plant, knowing it was useful put me on a mission to taste it. I couldn't smell much at first, but once the plant was dried, I started cooking with it, and I was floored.

The flavor starts out subtly, like elderflower—a sort of deep, sweet floral taste—but is quickly overtaken by notes of almond and marzipan, a flavor passed down through its heritage in the Rosaceae family; it's the same reason that apple seeds, and the pits of apricots and plums, taste of almond. In my opinion meadowsweet is superior to elderflower, but it doesn't get nearly as much attention. And as if the taste weren't good enough, the flowers keep their flavor after drying for year-round use. Meadowsweet can be used in just about any dairy-based dessert you can imagine, by warming cream and infusing with dried or fresh flowers wrapped in cheesecloth. It's also water-soluble, and is sold commercially as tea. Try it and become a convert. Note: People with sensitivity to aspirin or salicylates should probably avoid meadowsweet.

Meadowsweet or Elderflower Semifreddo

Serves 6–8, depending on whether you use an ice cream scoop or cut the terrine into slices

Semifreddo is essentially frozen custard that doesn't require an ice cream maker, and it is one of the very best ways to show off the flavors of meadowsweet, elderflower, and anything else you might use to flavor crème fraîche. Serve it with berries or a tart fruit sauce on the side. It will melt faster than ice cream, so I freeze my serving dishes in advance.

¼ cup (4 g) dried meadowsweet or elderflower flowers, or a few handfuls fresh
  (it's okay if there are a few small stems)

1¼ cups (300 ml) heavy cream
¼ cup (55 g) thick Greek yogurt
4 large egg yolks
¾ cup (150 g) sugar or maple syrup
¼ cup (60 ml) water (omit if you're
  using maple syrup)
Tiny pinch of salt
1 teaspoon vanilla extract, or
  2 teaspoons Galium Vanilla Extract
  (page 190)
A few scrapes of lemon zest,
  finely grated (optional)

Oil a loaf pan, then line it with cling film and put the pan in the freezer. Tie the meadow-sweet flowers in cheesecloth. Warm the cream. Allow the cream to cool to room temperature, then add the cheesecloth-wrapped flowers and yogurt, gently stir, cover, and leave out overnight at room temperature. The next day, warm the cream mixture gently and remove the flowers, carefully squeezing any excess cream back into the mixture. Chill the cream, then whip until it holds peaks. Chill the whipped cream and reserve.

  In a stand mixer, whisk the egg yolks. Meanwhile, heat the sugar, water, salt, and vanilla to a rolling boil, then slowly and care-fully pour the hot syrup down the side of the bowl in a thin stream while whisking the eggs (using a container with a pouring spout makes this easier). Be sure to add the hot syrup slowly, or you'll risk cooking the egg yolks. When all the syrup has been added, continue whisking until the yolk mixture reaches room temperature, about 5 to 10 min-utes. It will lighten in color and triple in volume. Mix in the whipped cream and the zest, then pour the mixture into the loaf pan and freeze until set, about 4 to 6 hours, or overnight. To serve, unmold the semifreddo and cut into slices, or scoop it out like ice cream, serving quickly in frozen dishes to avoid melting.

DIY Fermented Capers

When I had my caper breakthrough, I was walking on the edge of a forest in the spring, looking for mushrooms to bring to the restaurant, when I started to see all kinds of unopened dandelion flower buds. *I wonder what I can make with those?* I thought, and then I remembered that capers are just the unopened flower of a Mediterranean vine, which my mind turned into *Capers are just unopened flower buds!* After I worked out some dandelion capers I liked, I started applying the method to other plants and small, roundish-looking things. There are lots of different capers you can make—flowers are just the beginning—but generally, if I'm going to call them capers, I'm going to start with something in a green or unripe stage.

The method is easy: salt, water, and nothing else. I take a Mason jar and fill it with whatever ingredient I've foraged, along with enough water to cover, then I take the weight of the water and ingredients, multiply by 0.03, and add that much salt in grams, or just add 1.5 tablespoons of salt per quart (liter) jar. Then I screw the lid on and leave the contents at room temperature to ferment for a week or so, or until I like the taste. Afterword, I refrigerate them. Not every single unripe, green thing is worth capering, but there's a great number that are. To save you the trouble of experimenting, here are some of my favorite things to preserve unripe, in "caper form."

- Green gooseberries and unripe currants, especially black
- Nasturtium seedpods (arguably the best DIY caper, these have a flavor nearly identical to store-bought capers, but beware the aroma)
- Unopened dandelion flowers (get the tightest, youngest ones you can, and steam them until just tender before fermenting, or let them ferment first and then put them into canning jars and use a water bath to tenderize them)
- Green Szechuan peppercorns
- Unopened daylily flower buds
- Green ramp seeds, scapes, and wild onion bulbils
- Milkweed flower buds

Evergreens

The piney flavor of evergreens is a great aroma to add to your repertoire. There's a number of different parts of trees you can cook with—young cones, needles, and pollen, for starters—but my favorites are probably the young growing tips of spruce trees.

Spruce tips are widely available and easy to harvest; the only tricky part can be using them with purpose, since they can be overpowering. Their flavor can be incredible in the right place, but bitter and tannic when used in excess, so I use them sparingly, like an herb. Their flavor is a fascinating combination of pine and citrus notes, which can have a subtle or strong astringency depending on the particular species you're harvesting. Each tree I've sampled tastes different, but my favorites are white and Norway spruce. I don't care for balsam firs at all. Taste around and find some you like.

Spruce tips have been creeping into foods and beverages for a while. You'll find them on seasonal menus, brewed into beer, and infused into syrup for drinks, as well as on fancy wholesale price lists commanding more than $30 per pound frozen, year-round. Here are a few notes on cooking with them:

- First of all, the term *cooking* is misleading. I like spruce tips best added fresh to cold dishes, used as a garnish, or in desserts (my favorite), where they take on a flavor reminiscent of ripe honeydew melon and pine.
- Fresh green vegetables love conifer tips, especially asparagus, peas, fava beans, and green chickpeas.
- All true conifer tips should be edible, and some are delicious, but **yew tips (*Taxus* spp.) are poisonous.**
- Spruce tips are good just about anywhere you might use mint, and the two have a flavor affinity for each other.
- Tips like mild-flavored nuts, especially pistachios.
- Ripe fruit and berries, especially sweet ones like blueberries and strawberries, pair well with tips.
- For the best flavor year-round, do what restaurant suppliers do: Vacuum-seal your spruce tips and freeze them.
- Spruce tips are high in vitamin C—so high, in fact, that they can give some people a stomachache if they consume too many raw tips. That said, I've never heard of any issues caused by eating them after they've been puréed for desserts (as they are in every dessert in this book) or mixed in sugar for syrup.
- Choose mature, healthy trees. Harvesting from young trees could stunt their growth, especially harvesting the apical (top-most) tip.

Spring Vegetables with Spruce Tips and Lemon Oil

Serves 4–6

This is one of the best examples of how to use spruce tips in a savory dish, highlighting their affinity for fresh green vegetables. Many green spring vegetables are welcome here, but try not to miss the fiddlehead ferns, since the unfurled tops soak up the dressing especially well. Depending on the species of spruce you use, the taste of this side dish will range from quite mild to fairly powerful, so taste it after adding just a small amount of your tips to make sure you like the flavor, and go from there. My local Norway spruce (*Picea abies*) tips are pretty mild, but others might be a bit strong.

1 pound (455 g) mixed spring vegetables, especially asparagus, winter or spring radishes, and fiddlehead ferns
Up to ½ cup (28 g) young, small spruce tips, any papery husks removed

Serving
Lemon-Infused Oil, to taste (recipe follows)
Fresh lemon juice, to taste
Kosher salt and fresh-ground black pepper, to taste
Chopped fresh spearmint leaves, to taste
Chopped fresh parsley, to taste

Blanch the asparagus in boiling, salted water until just tender, about 1 to 2 minutes for chunky, homegrown garden asparagus, depending on size. Pencil-thin, cultivated asparagus will cook more quickly. Refresh the asparagus in cold water. Cut the tips off the asparagus, then cut the stalks diagonally into ½-inch (1.25 cm) pieces. Repeat this process for the fiddleheads, but don't chill them, or they may darken.

Trim a few of the radishes and, using a mandoline or a sharp paring knife, shave them into ¼-inch (6 mm) slices roughly the same size as the asparagus and fiddleheads. Small radishes can be quartered to add texture. If your spruce tips are long, consider cutting them in half or giving them a rough chop.

To serve, toss all of the vegetables, including the spruce tips, in a mixing bowl and season aggressively to taste with the Lemon-Infused Oil, lemon juice, salt, pepper, and fresh herbs. Allow the mixture to marinate for a few minutes. Taste again just before serving, adjust the seasoning as needed, and toss again to coat with the natural vinaigrette that forms.

Lemon-Infused Oil

Makes 1 pint (480 ml)

2 cups (480 ml) mild-tasting olive oil
Peel of 3 large, organic lemons
Small handful of lemon leaves (optional)
¼ teaspoon kosher salt

Pour the olive oil into a vacuum bag, set it into a container so that it's upright, and freeze. Peel the lemons, then mix the peel with the leaves, and massage a bit to bruise the peels and release their aroma. Toss with the salt, add to the bag with the oil, and vacuum-seal the bag. Juice the peeled lemons and save for another purpose. Allow the oil to sit in a bowl for 2 weeks in a cool, dark place, then strain and refrigerate. If you don't have a vacuum-sealer, you can use a clean glass jar. The oil will keep a good flavor for a month in the fridge.

Spruce Tip Key Lime Pie

Makes one 9½- or 10-inch (26 cm) pie

This recipe offers another fun way to show-case the affinity spruce tips have with citrus. This is a little different from traditional key lime pie, as it won't be as tart, but it's close, and the spruce flavor works really well with a simple graham cracker crust. Serve with stewed blueberries or your favorite fruit, and whipped cream.

Walnut graham crust

¼ teaspoon salt
¼ cup (150 g) sugar
1¼ cups (135 g) graham cracker crumbs
¼ cup (30 g) finely chopped black walnuts
   or regular walnuts
¼ teaspoon ground cinnamon
6 tablespoons unsalted butter

Filling

4 sheets silver gelatin, or 1¼ ounces (35 g)
   unflavored gelatin
2 cups (480 ml) heavy cream
1 can (14 ounces / 397 g) sweetened
   condensed milk
¼ teaspoon salt
⅓ cup (65 g) sugar
Scant ½ cup (28 g) chopped fresh or frozen
   spruce tips, any papery husks removed
A few generous scrapes of fresh lime zest,
   to taste
⅓ cup (80 ml) key lime juice or
   Persian lime juice

Preheat the oven to 350°F (180°C). Place all the crust ingredients except the butter into the bowl of a food processor and pulse until mixed. Melt the butter and pour it slowly into the food processor, pulsing just until the crumbs are evenly moistened and begin to stick together. Press the mixture into the pie pan, extending the crust up the sides. Bake the crust for 12 to 15 minutes or until lightly browned. Allow the crust to cool while you prepare the filling.

Soak the gelatin sheets in ice water, then squeeze them dry. Warm half of the cream with the condensed milk in a saucepan, then add the gelatin and whisk thoroughly until just dissolved (you'll want to purée it with a hand blender if you use powdered gelatin). Remove the saucepan from the heat and add the remaining cream, salt, and sugar. Set the saucepan in a sink or bowl full of cold water and whisk the mixture until it reaches room temperature. Pour the mixture into a blender, add the spruce tips, and purée for 30 seconds or so until well blended, then strain through the finest strainer you have. Whisk the lime zest and juice into the mixture well, which will cause the filling to thicken, then pour it into the crust and refrigerate until set, a few hours.

Spruce Tip Ice Cream

Makes 1 quart (945 ml)

One of my signature desserts, Spruce Tip Ice Cream had a cult following when it graced the dessert menu. One of my servers used to have her children pick them for me, with the promise of coming to the restaurant for a scoop fresh from the ice cream machine when it was done. It's great all by itself, but for some variation try it on a rhubarb crisp or with a handful of warm blueberries. Adding dark chocolate chips or shavings makes a nice play on mint chocolate chip ice cream, too.

6 large egg yolks
¾ cup (150 g) sugar
⅛ teaspoon salt
3 cups (720 ml) half-and-half
Scant ½ cup (28 g) chopped fresh or frozen spruce tips, any papery husks removed
1 teaspoon fresh lime juice

Whisk the egg yolks with the sugar, salt, and cream, then heat on medium-low, whisking occasionally to make sure the egg doesn't stick to the bottom of the pan.

When the mixture starts to steam and is hot to the touch, but not bubbling, remove it from the heat, whisking to help it cool until room temperature. Transfer the mixture to the bowl of a blender.

Add the spruce tips and purée, working up the power settings gradually until you get to high. It takes a bit of horsepower to break down the needles, and for the best flavor you really need them finely blended.

Pass it through a fine strainer, whisk in the lime juice, and refrigerate it overnight for the best texture. Finally, place the mixture in the bowl of an ice cream maker and process. My ice cream maker usually takes about 45 minutes. When the mixture looks thick like sour cream, transfer it to the freezer.

Spruce Tip Panna Cotta

Serves 4

Simple panna cotta is a great way to use spruce tips, and probably the most accessible thing to make for first-timers. Fresh fruit or a drizzle of berry sauce makes a good garnish.

2 sheets silver gelatin (2 teaspoons powdered)
2 cups (480 ml) heavy cream
Pinch of kosher salt
¼ cup (50 g) sugar
¼ cup (14 g) chopped fresh or frozen spruce tips, any papery husks removed
2 teaspoons fresh lime juice
Stewed berries, such as blueberries, or your favorite in-season fruit, for serving

Soak the gelatin sheets in ice water. Squeeze the gelatin dry, then add the gelatin (prepared sheets or powder) to the cream, salt, and sugar. Heat the mixture, whisking to dissolve the gelatin. If you use powdered gelatin, purée this with a hand blender to break up any lumps. Cool the pot in a sink or bowl half full of cold water until the mixture reaches room temperature. Pour the mixture into a blender with the spruce tips, then blend, working up the settings to high, for about 30 seconds or until well blended and light green. Strain through a fine strainer, then whisk in the lime juice. Pour evenly into four ramekins or custard dishes and chill 8 hours or overnight to set before turning out, garnishing with the berries or fresh fruit.

Spruce Posset

Serves 8

Posset is one of the easiest spruce tip desserts you can make, and I owe the idea to my old pastry chef Taylor Kollitz. A posset is an old-fashioned British custard; it's made without eggs and is a sort of cousin to panna cotta. It was often served to invalids, but the texture is so delicate that it would be a shame to serve it only to the sick. Think of the cooked cream as a clean canvas for whatever flavor you'd like to introduce. Traditionally citrus is used, as it helps the cream set, but I've modified a traditional recipe to be more versatile. Reducing the cream helps to stabilize it so you can use less citrus to set the mixture and is an important step in making sure the posset sets. These are a bit stronger than the other spruce desserts here, and a little goes a long way. I serve these in the smallest Mason jars—no more than 4-ounce (115 g) size. Different vessels can be used, but because the spruce flavor is fairly intense, I recommend decreasing the spruce tips by at least 25 percent if you plan on serving larger portions. Blueberries or whipped cream make a nice garnish.

3 cups (720 ml) cream
⅔ cup (130 g) sugar
⅓ cup (20 g) chopped fresh
  or frozen spruce tips, any papery
  husks removed
2 tablespoons lime juice
Tiny pinch of fine salt
Whipped cream, for serving (optional)
Fresh berries, for serving (optional)

In a high-sided pan that will resist overflowing, warm the cream and sugar and reduce on medium-low, stirring occasionally and watching carefully so it doesn't boil over, until it looks reduced by about a third and you have 3 cups (720 ml) of sweetened cream. Cool the cream to room temperature. Working carefully, purée the cream, the spruce tips, the lime juice, and the salt in a blender until well blended, then pass it through a fine strainer. Pour into the serving vessels, and refrigerate for 8 hours or overnight, uncovered. If you won't be serving the custard soon, cover them to prevent them from absorbing the flavors of nearby foods. Serve with a dollop of whipped cream, and maybe some fresh berries tossed with a pinch of sugar.

Mugolio

What tastes like pine trees and looks like maple syrup, but costs up to eight times as much? Mugolio. Technically, *mugolio* refers specifically to syrup made from young mugo pinecones (*Pinus mugo*) left to macerate with sugar. As time goes by, the sugar draws out liquid from the pinecones, absorbing incredible aromas in the process. A chef and specialty purveyor secret for years, mugolio has been gaining traction, since it's fun and easy to make, and since the current price is about $20 for a 3.5-ounce (100 ml) bottle (that's less than ½ cup)! All of this is nothing new, though, and a few good foraging references like Marie Viljoen's *Forage, Harvest, Feast* and Pascal Baudar's *The Wildcrafting Brewer* mention similar macerated creations.

The big takeaway here is that while pinecones are the simplest option, you can make similar macerated syrups out of lots of things that smell good, and probably plenty of things that don't come from conifer trees. Sweetfern nutlets, juniper berries, various herbs like wintergreen or mint—there are tons of possibilities. When the syrup is done (it takes a few weeks, minimum) you can put it on anything. For the purest flavor, drizzle it on something like vanilla ice cream or pancakes.

To get more creative, add some to glazes, drinks, and sauces, or use as an all-purpose substitute for maple syrup or honey in baking and desserts. I prefer to use one aromatic at a time for a pure flavor, as syrup made from taking a bunch of different things and stuffing them in a jar can taste busy, but that's just me. Use raw sugar or light brown sugar, since brown sugar has more water, which means more space for the aroma to infuse into, compared with recipes that use drier, plain white sugar. Raw or light brown sugar also imparts a more attractive light amber color. For a 100 percent wild version, try using maple syrup or honey instead of sugar.

Macerated mugolio syrup can be made from cedar cones, pinecones, and spruce tips. Each batch has a specific flavor.

Spruce Tip Syrup

Makes approximately 1½ cups (375 ml)

This is probably my favorite tree syrup. Once you've made it with spruce tips, try the green cones of eastern white cedar (*Thuja occidentalis*) or a similar tree. Two cups each of spruce tips and sugar will make a small amount of syrup to play with, but you can make batches to suit your needs using the same proportions of equal parts spruce tips and sugar by volume. As a general guideline, each packed pint jar of spruce tips and sugar will make around ¾ cup (80 ml) of finished syrup.

2 cups (115 g) spruce tips or cedar cones
2 cups (400 g) organic turbinado sugar
  (light brown sugar is fine in a pinch)

Combine the spruce tips and the sugar, and pack into a jar. If you want to follow some of the old recipes I've seen, you'll bury the jar in the ground (definitely optional!). Leave the jar for at least a month on a counter or in the pantry. The volume will decrease by about half. If you want, you can keep adding spruce tips and sugar in the same proportions to fill up the jar, because the volume decreases over time. After waiting at least a month—longer, if you like—scoop the mixture into a pot, cover, bring to a boil, then strain, bottle, and refrigerate it. If your syrup boils too hard, it may solidify when chilled; if this happens, simply warm it up and add a bit of water to correct the consistency.

Pinecone Syrup

Arguably the easiest tree syrup to make. Harvest young pinecones that are still green or can be cut with a knife, then combine in a jar with an equal volume of sugar, as in Spruce Tip Syrup (page 211). I like the tiny pinecones from red pine (*Pinus resinosa*), which are only the size of a quarter. You'll want to remove the lid and stir the contents to "burp" the jar every few days, as pinecones seem to have a lot of yeast on them and ferment vigorously. After a month pour the contents into a pot, bring to a boil, strain out the pinecones, and jar as you would for the Spruce Tip Syrup.

Red pine (*Pinus resinosa*) cones. Any of these sizes will make a good syrup, as long as they're green and soft enough to cut with a knife. Balsam fir (*Abies balsamea*) cones can be nice, too.

Wintergreen

Wintergreen (*Gaultheria procumbens*) is a very small, highly aromatic plant that thrives in sandy, acidic soil near pine trees and conifers. Its flavor is in the realm of mint, but different, and if you're wondering, it's the exact same plant used to flavor winter-green gum. It has thick, waxy-feeling green leaves, and eventually pro-duces small, red, aromatic berries. Some people harvest the berries, but I much prefer to just harvest the leaves, which can keep for a month or more in the refrigerator in a tightly sealed container. Wintergreen makes excellent tea but even better mugolio, which can be used just about anywhere you'd imagine. The plant's aroma is what I describe as heat-shy, so if you cook with it, know that the flavor may not last too long. In the right place, such as simmering with red fruit, it can be excellent.

Wintergreen Syrup

Makes 1½ cups (375 ml)

Some ingredients don't respond well to being cooked, and wintergreen is one of them. It took a few tries, but the process I devised for this wintergreen mugolio basi-cally entails making the standard mugolio recipe backward. Here, you'll make the syrup first and then infuse it with the aro-matics. The flavor is just as strong, but will weaken if it's cooked. Wintergreen is only one example of an aromatic you might use, but it's one of the best I've found. Try it drizzled over yogurt or labneh.

2 cups (425 g) light brown sugar
1 cup (240 ml) water
2 cups (60 g) chopped wintergreen leaves

Bring the sugar and water to a boil and cool, then combine with the wintergreen and allow to macerate at room temperature for a week. Strain out the leaves and refrigerate. The syrup will keep for a few weeks.

Pine and Cider Varenye (Pinecones in Apple Molasses)

Makes 1 generous cup (240 ml)

Varenye is a traditional preserve derived from immature pinecones in the Caucusus, made by cooking immature pinecones with sugar and water. The end product is a thick, jammy substance and is an acquired taste, to say the least. It can be good with the right partner, like fat, especially dairy such as goat cheese, but the taste can be a bit medicinal for a lot of people.

After making the original version, I came up with this one: a 100 percent forest product that tastes much better than most things with the same title I've sampled. The cider calms the flavor of the pinecones a bit, resulting in a milder finished product where the cones are less aggressive tasting than the pure sugar preserves I've made. It's also less sweet. It makes a great bite with rich cheese on a cracker, and the thick syrup is nice melted and added to drinks and sauces. As a side note, the apple cider molasses is a fantastic (and traditional) preserve by itself, without the pinecones.

1½ ounces (40 g) young pinecones (no larger than a dime)
2 whole cloves
¼-inch (6 mm) piece of cinnamon
8 cups (2 L) unfiltered apple juice or apple cider

Rinse and clean the pinecones, then blanch in a few inches of boiling water for a minute, drain, and reserve. Wrap the cloves and cinnamon in cheesecloth and simmer them with the pinecones and cider, discarding the spices and cheesecloth halfway through cooking. Reduce the liquid until it resembles warm honey. You should have a little more than 1 cup (240 ml) of liquid. Pour the piping-hot jam into a jar, cool, and store, tightly covered, in the fridge for a month or two. You can also process ½-pint (240 ml or similar-sized) jars in a water bath.

Cedar Cones

I always wanted to gather my own juniper, but the trees around me usually have very bitter-tasting berries. Cedar cones, especially those from eastern white cedars (*Thuja accidentalis*), are widely available near me because they're planted as ornamentals. These can be substituted for juniper and are typically used in their fresh form. I prefer to use them fresh or frozen (especially for cedar mugolio), but they do keep some of their flavor when dried and can be ground and used in dishes such as sauerkraut.

Cedar Cone Sauerkraut

Juniper can be a difficult seasoning to work with, as it can be overpowering, but it pairs well with submissive cabbage. This is an outline of my favorite kraut method, following the basic instructions for dry fermentation (page 26).

2 pounds (910 g) garden cabbage
   (1 large head)
2 ounces (55 g) fresh green cedar cones,
   or to taste, coarsely chopped (juniper
   berries can be substituted)
Kosher salt, 2 percent of the weight
   of shaved cabbage, or roughly
   1 tablespoon

Trim the root from the cabbage, then cut it into pieces that you can shred on a mandoline or cabbage slicer, or with a large chef knife. Shave the cabbage about ¼ inch (6 mm) thick, then toss with the cedar cones or juniper berries and the salt. Pack into a crock or other fermenting vessel.

Pound the seasoned cabbage with a mallet, pressing it down with a weight to keep it underneath its own brine that forms naturally for one to two weeks. Check on it occasionally to make sure it's kept underneath a thin layer of brine until you like the flavor, then transfer to a container with a tight fitting lid and refrigerate.

Variation:
Wild Seed Kraut

Another great way to spice up your kraut is with wild or other aromatic seeds in place of or in combination with the cedar cones or juniper. Some I like are angelica, caraway, and mustard seeds. Start with a teaspoon or two, and then follow your instincts.

Cedar Cone Aglione

Makes scant ½ cup (135 ml)

This is one of my most trusted ways to preserve garlic and a secret I've carried with me through kitchen after kitchen through the years. It's basically a concentrated preserve of Italian origin like pesto, but used with a lighter hand, and generally tossed in a hot pan to calm the garlic before other ingredients are added. The original recipe used juniper, but cedar cones make a great variation.

1 ounce (28 g) whole cloves garlic,
  roots trimmed (6 large cloves)
1–2 tablespoons cedar cones or
  juniper berries (whichever you prefer)
2 generous tablespoons chopped fresh
  rosemary, stems removed
1 teaspoon red pepper flakes, or to taste
⅓ cup (80 ml) cup cooking oil

Reserve 2 cloves of garlic. Process the rest of the garlic in a food processor until finely chopped. Take the 2 reserved cloves of garlic and whack them with the flat side of a heavy knife, then lightly crush the cedar cones in the same manner (crushing makes both easier to chop together). Mince the garlic, cedar cones, rosemary, and red pepper flakes, then combine with the remaining garlic and the oil. It will look a bit like garlic pesto. The aglione will keep a vibrant flavor for a week under refrigeration, covered, but will be usable for much longer. If it threatens to dry out, add a spoonful of oil to keep everything covered.

Variation:
Roasted Potatoes with Aglione

Make aglione just to eat these. Simmer some potatoes in lightly salted water until barely tender, then drain, cool, peel, and cut into bite-sized pieces. If you have leftover cooked potatoes from a previous meal, simply cut them up. Heat some oil (or preferably lard) in a heavy pan such as a cast-iron skillet, and sauté the potatoes on medium-high, turning occasionally, until golden and crisp all over. Stir some aglione into the pan, tossing to coat the potatoes. Cook for 2 or 3 minutes longer, to allow the heat to tame the garlic a bit. Use a slotted spoon to remove the potatoes from the pan, then season to taste. Serve hot.

Variation:
Pasta Aglione

Warm about a tablespoon of aglione per serving in a pan with a good glug of olive oil and a few anchovy fillets. Break up the anchovies as they cook, then, as the mixture starts to turn golden, add some cooked pasta, a splash of white wine, and red pepper flakes to taste. Toss quickly and serve. Pecorino or another grating cheese is a good garnish. Adding tomato sauce is another quick variation I often ate late at night after my shifts were over.

CHAPTER 4

Nourishing

Nuts, Grains, and Starches

This chapter is all about nourishing and hearty nuts, grains, and starches: tips and tricks, new ways of thinking about old things, trusty recipes I've developed and relied on, and special ingredients I've sought out over the years that you might like to explore. Some of the ingredients, such as black walnuts, I might harvest myself occasionally; others, like wild rice or acorn oil, I haven't, because they're available to purchase— allowing me to support local producers and spend more time getting lost in the woods hunting things I can't buy.

Even if I'm working with something I haven't har- vested myself, using the forager's eye that pushes me to search for the best ingredients has shown me new things in old places. Tasting a freshly shelled black walnut, rich with perfume and so full of oil it weeps when the nut is pressed between your fingers, is an experience you'll never get from store-bought walnuts, or even commercially harvested black walnuts, and the same goes for the incomparable aroma that wafts from a simmering pot of quality wild rice.

Real Wild Rice

Wild rice is an institution where I live in the Midwest. I grew up with it, but I never tasted high-quality wild rice until my late 20s. The only wild rice I knew was the same dark, shiny, musky-tasting kernels most people are familiar with. Technically, those black kernels are from the same group of aquatic plants (*Zizania* spp.), but in terms of taste they couldn't be more different from the good stuff. Unfortunately, unlike other traditionally protected foods around the world (Italian Parmesan, for instance), there's no regulation on labeling wild rice, so separating the good from the other can be challenging.

The good stuff is wild-harvested wild rice, often labeled as *natural*, *lake rice*, *hand-harvested*, or *manoomin*—the Anishinaabe name ricers might use to refer to a truly wild-harvested product. The other wild rice, often referred to as black paddy rice, will usually be labeled as *cultivated* or *farmed*, so it isn't actually wild at all. I knew I preferred natural wild rice to the farmed black paddy rice the first time I tasted it, as much for the depth of flavor as for the shorter cook time, but I didn't understand exactly why for years. The reason for the differences between the two is a bit complicated. As I understand it, most cultivated wild rice is allowed to stay damp for some time after harvesting to soften the hulls through decomposition; as that happens, the grain responds by hardening its seedcoat, which also makes the grains turn black. The blackening or "curing," and some fermentation that happens in the process, imparts a stronger flavor to the grain that I'd describe as musty, as well as making the grains tougher, increasing the cooking time. By contrast, manoomin will be dried quickly after harvesting and then parched over a fire, which decreases the cook time and water it will absorb in the process.

Another thing I find useful to consider is that farmed black paddy rice generally uses a ratio of 4:1 (or more!) water to rice, while natural wild rice (again, generally) uses a 2:1 ratio. That means the black paddy rice soaks up more liquid during its longer cooking time, making it heavier with water weight. Natural wild rice, on the other hand, has a light weight similar to other grains, as well as an enticing flavor and aroma, and is perfectly at home for any meal of the day—undiluted by "filler" grains as is common with black paddy rice. Taste some good wild rice drizzled with maple syrup, anointed with a pat of butter, and I think you'll agree.

Unfortunately, when the black "wild" rice started being commercially cultivated (in the 1960s), the wild rice most people became accustomed to seeing wasn't the best-tasting one. Like so many things companies would like us to buy, it was the one that was easiest to harvest and sell on a commercial scale. From there, the imposter seems to have become the only wild rice. For the life of me, I can't understand how natural, wild rice hasn't gotten its day. Even in Minnesota, where it's a source of local pride, entire books have been published specifically on wild rice without even a mention or suggestion that there is anything other than black paddy rice for us to enjoy. It's a culinary tragedy. On the bright side, all it takes is one bite of the real deal for most people to change their wild rice religion.

There are lots of different suppliers out there, but one of the most consistent is the White Earth Nation (realwildrice.com) in northern Minnesota. Whatever supplier you choose, I recommend purchasing from smaller suppliers, especially Indigenous peoples in the Midwest. The Bois Forte band of Ojibwe (nettlakewildrice.com) is another good supplier, as is foragersharvest.com.

As with so many things, you get what you pay for, and typically the best wild rice will cost the most. At the time of this writing, a fair price for natural wild rice could be anywhere from $12 to $20 per pound (455 g), whereas cultivated rice can cost $6 a pound or less, although there are exceptions. A few other things I find helpful in sifting through suppliers on the market are first, avoiding wild rice labeled as *cultivated*. Instead, look for wild rice labeled as *natural*, *lake rice*, *manoomin*, *wood parched*, or *hand harvested*. Use your eyes, too: If the rice looks dark or black, it's probably the black paddy rice. Also, be on the lookout for rice that contains many broken seeds; while blends with broken kernels can

cost less, the broken kernels absorb water more readily than whole ones and when cooked together can make wild rice mushy, although it's a bit of a first-world problem.

When I cook good wild rice, I like it most often cooked as is—less is more. I prefer black paddy rice, with its stronger flavor, for making into wild rice flour for baked goods and polenta or even dredges for meat. Mixed with some salt, pepper, and powdered, dried ramp leaves, it's one of my favorite dredges for panfish like sunnies.

Forms of wild rice, *clock-wise from the upper left*: natural wild rice, cultivated black paddy "wild" rice, larger particles leftover from sifting, and sifted wild rice flour.

Basic Wild Rice

Makes 1 pound (455 g) cooked wild rice

The basic recipe. I eat it for breakfast, toss it in soup, warm it up for dinner—whatever, you can't go wrong. Some recipes I've seen (from wild rice companies, no less), call for up to 6 cups (1.5 L) of water per cup of rice, instructing you to discard any aromatic liquid after cooking—the heresy! I even had one line cook who used to drink the cooking liquid. Cooked with minimal water, wild rice cooks in its own essence and, in turn, will flavor other dishes you add the cooked rice to, like soup.

The exact water-to-rice ratio is debatable. I usually use a ratio of 2:1, since I like my rice to keep its shape and not curl too much, but anywhere from 2 to 3 cups of water to 1 cup of rice will be fine, especially if you prefer it softer, as some people do.

1 cup (140 g) natural wild rice
2–3 cups (480–720 ml) water
½ teaspoon kosher salt, or more to taste

Rinse the wild rice well. Bring the rice, water, and salt to a boil. Reduce the heat to low and simmer, covered, for 20 to 25 minutes, or until the rice is just barely tender and tastes good to you. Drain the rice if needed, then cover the pot and allow the rice to continue steaming, off the heat, until serving.

Breakfast Wild Rice

This is one of the ways I most often eat wild rice. Follow the basic recipe, and then serve for breakfast with your favorite toppings. I tend to make versions with berries and maple syrup, but you can make a great savory version, too, as I've outlined below.

Sweet

Here are a few sweet ideas from which to pick and choose:

- Your favorite toasted nuts and seeds
- Diced raw or cooked apples, bananas, or other fruit, especially blueberries
- Maple syrup, birch syrup, or jam or preserves (thinned with a little warm water to make a quick fruit sauce)
- A good dollop of thick yogurt, for tang
- A dusting of ground cinnamon
- Some kind of fat: My favorites are aromatic nut oils (walnut, peanut, hickory nut, or acorn), but butter is fine, too

Savory

For a savory breakfast rice, I crumble some sausage, move it to the side of the pan, scramble an egg or two in the same pan, then toss in some cooked or fresh greens, cook off the water for a second, and add some cooked wild rice just to heat through. Adding ramp leaves or green onions is also good—just like fried rice. Serve with your favorite hot sauce on the side, or use something like Black Walnut Ketchup (page 258) or Tabasco-Style Ramp Hot Sauce (page 173).

Wild Rice with Black Walnuts, Green Garlic, and Wild Herbs

Serves 6 as a side

I came up with this dish to serve a few hundred guests at a dinner for Slow Food Minnesota, using young green garlic and our local wild bergamot (*Monarda fistulosa*) along with ground ivy (*Glechoma hederacea*). Most people know of ground ivy, or creeping charlie, as a common and aggressive garden weed, but historically the plant has been used in place of hops for brewing ale, among other things. The flavor is strongly herbaceous.

You can substitute other herbs as you like, but I encourage you to taste a spoonful with the ground ivy leaves. Although they taste strong fresh, combining them with other ingredients and heating them calms their flavor and is a good experiment in how flavors meld, mellow, and change depending on what you eat (chew) them with. Ramp leaves, garlic, or other scapes, or any young growing parts of onions are a good substitute for green garlic, if it's out of season.

1 cup (140 g) natural wild rice
2 ounces (55 g) black walnuts or other nuts, lightly toasted
3 ounces (85 g) green garlic or scallions, in ¼-inch (6 mm) dice
3 tablespoons unsalted butter
2 tablespoons chopped wild bergamot
¼ cup (10 g) (or so) creeping charlie leaves and flowers, if available, washed, cleaned, and coarsely chopped if large, stems removed, divided
Sea salt and fresh-ground black pepper

Cook the wild rice in 2 cups (480 ml) of lightly salted water until tender, roughly 20 to 25 minutes, then drain and reserve. Toast the walnuts in a 300°F (150°C) oven for 15 minutes, or until aromatic. Meanwhile, sweat the green garlic in the butter in a pan. Then add the cooked wild rice to the same pan, along with the toasted walnuts, bergamot, and half of the creeping charlie, and toss to combine. Check the seasoning and correct for salt and pepper as needed, and add some more creeping charlie if you think it needs it.

Wild Rice Corn Bread

Serves 6–8

I spent weeks developing this recipe to serve 200 people as the crowning glory of a wild-food-themed brunch at the Midwest Wild Harvest Festival—arguably the greatest wild food festival in the United States. Wild rice flour shines in simple corn bread, although *corn bread* is a bit of a misnomer since the recipe contains no corn. If you can't find commercial wild rice flour (realwildrice.com is the best), you'll need to make it yourself using a grain mill: Grind the wild rice through the mill's finest setting, then sift it. You can get a similar product using a spice grinder, but it isn't quite the same, and can create a gummy layer on the bottom of the cornbread. The larger particles left over from sifting can be saved for uses such as thickening soup.

1 cup (240 ml) water
1 cup (140 g) wild rice flour, or a heaping cup of cultivated black paddy wild rice, ground to a fine flour and sifted
1 cup (240 ml) buttermilk
2 large eggs
1 cup (120 g) all-purpose flour, or equivalent
⅓ cup (65 g) sugar
2 teaspoons baking powder
¼ teaspoon baking soda
¾ teaspoon kosher salt
½ cup (135 ml) melted butter or lard, for serving
Maple syrup, for serving

Preheat the oven to 375°F (190°C). Bring the cup of water to a boil, then pour over the wild rice flour, cover, and allow to cool (this step is optional, but recommended if you grind your own wild rice flour). Mix the remaining wet ingredients with the soaked wild rice flour, then whisk together the dry ingredients separately before folding them into the wet ingredients until just combined. Transfer to a greased 10-inch (26 cm) cast-iron skillet for tall, thick corn bread, or a 12-inch (30 cm) cast-iron skillet for thinner corn bread, and bake for 25 to 30 minutes, or until just set. Serve with plenty of butter and maple syrup.

Wild Rice Polenta

Serves 4 as a side

I used to know a farmer who would bring me the most incredible hand-ground grits made from flint corn (*Zea mays* var. *indurata*), which I happily bought for $50 a gallon. After I bought all he had, I needed to find something similar to fill the hole on the menu. It didn't take too long for me to start grinding up some broken / soup-grade parched wild rice and cooking it just like the flint corn. Cooked up as polenta, it's delicious for any meal of the day, and it pairs as well with meat or mushroom gravy as it does with butter and maple syrup.

1 cup (140 g) wild rice, any kind
2½ cups (625 ml) strong homemade
  chicken stock (substitute milk or nut milk
  for sweet versions)
2½ cups (625 ml) milk
3 tablespoons unsalted butter
¼ cup (25 g) high-quality grated Parmesan
  cheese (optional, for savory versions)
Kosher salt, to taste

Grind the wild rice in a grain mill, high-speed blender, or spice grinder. The mix shouldn't be complete powder like wild rice flour—some chunks here and there will give some texture to the finished product.

Bring the stock and milk to a simmer, then stir in the ground wild rice. Cook at a slow simmer, stirring occasionally, until the liquid is absorbed and the mixture has thickened to the consistency of oatmeal, about 15 minutes. If the mixture seems wet, continue cooking until more liquid has evaporated. Add the butter and Parmesan (for savory), stir to combine, taste and adjust the salt, and serve.

Wild Rice Polenta Cakes

Makes 12 slices or cakes (1 loaf pan)

Exactly like corn polenta cakes, but made with wild rice flour, these are a trusty, all-purpose side dish. They're great cut into thick slices, fried crisp, sprinkled with a little Parmesan cheese as well as a few tablespoons of sage butter, and baked until bubbling and browned.

2 cups (480 ml) water or stock
2 cups (480 ml) milk or half-and-half
4 tablespoons unsalted butter or lard
1 teaspoon salt
2 cups (280 g) wild rice flour

Bring the water, milk, butter, and salt to a simmer and gradually whisk in the wild rice flour, then reduce the heat to low and continue stirring. When the mixture tightens and becomes difficult to stir, switch to a wooden spoon and stir until the mixture is very thick and stirring is difficult, about 15 minutes. Transfer the mixture to an oiled bread loaf pan, banging the pan down on the counter to fill in the nooks and crannies. Cool, then chill completely. To cut the cakes, invert the loaf pan and remove the loaf of polenta, cut into ¾-inch (2 cm) slices, and pan-fry until crisp on both sides.

Wild Rice Bisque with Toasted Mushroom Croutons

Serves 2–4 as a light entrée

A crowd favorite, this bisque is a velvety rich soup that's all about the wild rice. Unlike the white rice or potato I'd use in something like lobster bisque as much for its thickening quality as its submissive flavors, wild rice is assertive, so if you use it to thicken soup, the flavor will come to the forefront. Since the soup is puréed, you'll want to garnish it with something that offers a different textural element; rehydrated, toasted mushrooms are great, as are gently sautéed green vegetables such as fiddleheads, asparagus, peas, and radishes. Like all bisques, this is a rich, creamy soup, so a little goes a long way.

Croutons (optional)

Scant ½ ounce (14 g) mixed, dried bolete
  mushrooms, or another dried mushroom
  of your choice
Oil
1 teaspoon finely minced garlic
Kosher salt, to taste
Pinch of fresh Italian parsley, sliced

Bisque

3 tablespoons lard, bacon grease, or
  cooking oil
½ cup (70 g) plus 2 tablespoons wild rice—
  any kind
2 ounces (55 g) celery, diced small
2 ounces (55 g) yellow onion, diced small
2 ounces (55 g) fennel or leek, diced small
Kosher salt and fresh-ground black pepper,
  to taste
¼ cup (60 ml) dry sherry
4½ cups (1 L) meat, mushroom, or
  vegetable stock
½ cup (135 ml) heavy cream (optional)

Good-tasting oil, such as Smude's sunflower
  oil or extra-virgin olive oil, serving (optional)

First, make the mushroom croutons. Rehydrate the dried mushrooms in cold water to cover for 20 minutes, then drain and press dry between towels. Sweat the mushrooms in a small amount of oil on low until crisp and toasted. Add the garlic and cook until just lightly browned, then season with salt, toss in the parsley, and cool. The mushrooms should be crisp, nutty, and addictive. They can be held at room temperature for a couple of days.

To make the bisque, melt the lard in a large skillet, then add the rice (use only ½ cup if you plan to omit the cream) and vegetables and sweat them on medium until translucent, about 10 minutes. Do not color. Add the salt and pepper. The mixture should smell nice and nutty. Deglaze the pan with the sherry, cook off the alcohol, then add the stock. Simmer on low, covered, until the rice is completely cooked, about 20 minutes. Add the cream (if you're using it), then carefully purée the mixture in a blender until very smooth. Double-check the seasoning, adjust as needed, then chill to room temp and refrigerate, or serve, topped with the mushroom croutons and drizzled with a thread of good-tasting oil.

Wild Rice Crepes with Wild Cherry Gastrique and Whipped Cheese

Makes 9 crepes (enough to serve 4 people 2 crepes apiece, if you don't mess up too many crepes)

When I was writing brunch menus and had a limited amount of savory dishes on the menu, or worried about something selling out, I would run these crepes to help balance things, since they're a guaranteed sell. There's just something about the way cream cheese combines with tangy, sweet cherry gastrique (or another berry of your choice—the recipe follows) that's irresistible. Think of the garnishes for serving as suggestions.

Crepes
½ cup (60 g) all-purpose flour

½ cup (70 g) wild rice flour, or black paddy wild rice ground to a very fine flour and sifted
2 large eggs
¼ teaspoon kosher salt
1 cup (240 ml) plus 2 tablespoons milk or water
2 tablespoons melted butter or lard, plus more for cooking

Filling
4 ounces (115 g) chèvre
8 ounces (225 g) cream cheese

Serving (optional)
Diced firm apples, such as Honeycrisp or Sweet Tango
Toasted black walnuts

Purée the all-purpose flour and wild rice, eggs, salt, milk, and butter. Allow to rest for 30 minutes. Grease an 8-inch (20 cm) nonstick pan or crepe pan, and heat until gently

smoking. Ladle scant ¼ cups (60 ml) of batter into the pan, swirling so the batter covers the bottom, then cook on one side only, until you can see browning around the edges—this will happen very quickly once the pan gets up to temperature. Transfer the finished crepes to a plate, stacking on top of each other to steam them and ensure they remain pliable.

Combine the chèvre and the cream cheese, mixing well. Fill each crepe with 2 tablespoons of the cheese filling, then fold them up into rectangular packets, storing them seam down. From here, the crepes can be made ahead of time and refrigerated, which is how I had cooks prep them for restaurant service.

To serve, brown the crepes gently in butter until heated through. Meanwhile, sauté the apples quickly and toss with the walnuts. Serve the crepes sprinkled with apples and walnuts, then drizzle the gastrique over each portion, or pass it on the side.

Berry or Stone Fruit Gastrique

Makes about 4 cups (945 ml)

One of my favorite fruit preserves is gastrique, a fancy name for a simple sweet-and-sour syrup you can make from all kinds of juicy fruit, but especially wild cherries, grapes, elderberries, highbush cranberries, or anything else that might need to be strained to remove seeds or pits. Oh, and it's so easy you don't even need a recipe.

The addition of vinegar is important here. Typically, only water and sugar are used in preservation methods like this, but the added acid gives you the flexibility to use the gastrique with game meat, as well as with desserts, pancakes, ice cream bases, drinks, and the like.

5 cups (1.25 L) small fruit: chokecherries, raspberries, wild grapes, aronia berries, elderberries, highbush cranberries, or other small berries with a lot of pits or skin and little juice
1 cup (240 ml) water
Pinch of salt
2 cups (480 ml) wine vinegar—white for lighter fruits, red for darker fruits
3 cups (600 g) sugar (approximately)

Wash the berries, then combine with the water, salt, and vinegar in a nonreactive saucepan. The berries should be just barely covered by liquid, with a few bobbing around here and there, known in the kitchen by the technical term *floating hippos*. Bring the pot to a simmer, cover, and cook for 15 minutes on low heat. Mash the berries, or use a hand blender to break them up, simmer for a few minutes more, then strain the liquid, measure it, and combine with an equal volume of sugar. Boil for another 5 minutes or until the syrup barely coats the back of a spoon, then transfer to jars and store. The syrup will be shelf-stable processed in small jars and kept in a pantry.

Corn and Beans

Eaten together, there aren't many foods as satisfying as corn and beans, especially if the corn has undergone nixtamalization, the process of treating corn with an alkaline solution that unlocks nutrients and improves digestibility, as well as making it possible for us to enjoy things like tamales, tortilla chips, and masa cakes. This section offers a few of my favorite things to do with these familiar staples.

But I've also included a couple of recipes featuring lupin, or lupine. You might be thinking, *Lupin? As in, the garden plant?* Kind of. There are roughly 200 plants in the genus *Lupinus*, which is in the larger family Fabaceae—the bean family. The lupins (or lupines—either spelling is acceptable) in your friend's garden,

and the ones I see here in Minnesota aggressively growing all along the North Shore of Lake Superior, will both make tiny, almost unnoticeable beans in a pod at the end of their yearly growth cycle. However, these are not the same species grown as a food plant, and even with the edible types, all of them need to be processed by extended leaching/soaking before eating, just like acorns.

The lupins grown for food are known in South America, Europe, and the Middle East and are widely available online or in Middle Eastern grocery stores, and instead of the size of a split pea, they're about the size of a dime. The flavor is interesting—a bit like olives or other briny foods, and a bit like nuts or seeds.

Below, Clockwise from top right: purple Hopi corn my father grew; lupin beans; Huun Ga'I, cob-roasted Pima corn; S-Chuuk Bavi, heirloom black tepary beans from Ramona Farms; and giant Mexican hominy.

Lupin Beans

Like olives, lupin beans make a great inter-active appetizer and they're excellent served together, drenched in aromatic olive oil, garlic, toasted fennel, and citrus peel. Lupin flour can also be used to make a very good version of Farinata (page 232).

Dried lupin beans
Water
Kosher salt

Soak the beans overnight in three times their volume of water. Drain the beans, then cover with at least three times their volume of fresh water and cook for 1 hour on low, covered. Do not let the water level get too low, or the beans will discolor. Drain the beans, cover with fresh cold water, and refrigerate. At this point you can taste a bean to judge the bitterness, which will diminish each day the beans soak. Con-tinue tasting a bean each day until they stop tasting bitter, discarding the water covering the beans and replacing it with fresh water every day. It should take almost a week to leach the beans. When the beans stop tasting bitter, drain their water one last time, replacing it

with 7 percent brine (7 grams of salt for every 100 grams of water, or roughly 4 tablespoons of kosher salt per quart of water) to cover. Bring the beans, in brine, back to a simmer, then cool and refrigerate. The beans will be a little al dente, and not soft or mushy—this is normal. To eat the beans, squeeze them to remove the skin, then eat the bean inside. Discard the skin. The beans will last for a month, refrigerated and covered in brine.

Variation: Lupin Beans with Olives
As they're interactive, lupin beans make a great addition to a bowl of marinated olives. Here's what I do: Slice a few cloves of garlic and sweat them in a generous glug of olive oil. Peel a few strips of zest from an orange and a lemon, bruise them with your hand, and add to the oil, along with some finely chopped rosemary. Heat the mixture on medium until it's very aromatic (a few minutes), then toss with your favorite blend of olives (with pits) along with about the same amount of lupin beans. Pack the mixture in a container and allow to marinate for a few hours or over-night, then serve warm as an appetizer.

Corn and Bean Terrine

Serves 6–8 as an entrée (1 loaf pan)

Cherokee author Nancy Plemmons said the three hallmarks of modern Cherokee cuisine were corn and bean bread, sochan leaves, and pork lard. I loved the idea of these three ingredients in a dish, and I wanted to make something that was a nod to that, but without the pork introduced by white colonists.

Traditionally, the corn and bean bread took the form of handmade dumplings, but here I use the same ingredients in a terrine reminiscent of polenta studded with cooked beans—which is what happens when you're inspired by Native American ingredient combinations, but were trained in Italian kitchens. I use corn flour, as it cooks twice as fast as typical polenta, with only a few minutes of vigorous stirring, instead of polenta's 30 or so. After the terrine chills, it's sliced and fried, and the beans give it a beautiful mosaic pattern, as well as lending starch to help make a delicious, crisp crust.

Adding crushed cracklings from rendering lard along with the beans is a great touch. A drizzle of maple syrup, especially with the crackling addition, is also good and evokes flavors of the pioneer era. To complete the Cherokee-inspired trio, serve it with sochan cooked in meat drippings.

¼ cup (60 ml) rendered animal fat or
  cooking oil, plus more for final cooking
4 cups (945 ml) meat or vegetable stock
1½ teaspoons kosher salt
2 cups (300 g) corn flour
4 ounces (115 g) cooked kidney beans,
  drained and rinsed if canned

In a 3-quart (3 L) or other tall saucepan, heat the fat, stock, and salt. While the mixture is heating, gradually whisk in the corn flour, continuing until the mixture is firm, then switch to a wooden spoon. Turn the heat down to medium-low and continue cooking for 10 minutes, until all the water is absorbed. When the mixture is very thick, gently stir in the beans, then transfer the mixture to a lightly oiled bread loaf pan. Smooth out the top as well as you can, and firmly tap (slam) the loaf pan on the counter to reduce any air pockets. Cool the terrine to room temperature, then cover and refrigerate. From here, the terrine can be made ahead and stored, covered, in the fridge. To serve, invert the loaf pan to remove the terrine, cut into ¾-inch (2 cm) slices, and pan-fry until nicely crisp and on both sides.

Three Sisters

Serves 8 as a side

The classic Native American combination of corn, beans, and squash is not only an incredibly sustaining dish but a testament to symbiotic agricultural practices, each plant playing an integral part in the whole. Corn grows tall, allowing the beans to climb up and get sunlight. The squash acts as ground cover, shading out weeds. Legumes add nitrogen back into the soil. It's a perfect example of ancient, native nutritive knowledge hidden inside a simple recipe. The bacon in this dish is more of a seasoning than a physical component, so resist the urge to add a lot of it.

4 ounces (115 g) slab bacon, in ½-inch
   (1.25 cm) dice (or ¼ cup / 60 ml
   rendered lard)
3 cups (385 g) diced squash, in 1-inch
   (2.5 cm) dice (preferably a custardy type,
   such as buttercup or kabocha)

15 ounces (425 g) cooked hominy, or 1 can
15 ounces (425 g) cooked heirloom beans,
   or 1 can
Kosher salt and fresh-ground black pepper
1 tablespoon chives or mixed herbs, for
   serving (optional)

In a wide pan such as a 12-inch (30 cm) cast-iron skillet, render the bacon on medium until it begins to brown and has given off a decent amount of fat, then push the bacon to the side, add the squash, stir to coat with the fat, and cook until just tender. Add the hominy and beans, then season to taste with salt and pepper. If the dish looks dry or if the bacon didn't give up a good amount of fat, add some melted lard or bacon grease, to taste. When the mixture is heated through, double-check the seasoning, toss with the herbs, and serve immediately.

Three Sisters Soup

Serves 6

Soup is one of the most traditional uses of the three sisters. Corn, beans, and squash are all mild tasting, so it's really important to use the best stock you can find, and to taste and season the soup multiple times until you're pleased with it.

4 ounces (115 g) bacon, cut into
  ½-inch slices
1 medium onion, in ½-inch (1.25 cm) dice
1 large clove garlic, minced
8 cups (2 L) meat stock, preferably from a
  leftover turkey carcass
12 ounces (340 g) white sweet potato
  (or winter squash, such as kabocha),
  cut into large cubes
15 ounces (425 g) cooked hominy, or 1 can
15 ounces (425 g) cooked heirloom beans,
  or 1 can
½ tablespoon chopped fresh sage
Kosher salt, to taste
3 tablespoons lard (preferably venison,
  bear, or pork), or use cooking oil
4 ounces (115 g) sochan, mustard, or turnip
  greens, cut into 1-inch (2.5 cm) pieces,
  stems removed
10 ounces (285 g) leftover turkey or chicken

In a large soup pot, sweat the bacon until crisp and the fat is rendered. Add the onion and garlic and sweat for a few minutes more, then add all the ingredients except the turkey or chicken and bring to a simmer. Cook for 15 minutes or until the sweet potato is tender, then add the turkey or chicken, heat through, double-check the seasoning for salt and correct as needed, and serve. The soup will taste better after it sits for 24 hours.

Farinata

Serves 4–6

Farinata is the easiest, cheapest, most satisfying Italian street food you've never had. Nothing more than chickpea flour with a good pinch of chopped rosemary, salt, and oil poured into a screaming-hot pan, it comes together in a snap and makes a great appetizer or side. Chickpea flour is traditional, and very good, but lupin flour (or any other legume flour) can be used, too. If you have a way to cook at very high heat (above 500°F/260°C), say with a pizza oven, this is a fun thing to make.

1 tablespoon good-tasting oil, such as
  extra-virgin olive oil
2 cups (480 ml) warm water
¾ teaspoon salt
Coarse-ground black pepper, to taste
1½ cups (140 g) legume flour, such as
  chickpea, pea, lupin, or lentil
¼ teaspoon (a generous pinch) finely
  minced fresh thyme or rosemary
1 tablespoon cooking oil

Pour the good-tasting oil into the water in a bowl with the salt and pepper, then add the legume flour and thyme or rosemary, beat with a whisk to break up lumps, and allow to hydrate for at least 15 minutes or overnight. Meanwhile, heat a well-seasoned 10-inch (26 cm) cast-iron pan (or other ovenproof nonstick pan) in the oven at 500°F (260°C). Carefully remove the (exceptionally) hot pan from the oven with a thick, dry potholder or other heavily insulated device, add the tablespoon of cooking oil, then pour the batter into the pan and return it to the oven to bake for 15 to 20 minutes or until lightly browned and cooked throughout. Cool for 5 minutes, then cut into wedges and serve.

French Corn Bread Wrapped in Wild Leaves

Makes one 10-inch (26 cm) pan

A sort of French sourdough corn bread that was traditionally wrapped in cabbage leaves. I wrap mine in wild, jagged cow parsnip leaves for a striking appearance. This is a hybrid between corn bread and typical yeast bread, with a slightly bouncier texture. The best part is the leaves. You can use any leaf you like to wrap the bread, but finding large, wild leaves like cow parsnip, ramp leaves, mature sochan, or a blend of your favorites makes the finished product a beautiful, portable conversation piece. This is one of my go-to recipes for bringing to wild food tastings, cutting into pieces, and dipping in flavored oils or eating with cheese. It travels well, and it likes to be toasted.

Large leaves for wrapping the bread (wild grape, sochan, dock, cow parsnip, or garden leaves such as sunflower, cabbage, or chard), as needed to cover a 10-inch (26 cm) cast-iron pan from top to bottom

2 cups (300 g) corn flour

1 cup (240 ml) buttermilk

2 teaspoons sugar

2 teaspoons chopped fresh rosemary (or thyme, savory, or dill)

2 ounces (55 g) freshly toasted black walnuts, walnuts, or pecans, coarsely chopped

2 teaspoons fine salt

¼ teaspoon fresh-ground black pepper

⅓ cup (80 ml) Smude's sunflower oil, walnut oil, or melted animal fat

1 pound (455 g) Pâte Fermentée (page 149)

Blanch the leaves in boiling water for a few seconds to wilt, then refresh them in cold water and lay on a towel to dry. If you use cabbage leaves, you'll want to blanch them for a minute or two to ensure they're tender and pliable. Toast the corn flour in a skillet in a 350°F (180°C) oven for 20 to 25 minutes, or until aromatic. Transfer the hot corn flour to a mixing bowl, then add the buttermilk, sugar, rosemary, walnuts, salt, pepper, and oil, and allow to cool for 10 minutes, or until it reaches 100°F (38°C). Cut the Pâte Fermentée into four pieces and work them together in the bowl of a stand mixer using the dough hook attachment for a minute or two. Gradually add the corn flour mixture to the Pâte Fermentée, ¼ cup (60 ml) at a time, allowing each addition to incorporate fully before adding the next.

Grease a 10-inch (26 cm) cast-iron pan, Dutch oven, or similar shallow baking dish, line it with the blanched leaves to cradle the dough, making sure to leave some hanging over the sides to be folded over the top of the bread. Add the dough, pressing it down flat to fill the pan, then fold the leaves over the top, making sure they adhere. The dough doesn't need to be completely covered. Cover the pan with cling film and allow the bread to rise for about an hour, until slightly puffed. Preheat the oven to 400°F (200°C), placing a second pan on the lowest rack; when the oven reaches 400°F and the second pan is searing hot, carefully pour a couple of inches of water into it to create steam, then quickly put the corn bread on a higher rack and shut the oven door. Bake for 10 minutes at 400°F, then reduce the heat to 350°F (180°C) and bake for 30 to 35 minutes more, or until a thermometer inserted in the center of the loaf reads 190°F (90°C). Remove the loaf from the pan to cool completely before slicing.

Hickory Nuts

For a while I thought black walnuts must be the most delicious, expensive, hard-to-source nut, and they were—until I met shagbark hickory (*Carya ovata*) nuts. Hickory nuts are like small, buttery, delicious pecans, and they'll cost you a lot more, upward of $30 per pound (455 g) retail—if you're lucky enough to find some. Ingredients a chef can't have are pure catnip, though, and, scoffing at the price, I purchased hand nutcrackers with the goal of teaching my dishwashers to shell hickory nuts I purchased unshelled, for a third of the price, in their "spare" time. I was going to outsmart the system with a skilled, crack team of professional nut crackers, and I would have my hickory nuts, for cheap.

I was soon to learn the error of my assumptions.

The dishwashers tried to crack the nuts for about 30 minutes, most of the nuts shattering, smashing the nut meats to bits, with tiny shell projectiles flying around the dish pit like meteors perfectly sized to fly into an unsuspecting eye. After this, they refused to handle—or even look at—the nuts, leaving me with useless nutcrackers and plenty of bags of whole nuts I had no clue how to work with. Frustrated, confused, and embarrassed that I, a chef, could be so ignorant of any foodstuff, I silently escorted the nuts to the compost.

If I only knew then what I do now! Although you can definitely shell and eat hickory nuts (they're excellent), my favorite cooking method is the one Indigenous peoples developed to get the most out of the nuts, without having to individually shell a single one. That means, to make any of the awesome recipes for hickory nuts in this book, you don't have to shell a single nut. Not *one*.

The traditional Native American method goes like this: Nuts—shell and all—are pounded in a hollowed-out log called a botagen with a giant pestle, and the resulting paste of nutmeats and shells is made into balls, then dropped into water to cook. After simmering for a while, the mixture is allowed to settle for a moment, and the hard shell fragments, being heavier than the nutmeats, sink to the bottom of the pan, and the nutmeats and liquid—a sort of nut milk—are ladled off for eating or cooking. It's an ingenious, labor-saving technique, and the liquid, which tastes and smells like the buttery soul of a pecan, is unlike any nut milk you've ever had.

As if that weren't cool enough, hickory nuts (like their cousins pecans and walnuts) are also an oil crop—another process that doesn't involve shelling and picking nuts. Similar to the Hickory Nut Milk, the nuts are pounded then simmered in water. Because heat makes oil and water separate, the oil floats to the top and is ladled off for later use. (This works with acorns, as well.) Sam Thayer introduced me to the process; his company, Forager's Harvest, sells bitternut hickory (*Carya cordiformis*) oil (take my advice and buy the large jug), breathing new life into an ancient food tradition that might have been forgotten.

In order to make Hickory Nut Milk and the recipes that require it here, you're going to need a way to do that. If you have a botagen or hollowed-out tree trunk—great! But if you're like most people, including me, you don't, and that's okay, too. There are probably other ways to get around it, but here's what works for me: Take your hickory nuts and crack each one individually with a hammer, then inspect each one diligently for spoilage or rancidity (it happens). Just a single rancid nut can ruin a batch of nut milk. Grind the nuts in a high-speed blender in a separate bowl dedicated to dried corn and other, similar things. It's loud, but the whole process is done in a few moments,

and I end up with a decent approximation of the traditional mashed nuts and shells.

As for acquiring nuts, the ideal scenario is to harvest them yourself, which, besides letting you channel your inner woodland creature (picking up nuts on the ground is a bit like finding money), is 100 percent free. But no one can harvest everything all the time, and if you don't have a hickory nut tree of your own, there are online sellers (browse around on eBay and Etsy) that will ship whole or shelled nuts to you. Although buying nuts isn't nearly as romantic as picking them yourself, it can be a good way to introduce yourself to them, especially if they don't grow close to you. If you eventually plan to hunt for them yourself, a bonus of starting with some you bought is that you'll learn how to work with them, and will be able to quickly identify any you come across in the wild—a process I call spoon-feeding identification, which I used to use ordering mushrooms I hadn't found, like matsutake, before I hunted them myself.

Here as elsewhere, you get what you pay for, and some sellers are better than others. Also keep in mind that some nuts may have been stored for years to be sold as decorations, rather than to crack and eat. When buying whole hickory nuts, I look for small shagbark nuts from the most recent season, and I avoid large-looking nuts, which could be king nuts or mockernuts—both much larger with hard, tough shells like black walnuts that won't work for pounding into a mash. If you have any doubt, ask the seller, and caveat emptor: If the seller doesn't know what type of nut they have, they may not be storing or treating them as food.

Whether purchased or foraged, hickory nuts are fascinating unto themselves, and the fact that they can be made into a foodstuff without cracking and picking individual nuts creates completely new, delicious, and exciting possibilities for the adventurous eater.

Hickory Nut Milk

Makes about 3½ cups (850 ml)

This is the mother recipe, and a culinary tradition spanning millennia. Alone, sweetened with maple syrup and cinnamon to taste, it makes a very special drink, but I like using it to make other things, harnessing the pure, unadulterated flavor. For the best results, you'll need a botagen, a high-speed blender, or another way to bash the nuts and shells into a coarse meal. A grain mill won't work, since the shells are too firm. Don't have a botagen or high-speed blender? There's one last method. If you have a hard surface, like a molcajete, or basalt mortar and pestle, you can bash the nuts with a hammer, pick out any large pieces of shells, and use only the smallest mashed and broken pieces of nuts and shell.

What follows is the beginner version of Hickory Nut Milk I developed and, compared with other recipes, it will seem like a small batch for the amount of work involved—and it is. Once you get the hang of cracking the nuts and inspecting them for off ones, I'd encourage you to make larger batches. And don't throw out the small amount of milk when you start getting down to the bottom—the remaining nutmeats are used to make a second wash. It's an important part of getting the most from the nuts, and the first and second milks have different cooking applications.

8 ounces (225 g) crushed hickory nuts and shells
4¼ cups (1 L) water

Crack each nut individually, inspect for (and discard) any that smell off, are hollow, or have dark interiors. Take the cracked nuts and put them in a high-speed blender and process into a coarse meal—it will be loud. Add the nut mash to the water and bring to a simmer, stirring occasionally. When the pan starts to simmer, a raft of frothy nut cream will form on the top. Virtually all of the shell particles sink, but inevitably some will be caught in the foamy cream, so I like to spoon this off and add it to the second wash for extra flavor, and to remove nut shells from the finished milk. After you've skimmed the foam, let the mixture simmer for another 15 minutes or so, then turn off the heat, wait a few seconds to let the larger shell pieces fall to the bottom, and start ladling off nut milk. There's a real art to ladling off the milk; you want to wait just long enough to let the large shell pieces settle, but not so long all the nut meats go with them. Gently swirl the pan a bit and you'll get the hang of it. Eventually you'll need to tilt the pan to continue scooping off nut milk, but don't try to get it all or you'll get shell particles. Drain and save the remaining nut meats and milk to make the second wash—a weaker nut milk that's perfect for cooking rice or polenta, or as the base of a soup, since it's not thick like the first milk. Squirrel soup cooked with nut milk is delicious, and makes me chuckle.

To serve as a drink, season this first wash to taste with a dash of maple syrup and a tiny pinch of cinnamon, lading out small hot cups. Drinking semisweet liquid with small nut chunks might seem a little different at first, but after you smell the ultra-rich, buttery pecan aroma and give it your first taste, you'll be sold. It's a great family activity for a cold winter evening.

To make the second wash, pour another 4 cups (945 ml) of water onto the leftover shells and nutmeats in the pot, bring it to a simmer, turn the heat down, and cook for another 30 minutes, then strain and reserve. Use the second wash as the base for a soup, or use it to cook wild rice or another grain.

Hickory nuts after being cracked and ground in a Vitamix blender.

Cooking the mashed nuts with water to make nut milk. The first cream that rises can contain shell fragments and is ladled into a separate bowl in the back.

The pounded nut shells after making nut milk. More water is added to make the second wash.

Finished nut milk (*left*) and the second wash for cooking grains or using in soup (*right*).

Wild Rice Cooked in Hickory Nut Milk

Serves 4–6 as a side

This is a very old method for cooking wild rice. It won't taste like hickory nuts, but you'll notice a weight to it as you eat. The extra solutes and rogue nutmeats make the rice more filling and sustaining than wild rice cooked in plain water, and just like the three sisters, it's a fine example of nutritional knowledge passed down, tucked away inside culinary traditions like a secret message. As tempting as it might be to cook wild rice in pure nut milk, don't do it—you'll end up with clumpy, sticky rice that's too heavy. And if you're thinking this is impossible to make without a hickory nut tree near you, don't worry: You can make a weak nut milk with a blender, simply by puréeing 2 cups (480 ml) of water or stock with 1 to 1½ tablespoons of nuts or seeds of your choice, sunflower seeds being the best-tasting, least expensive substitute. Toasting the nuts or seeds can add an extra dimension, and should be done if you store them in the freezer, as I often do.

2 cups (480 ml) Hickory Nut Milk
  (second wash) (page 238)
1 cup (140 g) wild rice
½ teaspoon kosher salt, plus more to taste
3 tablespoons hickory nuts, or others of
  your choice
3 tablespoons fat, such as hickory nut oil,
  or your choice
Chopped Italian parsley, for serving
  (optional)

Bring the Hickory Nut Milk, wild rice, and salt to a simmer, then turn the heat to low and cook until the milk is absorbed, about 20 to 25 minutes. Fluff the rice, adding the hickory nuts and oil, and allow to rest and steam to gently finish cooking the rice. Double-check the seasoning for salt, adjust as needed, toss in the parsley, and serve.

Variation: Dried Winter Fruit Pilaf

Add some sun-dried wild plums or blueberries, soaked or simmered in hot water until tender, along with a few good pinches of dried ramp leaves.

Variation: Sausage, Nut, and Mushroom Pilaf

Add some cooked, crumbled sausage, sautéed mushrooms, and fresh or dried ramp leaves or green garlic.

Hickory Nut Pudding

Serves 4–6

This dish was inspired by kanuchi, a sort of soup made by the Cherokee using hickory nut milk. The nut and shell balls are simmered in water, strained, and sometimes cooked with rice and sweetened. Edith Knight shares her recipe in a great YouTube video called "Cooking Kanuchi, A Cherokee Tradition." My version here isn't a soup like Edith's, but hers inspired me to develop a version using the same ingredients. It eats like a mousse or pudding, and tastes like pure, buttery, hickory nut heaven. It's rich stuff, so I like to serve small amounts in jelly jars or custard dishes. If you want to use other nuts and seeds, try substituting a different homemade nut milk made in a blender—pecan, sunflower seed, or pine nut are where I would start, and I'd toast them very gently beforehand.

2½ cups (625 ml) Hickory Nut Milk (page 238)
¼ cup (50 g) long-grain rice
¼ cup (60 ml) plus 1 tablespoon maple syrup, divided
1 teaspoon Galium Vanilla Extract (page 190) or vanilla extract (optional)
Tiny pinch of salt
½ cup (135 ml) heavy cream

Bring the Hickory Nut Milk, rice, ¼ cup of the maple syrup, vanilla, and salt to a simmer. Cook with a lid ajar for 45 minutes, or until the pan is nearly dry but still has some liquid. Turn the heat off, transfer the pudding to a bowl, and wrap with cling film, pressing it down onto the surface to prevent a skin from forming. Cool the pudding to room temperature, then refrigerate until completely cool. Whip the cream and the remaining tablespoon of maple syrup to soft peaks and fold half of the cream into the pudding just before serving. Spoon the pudding into bowls and garnish with toasted hickory nuts and spoonfuls of the remaining whipped cream.

Hickory Bark Syrup

Makes 2 pints (945 ml)

A low-cost substitute for maple syrup made from hickory tree bark, this tastes like hickory smoke. It's not the same as maple syrup—not by a long shot—but it's an interesting forest-inspired product with a bit of a following in the foraging world, and I know a couple of people who sell it or give it away as gifts. Some add corn syrup to stop it from crystallizing, but I don't find it to be too much of a problem—just heat it up a bit before using. To add even more smoky hickory depth, set a 2-inch (5 cm) piece of hickory bark on fire until it's engulfed in flames and add it to the preliminary tea.

6 ounces (170 g) shagbark hickory bark, preferably in pieces about 6 inches long and 3 inches wide (15 × 7.5 cm)
5 cups (1.25 L) water
4 cups (800 g) white sugar

If the bark is fresh, scrub and clean it to remove fungi, spiderwebs, or anything you may have missed. Soak the bark in water for 15 minutes. Meanwhile, preheat the oven to 375°F (190°C). Roast the bark for 30 minutes, cool it until you can handle it, then break it into pieces and add it to a pot. Add the 5 cups of water to cover the bark (it should barely cover it; if not, add a little more) and bring to a boil. Reduce the heat to the lowest possible setting, then cook another 30 minutes, uncovered. Strain this bark tea through a fine strainer or cheesecloth, discarding the bark. You should have about 4 cups (945 ml) of bark tea. Mix the sugar with the liquid, return it to the pot, and cook until reduced by half, or until it is heated to 225°F (110°C). To hot-pack the syrup, pour the boiling-hot syrup into a sterilized jar nearly up to the brim, screw on the lid, turn the jar upside down, cool, then store. For water-bath canning, leave ½ inch (1.25 cm) of headspace. Hickory syrup will keep for a long time. Refrigerate after opening.

Roasted hickory bark will add a smoky flavor to syrup, but also to things like alcohol and vinegar. I used to age vinegar in a charred spruce log for my restaurant house dressing, which was inspired by Chef Magnus Nilsson.

Hickory Ice Cream

Makes 4 cups (945 ml)

Inspired by one of my favorite ice creams served by Chef Joshua Skenes at Saison in San Francisco, this uses hickory bark syrup as the base flavoring and sweetener, along with a piece of the bark itself—which is set on fire and quenched in the dairy. You end up getting an ice cream that tastes smoked, and it's a roller coaster of flavor in the same orbit as desserts made with salted caramel. A little goes a long way.

2-inch (5 cm) piece of clean hickory bark, preferably left over from making syrup
3 cups (720 ml) half-and-half
6 egg yolks
1 cup (240 ml) hickory syrup
⅛ teaspoon kosher salt
1 ounce (28 g) toasted, chopped hickory nuts (optional)

Heat the piece of bark over a fire until it's engulfed in flames. Extinguish the burning bark in the cream, stir, and allow this to infuse for 20 minutes, then remove the bark and discard. Whisk the half-and-half, egg yolks, syrup, and salt, then heat on medium-high until the mixture thickens. Cool, and allow to rest overnight for the best texture, then process in an ice cream machine according to the manufacturer's directions. Stir in the toasted nuts, if you like, after spinning.

Hickory Nut Milk Ice Cream

Make 1 recipe of Hickory Nut Milk (page 238) and cook it down until 1 cup (240 ml) remains, then add 2 cups (480 ml) of cream, ¾ cup (150 g) sugar, and 6 egg yolks. Heat gently, whisking, just until the egg thickens the mixture slightly, cool overnight and proceed as for Hickory Ice Cream.

Hickory Nut Oil Silk

**Yields 6 small jelly jars
(each 3–4 ounces / 85–115 g)**

One year, when I was picking bitternut hickory nuts with Sam Thayer to press for oil, he told me he'd always wondered if he could take the oil, incorporate maple syrup somehow, and craft it into a frozen dessert for one of the holy grails of wild food: the "100 percent forest" product. Having made a few desserts to showcase extra-virgin olive oil in the past, I tinkered with the oil for a few weeks and eventually came up with this frozen dessert made only with Hickory Nut Milk, maple syrup, and hickory nut oil that feels like silk melting on your tongue. Served in small dishes, it can be made in advance, just like ice cream.

To make the pure hickory nut invocation, you'll need one recipe of basic Hickory Nut Milk (page 238), for which heavy cream can be substituted. What you *can't* substitute, though, is the hickory nut oil, which you'll have to order from Forager's Harvest (www.foragersharvest.com). Even if you don't have any hickory nuts or oil, the real beauty and big takeaway here is expanding the same concept to different nuts and their respective oils: black walnut milk with black walnut oil, sunflower seed milk and sunflower seed oil, pumpkinseed milk . . . you get the idea. The key to using nut and seed milk instead of heavy cream is that they need to be thick like heavy cream, so you'll need to cook them down a bit to concentrate the fat.

⅔ cup (160 ml) maple syrup
½ cup (135 ml) very thick, reduced Hickory
  Nut Milk (or heavy cream)
Pinch of salt
1 cup (240 ml) hickory nut oil
1 small handful lightly toasted hickory nuts,
  for serving (optional)

Before you begin, make sure all of the ingredients are well chilled. In the bowl of a Vitamix or other high-speed blender, purée the maple syrup, nut milk, and salt. Drizzle in the hickory nut oil in a steady stream to form an emulsion, as if you were making mayonnaise. When all the oil is added, immediately pour the mixture into the serving jars (or other small dishes) and transfer to the freezer to set for at least 3 hours. Sprinkle with toasted hickory nuts just before serving if you like.

Acorns

Oak trees. Are a food plant. Oak trees are a food plant. Say it a couple of times. That quick saying is a useful one, and a good soundbite I like to share with people. We may not think about oaks and the acorns they produce as food, but they are—just as much as hazelnuts or walnuts—and they have been for many cultures, for a very long time. Native Americans processed the nuts by leaving them to soak in a river, and similar processes were used in the Far East, especially in Korea, where the tradition of harvesting acorns (and eating acorn tofu, or dotorimuk) is so appreciated that acorn starch is produced and sold commercially, across the globe—making Korea the largest producer of acorn products in the world. Don't believe me? Go look on Amazon. It's not cheap, but after you shell and leach your first acorns, you'll understand.

And that's not even mentioning the sheer weight of food a mature oak can make during a mast year (the production is cyclical). On a good year, a really good oak could drop more than 1,000 pounds of acorns on the ground. Now think about the inputs oak trees require—or *don't* require. Trees need no pesticide, no chemical fertilizer, no tractors and gas to plow up the fields. In reality, oak trees, and other food trees, are like the giving tree from the classic children's book by that name: They give and give and give, and really need nothing in return from humans—a far cry from all the annual crops reliant on fossil fuels and chemicals to which most of the arable land in the United States is dedicated.

Cold-Leached Acorn Flour

Acorns are bitter, and need to be leached before being made into the culinary flour that I use for all the recipes here. No doubt about it, leaching acorns is time consuming, but most of that time is unattended. There are lots of resources online that explain the process, so I'm only going to outline what works for me: the cold-leach. First, I find oak trees giving the largest acorns I can find, preferably from white oaks (*Quercus alba*). I avoid harvesting any acorns with holes (which likely contain larvae) or with attached caps (which have been rejected by the tree)—as both of these generally mean the acorns aren't fit to eat.

Acorns can be cut right away with a heavy chef's knife, but the shell is rubbery and difficult to cut, so I dry them in a dehydrator for a day or two on low heat until the shells are brittle. This also allows me to crack and leisurely process them over the winter, since after drying the acorns are shelf-stable in a garage or pantry, at least until the next season, like other nuts. If the acorns aren't dried quickly, larvae can infest them and ruin the harvest.

After the shells are dry, I crack the nuts, remove as much clinging brown inner skin as I can (this step is optional but decreases leaching time), and soak the dried nuts in water overnight. Then I take the soaked nuts and grind them, a few handfuls at a time, in a high-speed blender like a Vitamix with 3 to 4 times their volume of water, until they're finely ground. If you don't have a high-speed blender, I'd recommend grinding freshly shelled, undried acorns with the same volume of water in a food processor, although it will take some time. I pour this slurry of water and nuts into a large container or pot and store it in the fridge or outside if it's cool at night in the fall, changing the water once a day for a week or more—as long as it takes for the nuts to not taste bitter (I've had red oak / *Quercus rubra* acorns take 10 days or longer). After the tannins are removed and the wet meal tastes mild, I strain out the acorn meal, discard the water, and dry the meal on silicone sheets in a dehydrator until cracker-dry—typically overnight at 145 to 150°F—then grind the flour one final time in the blender or a spice grinder and store in a jar until I need it. Any flour that won't be used within a couple of months, I freeze in vacuum bags; this keeps it fresh for a very long time.

Cracking dried acorns.

Shelling and removing the inner skin.

Acorns puréed with water after soaking.

Straining ground wet acorns after leaching and regularly changing the water.

Spreading the strained mash on silicone mats.

Dried acorn meal ready to grind fine in a spice grinder before use.

Acorn and Pine Nut Johnnycakes

Makes about 12 cakes

Everyone loves pancakes, and these are a little different—small johnnycakes inspired by the Native American tribes of California who harvested both pine nuts and acorns. For the best texture, I use a combination of corn flour, acorn flour, and all-purpose flour. The pine nuts are the crowning glory and add a beautiful pattern to the cakes. They're as good with shredded pork as they are with maple syrup, blueberries, and butter—or acorn oil.

3 tablespoons pine nuts
½ cup (70 g) acorn flour
½ cup (75 g) corn flour or fine cornmeal
½ cup (60 g) all-purpose flour or equivalent
1 teaspoon baking powder
1¼ cups (300 ml) milk or water
2 tablespoons unsalted butter, melted lard, or bacon grease, plus a little extra for greasing the skillet
1 teaspoon kosher salt
1 tablespoon sugar (optional)
1 large egg

Preheat the oven to 200°F (95°C). Lightly toast the pine nuts in a skillet and reserve. Toast the acorn flour and corn flour (or cornmeal) in a dry skillet placed in the warm oven for a few minutes. Mix the all-purpose flour with the baking powder. Heat the milk, butter, salt, and sugar until the butter is melted, then fold in the acorn-and-corn-flour mix and beat in the egg. Finally, mix in the all-purpose flour until just combined.

In a lightly greased skillet (a 12-inch / 30 cm cast-iron skillet is good), put down scant teaspoons of the toasted pine nuts, then pour scant ¼ cups (60 ml) of batter over each set of nuts. Cook until the edges puff, flip them over, and cook for a minute or two more. Repeat, transferring the cooked cakes to a baking sheet in the oven until all the cakes are cooked. Serve with your favorite pancake toppings, or as a savory side dish, as you would bread.

Sam Thayer's Acorn Oil

Just as with hickory nuts, Native American tribes processed acorns as an oil crop, as well as a nut product, cooking the pounded acorns with water until the oil floated to the top and could be ladled off and saved for cooking—the tannins in the acorns aren't fat-soluble, so the oil isn't bitter. Also like hickory nut oil, the flavor is good (even better, in my opinion), but the most fascinating part is the deep red-orange oil produced from water oak (*Quercus nigra*) trees. Made in limited quantities, at a cost of about $50 per pint, it resides in the Mount Olympus of luxury foods. You can order some for yourself from foragersharvest.com.

Acorn Grits

Serves 4

A steaming-hot bowl of buttered, maple-syrup-kissed acorn grits is one of the most economical ways to use acorn flour. Corn grits are rich on their own, but adding acorns means they're even more so—this is super-rich stuff, and a little goes a long way. To stretch the acorn meal, and to provide the texture of grits that I love, I combine acorn flour with hand-ground cornmeal from either flint or dent corn that I grind myself—just simple cornmeal won't give you the right texture. To buy the right cornmeal for the job, look for stone-ground grits with the longest cooking time you can find—60 minutes is a good place to start, and will mean that the corn is a little coarse, which translates to better texture in the finished product.

⅓ cup (48 g) acorn flour
4 cups (945 ml) water
⅔ cup (115 g) coarse-ground corn grits
Kosher salt, to taste

Preheat the oven to 250°F (120°C). Lightly toast the acorn flour. Combine the water, corn grits, and acorn flour in an oven-proof pan, such as a Dutch oven, and heat until simmering, whisking constantly (you can also make larger batches in a crockpot, which is easier). When the mixture thickens, transfer it to the oven, cover, and cook for 1 hour, or until the corn and acorn particles are tender. If needed, heat on the stove to evaporate extra water and thicken it to your taste. Season to taste with salt, and serve with your favorite garnishes, such as butter, maple syrup, fruits, or nuts.

Acorn Crepes

Makes 9 crepes (enough to serve 4 people 2 crepes apiece, if you don't mess up too many crepes)

To make crepes, follow the directions for Wild Rice Crepes (page 226), substituting finely ground, sifted acorn flour for the wild rice flour.

Maple-Acorn Torte

Makes one 8-inch (20 cm) cake

Northern Italians have long cooked with a naturally sweet flour made from chestnuts, and that was the inspiration for my acorn crepes as well as this, my favorite acorn dessert. It's a lesson in simplicity: a dense cake made with nothing more than acorn flour, eggs, maple syrup, and a little bit of technique. Instead of using acorn flour raw, I hydrate it by cooking it into a mash beforehand. The flavor is slightly reminiscent of coffee cake, but don't expect a light, airy fluff—the acorns add a certain weight to it you'll feel. It's something to behold, simply sliced, possibly warmed, with a dollop of whipped cream and a cup of coffee. You could probably substitute other nut meals for acorn, but I haven't tried.

4 ounces (115 g) unsalted butter,
  plus extra for greasing the pan
1 tablespoon maple or white sugar,
  for dusting the pan
1 cup (140 g) acorn flour, finely ground
  and sifted
1 cup (240 ml) water
1 cup (240 ml) maple syrup

5 large eggs
1 teaspoon vanilla extract
½ teaspoon ground cinnamon
1 teaspoon baking powder
¼ teaspoon salt

Preheat the oven to 350°F (180°C). Butter an 8-inch (20 cm) springform pan, then sprinkle with sugar. Toast the acorn flour lightly in a skillet or oven until just beginning to darken—don't allow it to burn—then set aside to cool. Meanwhile, mix the water, butter, and maple syrup and bring to a boil, then add the toasted acorn flour and cook just until it thickens and a paste forms. Transfer the mixture to a bowl, cover it with cling film, and cool to room temperature. Beat the eggs until light-colored, add the vanilla and cinnamon, then gradually add the acorn paste. Mix until combined, then beat the mixture for another minute or two until you get a fluffy batter. Finally, beat in the baking powder and the salt. Pour the mixture into the prepared pan and bake for 25 to 30 minutes, or until just cooked through. Serve with whipped crème fraîche, whipped cream, or sour cream. The cake will keep, covered and refrigerated, for 3 to 4 days.

Black Walnuts

When I was growing up in west-central Minnesota, fall was the season when black walnuts (*Juglans nigra*) littered our yard, starting out as round, hard, dangerous obstacles I'd trip over, then slowly transforming into black, mushy orbs. I disliked them, especially when I had to clear them away to mow the lawn. When I bent down to examine one of the black orbs one day and found the outer husk full of larvae, my brain registered black walnuts as disgusting—although they were called walnuts, they certainly couldn't be food. Years later, in the professional kitchen where I had my first taste of them (and saw their price tag), I was hooked. When I started foraging and studying my surroundings, I learned to love the tree even more.

Now I see black walnuts not as a nuisance but as fascinating trees that offer a large variety of ingredients throughout the year. While the leaves are young and tender, they hold some of the same citrus-esque aroma as the green, immature nuts, and have been used in the past to flavor vinegars and old-fashioned condiments such as Black Walnut Bay Sauce (page 255).

The immature, green nuts, famously used to infuse alcohol in France and Italy, can also be eaten, and are actually good—although it took me years to find the right preparation. Finally, the mature nuts, stored and cracked by hand, are the most aromatic nut I've ever tasted, but you'll have to work for them. Like a lot of other nut-bearing trees, black walnuts are also an oil crop; they create a mild-flavored walnut oil without the strong flavor of the nuts. I order black walnut oil through Hammons Black Walnuts (black-walnuts.com).

Black Walnut Preserves

**Makes a 1-quart (945 ml) jar
or 2 pint jars (each 480 ml)**

If you've ever made Italian nocino or French Vin de Noix and wondered if there's anything else you can do with green walnuts, or if you've tried to make the reasonably well-known (among foragers) British pickled walnuts and found the texture unpleasant (or even horrible, as I did), this is for you. Walnut preserves are literally green walnuts preserved in syrup—a treat for after dinner, or something you could mix into all sorts of desserts. I'm not the first to make it—that honor probably goes to the people of Greece and Armenia, where it's also known as walnut jam.

There are a few keys to success here, the most important being that the walnuts must be picked at a specific stage—about the size of a ping-pong ball. Picked too early, or around the size of large almonds, they'll be too young, a crucible to peel, and, even after peeling, composed of too high a proportion of outer green husk. If the walnuts are too old, however, the inner shell will have formed and they'll be tough, like eating a walnut shell. If you're not familiar with walnut shells, they are also used as a natural abrasive for polishing gun casings and other metal parts. Chew on that.

Besides the stage of growth, the other paradigm-shifting technique for me was peeling. Yes, you peel them, preferably with a Kuhn Rikon or other heavy-duty Y-shaped peeler. *Easy* is not a term that will come to mind during the peeling process. The outer husk is what I always thought cooked, unripe black walnuts must be destined to taste like, but it isn't. This grainy husk, with its hypnotic, citrusy scent you'll dream of ways to capture as a seasoning, is just a shield protecting the finished product: a soft, tender interior that almost makes me think of softly cooked bone marrow or cheese.

They're shelf-stable till the reckoning and, if nothing else, make a jaw-dropping conversation piece. Peeled, the nuts flaunt shiny facets like a cut black gem, looking more like knapped obsidian jewels than an after-dinner snack with cheese, or garnish for a dessert. If at all possible, use a handful of dried galium leaves, meadowsweet, or the husk of a vanilla bean, or even just some vanilla extract, when making the syrup—the flavor seeps into the nuts during their hibernation.

1½ pounds (680 g) (roughly 30–35) green black walnuts, the size of ping-pong balls
Handful of dried galium leaves, a vanilla bean (seeds removed), or a teaspoon or two of vanilla extract
4 cups (800 g) sugar
4 cups (945 ml) water
¼ cup (60 ml) fresh lemon juice

Cover the black walnuts in water in a container and allow them to ferment for a week, burping occasionally and changing the water a few times, or as often as you can remember. After a week, drain the walnuts and, using a sturdy vegetable peeler and gloves to prevent staining your hands, peel them, which will be more difficult than it sounds. Tie the galium in cheesecloth for easy removal if you're using it. Pierce each peeled walnut twice with a fork, then combine with the sugar, water, and galium or vanilla. Simmer for roughly 1 hour on low, or until the walnuts are soft. Skim off and discard any scum or foam that rises to the top to ensure a clear syrup. Discard the galium leaves; if you used a vanilla bean, save it to pack in the jar(s). After an hour, turn up the heat, bring the syrup to a boil, and reduce until it looks like warm honey and coats the back of a spoon, about 15 to 20 minutes, then turn off the heat, stir in the lemon juice, and transfer the nuts to Mason jars with tight-fitting lids (I like quart jars here) to cool. You'll probably have some syrup left over. The jars should seal naturally from the heat of the syrup, but any that don't can be processed in a water bath. Allow the walnuts to age for at least a month before enjoying. Harvested at the right stage, I guarantee you they're worth the wait.

Really Good Granola

Makes 10 cups (1.1 kg)

One of my favorite things to put walnuts or other nuts in is granola, and this is the one granola to rule them all. This is my home batch of the granola with a cult following we used to sell by the bag at Lucia's To-Go. It's irresistible eaten out of hand on a trail or mixed with yogurt and fresh berries or bananas for breakfast—or, after your family and friends taste it, traded for goods and services.

Peanut butter–maple mix
½ cup (135 ml) cooking oil
½ cup (135 ml) maple syrup
½ cup (135 ml) honey
½ cup (135 g) peanut butter
2 tablespoons vanilla extract
1 tablespoon ground cinnamon

Toasting
5 cups (500 g) rolled oats
1 cup (85 g) shredded coconut
1 cup (60 g) flaked coconut
2 cups (480 ml) nuts or seeds (my favorites are pumpkinseeds, almonds, walnuts, and sunflower seeds, but mix and match your favorites to taste)

Fruit (optional, added at the end)
2 cups (480 ml) mixed dried fruit (raisins, cranberries, chopped apricots, et cetera)

Simmer the peanut butter–maple mixture ingredients, whisking to emulsify. Meanwhile, in a large bowl, mix the oats, shredded and flaked coconut, and nuts or seeds together. Pour the peanut butter–maple mixture into the bowl with the oat-nut mixture, stirring to coat evenly. It will be a little wet. Spread the mixture onto a cookie sheet and cook at 300°F (150°C) for 1 hour, rotating the pan 180 degrees once during baking. After an hour, turn the heat off, open the door and hold for a five-count, then close the oven door and continue cooking with the residual heat. I like it cooked quite dark, and I think you'll find light-colored granola bland in comparison after you taste this cooked to a darker hue. When the granola is cooked and dry, allow it to cool, then break it into clusters add in the dried fruit (if you're using any). Store in an airtight container at room temperature.

Variation: Maple Granola with Acorn Butter
The scent of cooking granola is always good, but this one is mind bending. To make it, substitute 1 cup (140 g) very finely ground, cold-leached acorn flour for the peanut butter. In the bowl of a high-speed blender, blend the maple syrup, honey, and acorn flour until smooth, about 30 seconds on high, then proceed as in the basic recipe.

Black Walnut Bay Sauce

Makes 2½ cups (625 ml)

From a nearly 150-year-old cookbook called *Housekeeping in Old Virginia*. The original recipes don't use proportions and were essentially thin, infused vinegars, but you can make a punchy condiment along the lines of the traditional Black Walnut Ketchup (page 258) by puréeing the mixture after it has infused for a few months, straining it to remove any fibers, then thickening by puréeing again with ⅛ to ¼ teaspoon xanthan gum. The sauce really does benefit from mellowing, so plan on forgetting about it in the cupboard until it gets cold outside. But if you're in a hurry, infusing for just a month or two is okay, as the tannins seem to mellow more quickly in the leaves, used here, than in unripe nuts. Use the finished sauce dashed on cooked greens or oysters; or you can warm it up, whisk it with butter, and reduce it a bit to thicken as a sauce for poultry or fish. It's also nice added to salads and dressings.

2 ounces (55 g) young black walnut leaves
1 teaspoon black peppercorns
½-inch (1.25 cm) piece stick cinnamon
¼ teaspoon whole allspice berries
¼ teaspoon whole cloves
1 tablespoon kosher salt
1 tablespoon minced fresh ginger
2 ounces (55 g) sweet yellow onion, finely chopped
1 large clove garlic, minced
¾ ounce (20 g) grated fresh horseradish
3 cups (720 ml) raw apple cider vinegar

Massage the black walnut leaves with your hands a bit to release their aroma. Toast the peppercorns, cinnamon, allspice, and cloves, then crush in a mortar and pestle. Combine all ingredients into a nonreactive container and allow to sit for a few months, then strain and bottle.

Black Walnut Honey

Makes 1 generous cup (240 ml)

I adapted this gem from *Recipes of the Highlands and Islands of Scotland*. It has the consistency of thick honey infused with walnuts and it's an interesting substitute in places you would use honey: on yogurt, with cheese, on toast, and so on. If you've ever made stovetop mustard in a double boiler, the process will be familiar. Instead of maple syrup, you can substitute ½ cup brown sugar, decreasing the egg yolks to 1, if you like.

¾ cup (180 ml) maple syrup
1 ounce (28 g) black walnuts, lightly toasted
  and crushed
¼ cup (60 ml) dry white wine, preferably
  infused with a few dried galium leaves
  beforehand
¼ cup (60 ml) orange juice
Zest of ½ orange
A few scrapes of lemon zest
2 large egg yolks
1 tablespoon unsalted butter
Pinch of salt

Bring the maple syrup to a boil, then turn the heat to medium-low, reduce by a third, set aside to cool a bit, then whisk in the remaining ingredients (the butter will melt as the sauce cooks). Put the mixture in a metal mixing bowl above (not touching) simmering water, and cook for 30 minutes, stirring occasionally with a wooden spoon, until the mixture thickens and the egg has activated. Cool, cover, and refrigerate. The sauce will last for a week, and will set up and thicken as it cools. A dash of lemon juice will refresh it if needed.

Vin de Noix (Walnut Wine)

Makes 1.4 L

The French cousin to nocino, the strong Italian liqueur infused with green walnuts. While nocino is high in alcohol, walnut wine is more mellow and sippable, and far less sweet, which I prefer. Sometimes I might add dark fruit to age with it after straining—a handful of wild cherries or other berries can be a nice addition. This is a traditional style Vin de Noix, which means you'll taste some tannins from the red wine in the finished product. If tannins aren't your thing, or you want some variation, you can use white wine instead of red, which will taste more like a walnut-infused sherry.

285 g (10 ounces) green, unripe black
  walnuts (about 12 medium-sized nuts)
225 ml (scant cup) brandy
1125 ml red wine (1½ standard bottles)
3 whole cloves or allspice berries
100 grams (roughly ⅓ cup / 80 ml) honey
  or maple syrup, or to taste

Aromatics (can be varied to your taste)

Small handful of dried or fresh *Galium
  triflorum* leaves
Small handful of dried meadowsweet flowers
3-inch (7.5 cm) piece angelica stem
3 strips orange peel
3 strips lemon peel

Halve the walnuts, then combine with all remaining ingredients in a ½-gallon (2 L) jar and allow to macerate for 30 days. Strain, store in jars or corked bottles, and keep in a cool dark place for at least 6 months. It makes a nice sip near the end of winter.

Black Walnut Ketchup

Makes about 4 cups (945 ml)

An old and fascinating recipe known in Europe for using unripe walnuts; I was inspired to try this after seeing a version in *Recipes of the Highlands and Islands of Scotland*. The end result is a sharp condiment that at first tastes the way black walnuts smell, although it will change and mellow with time. My journey to victory—including waging an epic fruit-fly battle that resulted from having multiple gallon jars of fermenting walnuts in my apartment test kitchen during the peak of summer—took some determination. Recipe tester Blair Miller recommended using miso instead of the anchovy for a vegetarian version, and I borrowed the genius idea of thickening the ketchup with xanthan gum from Hank Shaw. It makes a very interesting condiment for grilled meats, fish, and vegetables.

1 pound (455 g) young black walnuts
1 tablespoon black peppercorns
½ tablespoon whole allspice
½ tablespoon whole cloves
3 cups (720 ml) apple cider vinegar
1 cup (240 ml) red wine
Scant 2 ounces (55 g) kosher salt
1 ounce (28 g) fresh horseradish
1 medium yellow onion, chopped
1 large clove garlic, crushed
1 ounce (28 g) fresh ginger
2 ounces (55 g) anchovies in oil, rinsed
¼ teaspoon xanthan gum

Soak the walnuts in water for 7 days, without changing the water. The walnuts will ferment and bubble. After 7 days, wearing gloves to prevent staining your hands, drain the walnuts, crack them, and spread them out on a tray until they oxidize and darken, about 24 hours. Toast the peppercorns, allspice, and cloves on the stovetop, then grind to a fine powder. Chop the walnuts coarsely, then transfer to a saucepan with all remaining ingredients except the xanthan gum. Bring to a simmer and cook for 15 minutes, covered, until the onion is soft. Transfer the mixture to a high-speed blender, pureé, strain (optional; a high-speed blender can usually make it pretty smooth), then combine with the xanthan gum and purée again to thicken. The sauce can be stored in the refrigerator or processed in a water bath.

Georgian Nut Pesto (Phkali)

Makes a generous ½ cup (130 g)

Highly spiced, aromatic, and exciting, Phkali is a highly seasoned nut paste from the Caucasus, usually mixed with spinach to make a kind of dip, or mixed with cooked greens into balls. The herbs and spices in mine are traditional, but you can mix and match some of your favorites. The more herbs you use, the more interesting it will be. Any nuts or seeds can be used, but my favorites are walnuts, sunflower seeds, cashews, or others easily turned to a paste or butter. Consider making a double batch, especially if you have a powerful blender that can purée it smooth.

Traditionally, you'd mix the walnut paste to taste with cooked greens, which is a fun experiment. To try the traditional version, take 2 cups (455 g) of greens you've steamed tender, cool, then chop them fine and mix with ½ cup (130 g) of the nut pesto and lemon juice to taste. Taste and adjust the seasoning, form into balls, decorating with pomegranate seeds on each, and serve as a rustic, hand-to-mouth appetizer.

I've enjoyed Phkali as a spread for sandwiches, and spread on slices of grilled eggplant that were then rolled up and served with apple molasses mixed with tahini, as you would pomegranate molasses. It's also good tossed with pasta.

4 ounces (115 g) toasted black walnuts, English walnuts, hazelnuts, or sunflower seeds
1–2 large cloves garlic, or 1–2 tablespoons minced, to taste
½ teaspoon fresh-ground fenugreek
½ teaspoon kosher salt
Fresh-cracked black pepper, to taste
½ teaspoon red pepper flakes, or to taste
1 teaspoon ground fresh coriander
2 tablespoons water
¼ cup (15 g) chopped cilantro
2 tablespoons chopped mint
2 tablespoons chopped dill
¼ cup (60 ml) good-tasting oil, preferably walnut (cooking oil will do, in a pinch)

For the smoothest purée, grind the nuts to a fine meal in a spice grinder first, or use a rotary cheese grater. In the bowl of a food processor, grind the garlic, fenugreek, salt, pepper, red pepper flakes, coriander, and nuts to a meal; add the water and continue processing until the mixture smooths out a bit (at least 5 minutes), scraping down the bowl occasionally. Add the herbs and pulse a few times, then drizzle in the oil to get a smoothish paste. If the mixture breaks and looks very oily, process it with another tablespoon of cold water to bring it back together.

Phkali Dip

Makes 1½ cups (200 g)

One of the traditional ways the nut paste is used. Just think spinach-artichoke dip, without artichokes or dairy . . . kinda. Since the dip is served at room temperature, or cool, the most important thing is to make sure the greens are tender, soft, and taste good to you before you start mixing them with the nut paste. Depending on the age of your greens, this might take 5 or 10 minutes of gentle simmering, or less if you're using blanched, frozen, or very young greens.

8 ounces (225 g) cooked wild or cultivated
  greens (especially spinach, violets,
  and chard)
½ cup (130 g) Georgian Nut Pesto
  (Phkali, page 259), or to taste
1 tablespoon water
2½ tablespoons neutral-flavored cooking oil
Fresh lemon juice, to taste
Kosher salt, to taste

Pomegranate seeds, for serving (optional)
Olive or walnut oil, for serving (optional)

Before you begin, taste the greens to judge their tenderness. I often make this with blanched frozen greens, and depending on how long they were originally blanched, they usually need to be cooked a bit longer to ensure they're soft. Drain the greens, then cool and squeeze out as much water as possible, then cut in the crosshatch pattern or chop fine to ensure there are no long stems. Blend the greens and nut paste in a food processor, slowly drizzling in the water and then the oil, as you would with mayonnaise. Taste the mixture and correct the seasoning for lemon and salt; it should be smooth and spreadable. Transfer to a shallow bowl or plate, smooth out the dip, and gently press the blade of a knife down to make a crosshatch pattern in the greens. Sprinkle with pomegranate seeds, if you like, and olive or walnut oil before serving.

Bird Cherry Flour, Wojapi, and Mahlab

Although bird cherry flour, wojapi, and mahlab are all made from different species of cherries in the genus *Prunus* (*P. padus*, *P. virginiana*, and *P. mahaleb*, respectively), these three terms all refer to the same general thing: a sort of seasoning or foodstuff made from pounding, drying, or cooking wild cherries, yielding an end product that tastes strongly of almond and, in the process of drying and cooking, denaturing the cyanogenic glycosides people associate with bitter almond flavor. My favorite is bird cherry flour. To make it, dry whole wild cherries until cracker-dry in a dehydrator on high 140°F + (60°C)—it will take days—then grind to a powder, sift, and bake with the sifted flour. The excess stones and shells can be used to infuse alcohol or other liquids, like a wild cherry schnapps or noyaux infusion.

Dried, ground wild cherries are used in Native American, Russian, and Middle Eastern cuisines.

Bird Cherry Cake

Serves at least 10

Taste it once, and I can guarantee you'll be gathering wild cherries to dehydrate every year. Bird Cherry Cake is a traditional Siberian dessert made from equal parts ground, dried wild cherries and wheat flour. Not only does it taste incredible—a combination of rich cherry and almond—but alongside mahlab and wojapi it's a fascinating ethnobotanical example of how different cultures around the world independently developed similar ways to safely use wild cherries, stone and all, which contain cyanide-producing amygdalin in their raw state.

The dense crumb, the result of using half wheat flour and half ground, sifted dried wild cherries, wards off the elements, giving this cake staying power where traditional cakes would be stale after a few days. It's as good as the finale to a meal as it is with a cup of coffee or tea the next day. Bird cherry flour can be purchased online if you don't feel like collecting and drying your own, but

what's even better is that you can make something similar with a cup of any type of naturally dried fruit flour you like. Sifted grape flour makes the most purple cake I've ever seen, while flour made from wild plums is a rich maroon, with a gentle tartness. Cranberries, as they're seedless, make a decent substitute if you don't have access to wild cherries or other fruit. For a pure cherry theme, add a few spoons of cherry gastrique or syrup to turn the frosting pink. The subtle texture you'll find here and there from tiny pieces of cherry shell is traditional and will grow on you.

1 heaping cup (150 g) dried wild cherries
  (chokecherries, black cherries, or
  bird cherries)
1 cup (120 g) all-purpose flour, or equivalent
⅛ teaspoon kosher salt
1½ teaspoons baking powder
2 large eggs, room temperature
¾ cup (150 g) sugar
1 cup (220 g) full-fat sour cream
2 teaspoons vanilla extract or Galium Vanilla
  Extract (page 190)

Cherry frosting
12 ounces (340 g) full-fat cream cheese
4 ounces (115 g) unsalted butter
4 ounces (115 g) powdered sugar
Pinch of kosher salt
3 tablespoons cherry gastrique (see Berry
  or Stone Fruit Gastrique, page 227)
  (optional; this is mostly for color)
3 ounces (85 g) sliced almonds, toasted,
  for serving

Grind the cherries as fine as possible in a spice grinder or high-speed blender. If you use a spice grinder for the cherries, it will be very loud, and you'll want to grind 2 or 3 tablespoons at a time. Sift the cherry flour, saving the shells to make Wild Cherry Liqueur (page 264). Sift the all-purpose flour, salt, and baking powder together, then mix thoroughly with the cherry flour and reserve. Preheat the oven to 350°F (180°C) and butter an 8-inch (20 cm) springform pan. Whisk the eggs and sugar until doubled in volume, about 5 minutes, then whisk in the sour cream and vanilla extract. Fold in the cherry flour mix until completely combined. Pour the batter into the pan, making sure it's evenly distributed (I use a small offset spatula to smooth the top, but a wet spoon also works). Bake for 25 minutes or until just set. Remove the cake and cool.

To make the frosting, whip the cream cheese, butter, powdered sugar, salt and cherry gastrique until light, fluffy, and doubled in volume, about 5 minutes.

Now you're ready to assemble your cake. Using a long knife, preferably 10 inches (26 cm) or longer, carefully cut the cake in half horizontally, keeping the layers as equal as possible. Spread a generous amount of the frosting on the bottom layer of the cake (you're looking for a good ½ inch / 1.25 cm here) then put on the top and spread on the rest of the frosting using an offset spatula or a spoon. Gently press the almonds into the sides of the cake to help cover up any lightly frosted areas or exposed seam, then slice and serve.

Wild Cherry Liqueur

After dehydrating cherries, grinding them into flour, and sifting the results, you'll have a by-product of leftover stones and shells. There's still power in them, and alcohol is a great way to harness the flavor and stretch your harvest. One technique I like is a noyaux-inspired cherry liqueur, which comes out so strong it can also be used like an almond extract. Since cherry stones contain amygdalin, to be overly cautious, if you're using whole dried cherries, heat them in a 300°F (150°C) oven for 10 minutes before grinding. (I've been told by authorities on the subject I trust that amygdalin is denatured simply by breaking open the dried cherry stones and exposing them to air, too, but it's good to be overly cautious.)

To make the liqueur, take the shells and small pieces of stone left over from sifting the cherry flour (or just make a powerful version with unsifted cherry flour) and combine them in a jar with twice their volume of flavorless liquor, such as a good vodka. For each cup (240 ml) of vodka and cherry stone debris, you might add a teaspoon or two of unsifted cherry flour to help boost the flavor and color. Allow the mixture to sit and macerate for a month, then strain out the finished liquor and sweeten to taste with maple syrup. Because it's very strong, I use it as an almond/cherry flavoring agent to add to other alcohols, such as Vin de Noix (page 257) cocktails, and desserts. I can guarantee you've never tasted a cherry liqueur like it.

Kissel

Serves 4

Born from working with cherry flour, my version of this Russian classic is all about layering flavor using a specific fruit. Cherries are just an example here; grapes and plums would be excellent, too. Using dried fruit flour is only a suggestion, but with the cherries in particular, the flavor it adds is remarkable, and making a version with wild grape flour or blueberries would be delicious, too.

3 tablespoons cornstarch
½ cup (135 ml) water
1 pound (455 g) sweet Bing or other cherries, stoned to yield 12 ounces (340 g) fruit, or 12 ounces (340 g) frozen cherries
¼ cup (35 g) ground, dried wild cherries
½ cup (135 ml) cherry juice
3 tablespoons maple syrup, or to taste, depending on the sweetness of your fruit
Dash of fresh lemon juice, to taste
Whipped cream or crème fraiche, for serving

Mix the cornstarch and ½ cup water and reserve. Heat the cherries, ground cherries, cherry juice, and maple syrup on low heat, covered, until soft. Purée the cherries and their liquid in a blender, strain to remove the cherry flour and any residual stones, then return the mixture to the pan, whisk in the cornstarch slurry, and simmer on medium-low until thickened, about 4 or 5 minutes. Turn off the heat, whisk in the lemon juice to taste, and carefully pour the kissel into whatever serving vessels you're using. Cover and chill. Just before serving, top the kissel with whipped cream or crème fraîche.

Acknowledgments

Without the help and advice of a lot of people, reaching back years, this book wouldn't be here.

First, to Pilar, a woman whose beauty is only matched by her intelligence and acutely refined palate, thank you for your love, honesty, and patience putting up with the more difficult parts of this.

To all my family, thanks for all the support. Special thanks to Tom DuFresne, my grandfather, whose woodworking skills have graced so many of the images in this book. To everyone at Bubbling Springs, thanks for being my adopted family, and putting up with me rooting around in your yards, gardens, and fields all the time.

I've had many teachers in the kitchen, but two stand above the rest. To Chef Lenny Russo: Thanks for not firing me during my first six months on the job. To Chef Andy Lilja: Thanks for not firing me during my first six months on the job. Your guidance and friendship changed my life. To Chefs Angelo Volpicelli, William Salvadore, and Jeff Laumb, thank you for giving me a chance, and for all the lessons you taught a young, insubordinate, mouthy cook. To the friends I met on the line, Chefs Brandon Randolph and Amy Buckmeier. To Chefs Jeremy Betchtold and Matt Griffin, for fearlessly opening and closing restaurants with me, and sticking by my side through the great, the bad, and the ugly. To Chefs Jacques Chibois and Jean Louis Palladin, for the inspiration.

To Samuel Thayer and Melissa Price, for your endlessly inspiring work that helped change my life, giving the manuscript a technical edit, and your friendship. To Dorothy Kalins, for the invaluable advice. To Hank Shaw, for all the groundwork you've laid for the wild food community, and the invaluable advice over the years. To Ellen Zachos, for the lampascioni. To Mike Rasmussen: If we never played disk golf together, this book might not be here. To Dan Rasmussen: Thanks for pushing me to start the website, and putting up with me living in your basement.

All the recipe testers—the recipes in this book are better because of you: Tim Vizino, Stephanie Kochlin, Carla Beaudet, Barry Nelson, Twyla Carolan, Alison Krohn, Peter Parsons, Gordon Hester, Judy Krohn, Nicki and Brian Shaban, Barbara Ching, Blair Miller, Mark E. E. Sprinkle, Cathy Cagle, Mika Turner, Betsy Nelson (That Food Girl), Jade Stone, Kara Doucette, Steve Breschuk, Aaron McFarlane, Trudy Born, Dr. Michael Neely, Kari Witthuhn, Jan Wirth, Chris Gunthert-Hinz, Nicole Novak, Anita Wotiz, Daniel Whittington, Alexandra Woods, Emily Inwood, Jessi Peine, Corinna Gries, Jim Neevel.

To my editor Michael Metivier and everyone at Chelsea Green: Thanks for your patience and help making this come together.

To Betsy Lane Lancefield, for working under the gun to edit the manuscript in the middle of the 2020 wildfires.

Finally, to the readers who've been with me over the years through all the typos, accidental posts, and odd experiments, but especially Dan Farmer and Jacqui Shykoff.

Index

Note: Page numbers in *italics* refer to photographs.

milkweed (*continued*)

capers from, 203

in Cornmeal-Fried Milkweed Pods, *118*, 119

in Creole Milkweed Pod Stew, 122, *122*

in Dried Milkweed Buds or Fiddleheads, 117

harvesting in the wild, 70

in Milkweed Bud Fettuccine, 120–21, *120*

in Milkweed Flower Shrub, 121

in Milkweed Leaf Pasta Dough, 121

in Milkweed Shoots Milanese, 119

raabs (buds) of, *62*

safety considerations, 6

in Steamed Milkweed Buds, 117, *117*

using entire plant, 115–16, *116*

Milkweed Bud Fettuccine, 120–21, *120*

Milkweed Flower Shrub, 121

Milkweed Leaf Pasta Dough, 121

Milkweed Shoots Milanese, 119

Miller, Blair, 258

miner's lettuce (*Claytonia perfoliata*), *19*

Minestrella (Tuscan Soup of Many Greens), 32–33, *33*

Minestrella di Gallicano, 2

mint

in Carrot Cakes with a Salad of Carrot Leaves, 78

in My Favorite Marinated Eggplant, 96

in Stuffed Leaves with Fruit, Rice, and Nut Filling, 27

mirepoix, 73

mitsuba (*Cryptotaenia canadensis*), *19*

in Braised Cabbage with Bacon and Caraway, 89

in Carrot Family Salad, 79

in Parsley-Family Tabouleh, with Toasted Barley, 81

Molohkia, *52*, *53*

Monarda spp. (bee balm), *144*, 147, *197*

Monarda fistulosa. *See* bergamot (*Monarda fistulosa*)

mountain ash (*Sorbus americana*), 4

mugolio, 210, *210*

Muscari spp. (musk and grape hyacinth), 129

mushrooms

in Braised Burdock and Mushrooms, 139

croutons from, 225

in Prickly Ash Chili Sauce, 156

with Ramp Leaf Pierogi, *162*, *163*

in Sausage, Nut, and Mushroom Pilaf, 241

with Steamed Milkweed Buds, 117

in Vegetable Soup with Burdock Flower Stalks, 141

mustard family. *See* Brassicaceae (mustard family)

My Favorite Marinated Eggplant, 96, *96*

My Favorite Stinging Nettle Soup, 49, *49*

Myricaceae family, overview, 192

See also specific types

Myrica gale. *See* sweetgale (*Myrica gale*)

N

nasturtium (*Tropaeolum* spp.), *197*

capers from, 203

fermentation of seeds, 25

Native Americans. *See* Indigenous North American peoples

Nelson, Betsy, 142

nettles. *See* common nettle (*Urtica dioica*); wood nettle (*Laportea canadensis*)

nightshade family (Solanaceae), 92, *92*

See also specific types

Nilsson, Magnus, 201, 243

nixtamalization, 228

The Noma Guide to Fermentation by (Redzepi and Zilber), 24

Norway spruce (*Picea abies*), 7, 204

nut and seed milks

in Hickory Nut Milk Ice Cream, 244

in Hickory Nut Oil Silk, 245

in Hickory Nut Pudding, 242

from hickory nuts, 237, 238–39, *239*

varieties of, 242, 245

Wild Rice Cooked in, 241

in Wild Rice Polenta, 224

nut and seed oils

acorn oil, 47, 57, 65, 117, 217, 248

hickory nut oil, 39, *47*, 79, 87, 237, 245

pecan oil, 87, 237

pumpkinseed oil, 39, 41, 87, 245

varieties of, 245

walnut oil, 17, 87, 220, 235, 245, 259, 260

See also Smude's sunflower oil

nuts

about, 217

in DIY Gomae, 39

in French Corn Bread Wrapped in Wild Leaves, 235

in Green "Meatballs" Stuffed with Chèvre, 16

in Simple Wild Greens Saag, 22

in Stuffed Leaves with Fruit, Rice, and Nut Filling, 27

See also specific types

O

oak (*Quercus* spp.), 246, 247, 248

See also entries beginning with acorn

Oaxacan Squash Vine Soup with Masa Dumplings, 98

olives

in Bakoula, 44

in Lupin Beans with Olives, 229

in Stonecrop Salad with Tomatoes and Olives, 124

Olney, Richard, 38

onion

caramelized, 66

in mirepoix, 73

onion, wild

capers from, 203

flowers of, *196*

as member of the *Allium* family, 73, 146, 159

in Ramp or Wild Onion Leaf Butter, 172

in Spring Greens Dumpling, 36

in Tjeremsha, 169

orache (*Atriplex hortensis*), 2

Orrechiette alla Barese with Sausage and Wild Raabs, 63

ostrich fern (*Matteuccia struthiopteris*), pickled, 112

oxalate concerns, 13, 129

P

Palmer amaranth (*Amaranthus palmeri*), 2

panna cottas

Spruce Tip, 208

Sweet Galium, 189, *189*

parsley

in Braised Cabbage with Bacon and Caraway, 89

in Brussels Sprout Slaw, 87

in Carrot Cakes with a Salad of Carrot Leaves, 78

in Carrot Family Salad, 79

in Carrot Family Soup, 80

in Carrots (or Beets) Glazed in Their Juice, 82

in Goddess Herb Dressing, 43

in Green "Meatballs" Stuffed with Chèvre, 16

in Parsley-Family Tabouleh, with Toasted Barley, 81

in Spring Greens Dumpling, 36

in Wild Green Cakes, 15

in Wild Oregano Salmoriglio Sauce, 150

Parsley-Family Tabouleh, with Toasted Barley, 81

parsnip

in Carrot (or Parsnip) Leaf Salad, 79

in Carrot Family Salad, 79

harvesting in the wild, 70

See also cow parsnip (*Heracleum maximum*)

parts of plants, understanding properties of, 3

Pasta Aglione, 215

pasta dishes

Italian Nettle Soup (Zuppa di Ortiche), 50

Milkweed Bud Fettuccine, 120–21, *120*

Milkweed Leaf Pasta Dough, 121

Orrechiette alla Barese with Sausage and Wild Raabs, 63

Pasta Aglione, 215

Ramp Leaf Pierogi, *162*, *163*

Pastry Crust, 54

Pâte Fermentée, 148, 149, 235

pecans

in French Corn Bread Wrapped in Wild Leaves, 235

nut milk from, 242

oil from, 87, 237

About the Author

Adrian Danciu

Chef Alan Bergo is one of America's leading culinary authorities on mushroom hunting and foraging. A veteran of the restaurant industry, he spent nearly two decades as a professional chef specializing in local and wild foods at St. Paul's fabled Heartland Restaurant, The Salt Cellar, and Lucia's Restaurant in Minneapolis. He's best known for his blogs, recipes, and photography, all featured at his site, foragerchef.com—the web's largest resource on wild-mushroom cookery.